D0985092

FLORIDA STATE
UNIVERSITY LIBRARIES

JAN 17 1997

TALLAHASSEE, FLORIDA

CHANGING EUROPE

Changing Europe

Some aspects of identity, conflict and social justice

Edited by
ANGUS ERSKINE

With
MARK ELCHARDUS
SEBASTIAN HERKOMMER
AND JENNY RYAN

Avebury

Aldershot · Brookfield USA · Hong Kong · Singapore · Sydney

© Angus Erskine and contributors 1996

All rights reserved. No part of this publication may be reproduced, stored in a retrieval system, or transmitted in any form or by any means, electronic, mechanical, photocopying, recording or otherwise without the prior permission of the publisher.

Published by
Avebury
Ashgate Publishing Ltd
Gower House
Croft Road
Aldershot
Hants GU11 3HR
England

Ashgate Publishing Company
Old Post Road
Brookfield
Vermont 05036
USA

HN
373.5
C475
1996

British Library Cataloguing in Publication Data

Changing Europe : some aspects of identity, conflict and
        social justice. - (Perspectives on Europe)
        1. Europe - Social conditions - 20th century 2. Europe -
        Politics and government - 1989- 3. Europe - History - 1989-
        I. Erskine, Angus
        940 . 5 ' 59

        ISBN 1 85972 374 8

Library of Congress Catalog Card Number: 96-84026

Printed and bound by Athenaeum Press, Ltd.,
Gateshead, Tyne & Wear.

Contents

Tables and figures

Acknowledgements

This book is the product of an ERASMUS funded programme which organised five annual intensive courses bringing together students from twelve Universities in Europe. The editors would like to thank Mart-Jan de Jong and Marianne Otte of the Erasmus University, Rotterdam for creating and sustaining the network. Without their commitment to the network, this book would never have been written.

The students who have participated in the intensive courses have informed this book through their criticisms and feedback during the courses and we would like to thank them.

We are also indebted to Paul Littlewood and Oron Yoffe for their assistance in the preparation of this book.

Contributors

Mark Elchardus is Professor of Sociology at the Vrije Universiteit Brussel, Belgium and Director of the Centre for Sociology at that University. His main areas of interest are the sociology of culture, political culture and the sociology of time. His most recent books are *Op de ruïnes van de waarheid. Lezingen over tijd, politiek en cultuur* (On the ruins of truth. Lectures on time, politics and culture - Kritak 1994) and *Niet aan de arbeid voorbij* (Not beyond work - VUB Press 1995).

Angus Erskine lectures in Social Policy at the University of Stirling. His research interests are in poverty and social security in a comparative setting.

Sebastian Herkommer has been a Professor at the Institut für Soziologie, Freie Universität Berlin since 1971. He has conducted empirical research in various fields and published books and articles on political consciousness and education, on class analysis and social inequality, industrial sociology and the theory of ideology.

Ingrid Jönsson is an Associate Professor in Sociology at Lund University, Sweden where she specializes in the sociology of education. Her main research field is social class and gender selection processes in the school system. She will shortly complete a longitudinal study of the passage of an age group through the Swedish school system and the transition to working life. She is also currently working on a study of the transition from a centralized to a decentralized school system being implemented in Sweden.

Gerrit van Kooten is an Associate Professor of Labour and Organisation in the Department of Sociology, Erasmus University, Rotterdam. His main fields of interest are in labour market policy, quality of work, industrial relations, collective bargaining and industrial conflict.

Paul Littlewood lectures in Sociology at Glasgow University where he specializes in the sociology of education. He has previously published on Mediterranean rural social structures, child incarceration and the role of parents in schools. He is about to publish an account of the Scottish education system and is currently conducting research into patterns of access to and performance in higher education in Scotland.

Mike McGuinness is a Senior Lecturer in Politics at the University of Teesside, Middlesbrough, UK and is responsible for the exchange links under the ERASMUS programme. His main interest is in the impact of integration and the growing threat of racism, nationalism and xenophobia in Europe generally.

Jan Petersson is an Associate Professor of Social Policy and Economics at the School of Social Work, Lund University, Sweden.

Roswitha Pioch studied Political Sciences, Sociology and Theology at the University of Marburg. She is currently Lecturer in the Department of Sociology at the University of Leipzig. She has researched and published articles on social policy, social Justice, sociology of interest groups and interpretative methods. She is co-author of *Gerechtigkeit im Wohlfahrtsstaat*, Schüren Verlag: Marburg 1995.

Jenny Ryan is a Principal Lecturer in Sociology at Manchester Metropolitan University, England. In addition to comparative aspects of gender relations her teaching, research and publication interests also include those of gender, sexuality and the city/urban consumption patterns. Recent writings in this field can be found in the journal *Theory, Culture and Society* and in the forthcoming book *From the Margins to the Centre* (Wynne, D. (ed.) - Ashgate, Avebury).

Georg Vobruba is Professor of Sociology, University of Leipzig. His main areas of research are in social policy, political sociology and social theory. His latest publications include *Gemeinschaft ohne Moral* (Passagen, Vienna 1994), 'Social Policy on Tomorrow's Euro-Corporatist Stage', *Journal of European Social Policy*, Vol 5, No 4, 1995 and 'Self interested aid' in *Crime, Law and Social Change* (Forthcoming 1996).

Changing Europe?

Angus Erskine, Mark Elchardus, Sebastian Herkommer, and Jenny Ryan

European societies have always been in flux, but the period we are living in maybe one of the most stable in the past three hundred years. Yet, we stand at a crossroads. The processes of change currently taking place in Europe may lead to new threats to social cohesion or new opportunities for developing inclusive policies for the people of Europe. Social, political, cultural and economic changes are taking place which have a profound effect upon how people live their lives and how they see themselves.

We can discern two opposing directions in which Europe might be moving. On the one hand, there may be a continued development of existing social welfare provision, improving living and working conditions, enhanced democratic structures at regional, national and European levels, and a widening of prosperity based upon sustainable economic development. On the other hand, there are forces leading in the opposite direction. Unchecked economic competition amongst European states and between Europe and the rest of the world may lead to deteriorating living and working conditions for many, while at the same time pressure on state budgets decreases welfare provision. A more deregulated labour market, combined with alienation from existing political structures, may produce a Europe dominated by market relationships between people and, for those excluded from the market, increased impoverishment and a discipline, rather than welfare, state. The consequences of exclusion for a significant section of the population, in particular older workers, young people and migrant workers, may take a number of forms: economic exclusion through a restructured labour market and the privatising of welfare services; social exclusion as a consequence of the breakdown in social relationships and networks; and political exclusion from a civic society which reflects only the political and economic aspirations of the majority. This polarization through exclusion may be reinforced as new social divisions develop, leaving the children of the most excluded themselves excluded from educational opportunities, from paid work and from participation in society and politics.

1

The directions that European societies take will be partly determined by the forms of European institutional structures which are created. Increasing political powers at the level of the Union and growing competence in areas such as social policy will enhance or inhibit trends developing at a national level. But European history since the Treaty of Rome illustrates the resilience of the specificities and singularities of the countries of the Union. The coordination and harmonization of social policies as envisaged in the Treaty has yet to come about and there is no reason to suppose that the specificity of national cultural, institutional and social forces will not continue to act as an obstacle to unification. Differing cultural and social attitudes towards the nation and the family as well as different commitments to corporatist institutions as opposed to a belief in the free market, are reflected not only in the political ideas generated and dominant within different European nations, but also in the ways in which their economies are organized. In this sense, we should not uncritically accept the nostrums of those who argue that we are becoming part of one global market. Globalization implies that there are forces integrating the world in a new way, into one economic system and through that, dictating relations of production and consumption across the world. But the experience of Europe since the second world war, and earlier, illustrates the way in which the economic strength and organisation of different countries is embedded in their specific cultural, social and institutional arrangements.

How the key changes that are taking place are identified, in part, determines how they are understood and how their implications are analysed. In this book, we have largely concentrated, given the background of the authors, upon trends taking place in North Western Europe, although many of the issues raised are relevant in other parts of the continent. The articles revolve around three key themes: Identity; Conflict; and Justice. These reflect central pre-occupations within social science about the ways in which the processes of social change impinge upon the individual and society. Recent developments in Europe have led to profound changes in identity, not only in the relative importance of national, regional and ethnic identities, but also, and even more so, in the meanings of identities derived from class, gender and belief. This process has rekindled old, and fuelled new, kinds of conflicts. What this means is that individuals face a more differentiated and fragmented sense of who they are, and where they belong, as the social institutions of work, the family and political organization become transformed and new conflicts and contradictions develop. Social justice has been central to the concerns of social policies and European welfare states through the second half of the twentieth century. The emerging structures of the European Union and the changing social, political and demographic shape of European societies lead to new questions for social policy. Hence in relation to all three themes, this book is about key areas of experience in Europe and about how sociology and social policy respond to them in analysing the changes that are taking place.

The political and institutional context within which change in the societies of the European Union is framed is set by the Treaty of Maastricht which represents a major development in the political history of Europe. The Treaty contains institutional measures which aim to enhance the political, economic and social cohesion of the Union. However, whether the future direction of the Union is towards an ever deepening integration (as envisaged in Maastricht) or towards a widening of an economic union containing more European states, there are associated political and social tendencies both across Europe and within member states which lead towards social fragmentation rather than uniformity.

The countries of the European Union exhibit some political, economic and social trends towards homogeneity. There are political forces within member states and at the level of the Union, encouraging the fulfilment of the European project and the greater integration of the political structures of the Union and member states. Increasingly the mainstream of social and christian democratic parties are becoming committed to the European project and, with the gradual development of a more powerful political role for the European Parliament, the issues and implications of political integration become a major issue of debate within the political life of member states. Alongside this political unification process, social, economic and cultural changes are occurring to which political parties do not always have clear responses and whose impact upon the process of European unification is as yet unclear.

Current global economic developments such as the GATT agreement and the increasing internationalization of production mean that member states are faced by similar global economic pressures. One of the specificities of European societies reside, in their welfare states, their social security systems and their accompanying styles of political and economic decision making. This specificity is challenged by current economic and social trends. Within the current economic developments member states are faced with new kinds of economic pressures and their social consequences. These developments raise specific problems in the areas of organization, labour relations and political conflict, but also raise the issue of a new European and global perspective based on the internationalization of the welfare state and of social justice.

But it is not only European economies which share common changes; the social and demographic structure of European countries are also changing: in particular, the role of women in the workforce, and in the home, and the changing age profile of the population. While the extent of these trends is not uniform, the direction of the trends is similar. The changing position of women in the labour market and changing household and family structures along with an ageing population lead to new challenges to labour market policies.

Understanding the changes taking place requires a reexamination of some of the traditional categories of sociological analysis. Herkommer examines recent changes in class composition. He demonstrates that the idea of other lines of cleavage cutting across those of class is one of the major issues of post war sociology. One can see that the tendencies towards levelling out differences between countries is not primarily a consequence of the institutional preconditions of the European Community, but rather, of general modernization processes taking place in capitalist societies. On the one hand, new identities stimulated by the process of individualization and by a plurality of lifestyles and, on the other, divergence within societies and between some of the European countries, make for a picture of variety and heterogeneity, including new forms of polarization and cleavages in all advanced societies. The main thesis is that the plurality of lifestyles and an ever growing degree of individualization is not contradictory to a capitalist economy and its underlying fundamental class dichotomy.

Ryan in a different way takes up this theme by focusing upon a comparative examination of statistical and social attitude data concerning the changing position of women in the family and in the workforce. She suggests ways in which these changes are being integrated into changing gender identities for women. She discusses the continued significance of gender differences in the opportunities and risks that individuals face in the formation of their identities. The changes in attitudes and behaviour that she describes in relation to marriage, parenthood, family and work have to be understood not necessarily, she argues, as evidence of increased gender equality but as a restructuring of life styles, experiences and interests which are still crucially gender mediated.

Elchardus investigates the political growth of the extreme or populist right by concentrating upon the case of Flanders. He examines the thesis that changes in class structure and class identity have made class obsolete as a basis for analysing political and cultural change. He rejects this thesis and shows how class conflict has both changed and intensified.

These three chapters, by Herkommer, Ryan and Elchardus, provide a context within which the developments analysed in other parts of the book can be placed. This is not to imply that alone they are sufficient to fully understand the nature of the changes taking place. For example. the important areas of ethnic identity and patterns of migration have not been considered. Nor do all the subsequent chapters share the different perspectives being developed in these first chapters. But as they stand, these three chapters represent some of the key issues and developments necessary for the understanding of change. Changes in gender, age and class identities inevitably lead to changes in the conflicts that are based upon those identities. Old and new identities give rise to changing conflicts. Some commentators point to patterns of fragmentation and individualization as old identities are fractured by economic and social changes.

McGuinness examines the role of nationalism within the emerging political framework of the Union. He points to the risks of relaxed border controls between member states being compensated for by much more stringent controls on entry into the Union itself and the development of new forms of European nationalism as Europe attempts to avoid the developing violent ethnic conflicts, which are taking place beyond its borders, spilling over and igniting nascent ethnic conflicts within the Union.

Herkommer, in his second contribution to this book, provides a context within which we can understand the development of new forms of industrial production. In the concept of 'lean production' emphasis is laid upon a fundamental change in the labour process. Whether the new organisational paradigm will be able to change the central conflict between employers and employees, and whether the shop floor will lose its classic character of a contested terrain are discussed. The risks and chances of the new mode of production are dealt with, emphasizing the decisive power and the relative strength of capital and labour within the corporation and in society as a whole.

Van Kooten comments upon trends in traditional industrial conflicts in the form of strikes. Comparing strike activities in several European countries, he illustrates marked differences between as well as within these countries according to different periods after the war. He contrasts two approaches in the study of industrial relations. Whereas the manifestations of industrial conflicts are manifold, national strike patterns seem to be influenced by the characteristics of systems of industrial relations.

Historically in European states, welfare has played an integrative role attempting to overcome the conflicts which arise from differing identities and interests. An appeal to social justice through state organized welfare has been a central plank of social and christian democratic politics. Littlewood and Jönsson examine the convergences and divergences in the ways in which education systems are responding to social, economic and political changes. They examine a number of key themes which educational systems in European countries have been addressing and compare their responses and changes.

The fate of an ageing population at a time of high unemployment is explored by Petersson through examining the need and interests of older workers in the labour market and how public policy and employers have responded. For Petersson, this has to be understood through the different participation of the firm, the state and the individual in structuring the transition from employment to retirement. Petersson examines the constraints imposed by different systems of post retirement employment and pension support systems on older workers.

The last two essays in the book open up the issues of social justice and social policy intervention into wider questions which affect individuals regardless of class, age or gender. The first of these, by Pioch, couches questions about the role of state income maintenance policies in the face of declining employment and interruptions in income from wages. Pioch proposes a form of social security which she argues would address the social and economic changes taking place, while providing a basic income to its citizens. By dissociating basic income needs from employment status, the solution she provides provokes questions about how different categories of citizen might benefit from the radical change in the nature of income maintenance programmes: groups such as women, elderly people and other economic and socially excluded sections of society.

Vobruba argues that there are additional uses to social policy which are relevant to the transitions taking place in Eastern Europe. Social policy has an important role to play in ensuring that the economic upheavals during the transition to market economies do not take place at the expense of democracy. Whilst Vobruba's essay looks to changes taking place in Eastern Europe, the perspective it provides could be integrated into our understanding of the role of social policy in Western Europe. It reminds us that social justice is a matter of economic as well as social and political equity and that social policy can play a crucial role in economic change. In this essay, Vobruba locates a concern for understanding societal change at the macrolevel

This macrolevel can be usefully explored to frame our understanding of the transformations that simultaneously are taking place at the microlevel of identity and the group level of conflict. It is with the juxtaposition of these different kinds of understanding, mirrored in the particular substantive issues, that the different essays are concerned. Whilst they offer only partial accounts of some aspects of the changes taking place, they contribute to an agenda that constructs problems of identity, conflict and social justice as a concern of both social science analysis and social policy.

In this book we have tried to go beyond the truism of a changing Europe. Apart from describing and analysing some aspects of change in various fields of social life and drawing attention to trends towards homogeneity and heterogeneity, we emphasize an active as well as a critical function for sociological analysis. Europe should be changed through improving living and working conditions, protecting and enhancing welfare state provision, ensuring cultural diversity and developing individuality. These are threatened by economic recession, deregulation and the exclusion of many from the wealth of their nations.

1   Changes in the class structure

Sebastian Herkommer

Introduction

One of the major manifestations of radical change in modern Europe is seen in the erosion of its former class structure. Ever growing numbers of social scientists are proclaiming a society 'beyond class and status' (Beck 1983, Beck 1992, Berger 1986, Hradil 1987, Berger and Hradil 1990). In their eyes, neither the concept of stratification nor the concept of class reflects the reality of the social structure. A steady process of individualization is leading us towards a 'capitalism without classes', and instead of sticking to the idea of antagonism between the classes of capital owners and wage labourers, or conceiving social structure in terms of a stratum-like order according to income, education and prestige, it would be much more adequate to describe a pluralized structure of inequalities among members of society.

There are other scientists who would not go that far, and who would not replace class analysis altogether with a sociology of multidimensional inequality (Giddens 1973, Bourdieu 1979, Therborn 1987, Bader and Benschop 1989, Kreckel 1990, Crompton 1993, Esping-Andersen 1993, Koch 1994). They use class as a basic dimension of social structuration, which does not necessarily exclude the existence of other forms of differentiation (by gender, race and ethnicity, and distinguishing a vertical dimension and a horizontal one, or by distinguishing the centre from the periphery). They, too, emphasize change, but they are emphasizing differentiation and changes in inequality within the class structure. They would not announce the erosion and abolition of class altogether.

We have to bear this in mind when we try to give a general view of the changes in the social structure in Europe. Very often the findings of empirical studies on social class, stratification and inequality depend upon the theoretical approach used when designing the research and when interpreting the data. Therefore, to some

7

extent we are confronted with different results whenever we compare studies working with the concept of either class, or stratum, or inequality.

There is yet another problem to be aware of. Although there exist a large number of empirical studies and a lot of empirical data and statistics for single countries and for Europe as a whole, there are not many studies which use a concept which is directly comparable for each country in the European Union, and which deal with class differences and changes in class composition at the same time.

Fortunately, however, there are three examples of a fairly comparable character, which might serve to demonstrate the general trends of convergence and divergence in social structure, as well as the obvious diversity in the comments on these developments. Although written at different times and with different theoretical approaches, these contributions share in common a view of converging tendencies in all European countries. But they also put stress on variations of different types. The examples are, an essay by Dahrendorf published in the early 1960s (Dahrendorf 1964), an empirical study by Hagelstange published in the 1980s but also examining earlier developments (Hagelstange 1988), and, a recently published article by Hradil (1992).

Having presented these contributions, we shall give a short sketch of a structural model which for further studies could provide an integrative approach. The thesis is that the tendencies of individualization and of a pluralization of lifestyles in modern society can still be related to class analysis and to some extent be explained by class theory.

The service class society - Dahrendorf

Thirty years ago, Ralf Dahrendorf in his essay 'Recent Changes in the Class Structure of European Societies' argued 'that the trend toward the service class society is a fact in many parts of Europe'. He was convinced of the 'increasing reality of Europe as a unit. ... Western Europe is today more than a geographical concept. But this political fact must not deceive us about the variations within the continent.' (Dahrendorf, 1964, p.266). Relying on statistical data from most European countries, especially Britain, France and Germany, he tried to show both the general tendencies and the variations.

Due to the concept of class and class conflict which he had developed earlier (Dahrendorf 1959), Dahrendorf claimed that 'the Marxian notion of a society split into two antagonistic classes growing out of the property structure of the economy is no longer a correct description of European reality.' (Dahrendorf, 1964, p.227) He argued that:

> In any case a new type of class structure is emerging in Europe which differs in many respects from the old... For Europe as a whole, the society described by Marx is by now an Old Order... its demise was effected, or at least accelerated

by three sets of factors: social, economic, and political. (Dahrendorf, 1964, p.228)

These sets of factors were the extension of citizenship and civil rights (the 'social miracle'), higher income and shorter working hours (the 'economic miracle'), and changes in power structures.

This indicates a very special notion of class promoted by the author. Indeed, he defines the class structure of a society as 'the relationship of its members to the exercise of power'; 'class is about power'; and 'power is about politics'. It is not related in the last instance to the 'property structure of the economy'. (Dahrendorf, 1964, pp.225, 232, 263) Thus Dahrendorf in his essay refers to four groups or classes: the ruling groups, the service class, the ruled or subjected groups, and the intellectuals.

It was common in post war sociology to point to the absence of a revolutionary class consciousness among the workers in Western Europe. As an early representative of the embourgeoisement thesis, Dahrendorf insists on the intervening effects of non-economic institutions and of mentalities when he tries to explain the phenomenon:

> Our thesis in this essay is not that the economic miracle has by itself converted class-conscious workers into bourgeois conservatives. We have placed great emphasis on the social miracle and on changes in the structure of power which may be of much greater importance than a decade of prosperity. Above all, the crucial change in attitudes seems to me to lie in the fact that feelings of solidarity, and of the desirability of collective action have given way, for many workers, to the desire to advance their position individually. (Dahrendorf, 1964, p. 258)

This shift from solidarity towards individualism remains of general interest in contemporary debates.

Dahrendorf estimated that about 85 per cent of the people in Europe belonged to the 'ruled groups', consisting of three vastly different social categories - the old middle class, parts of the new middle class (which are not the service class) and the working class, heterogeneous itself. The proportion of self-employed people (old middle class) varied between 15 and 25 per cent. The greatest variations within Western Europe existed, like today, in the proportion of the population who were peasants.

These findings about the quantitative distribution of social groups relate to an important thesis, the thesis of embourgeoisement and individualism:

> Although only a fraction of the population can be counted among the service class proper *[top bureaucrats and administrators]*, the values of this category have spread to all other groups. Paramount among these values is the

9

replacement of cohesive feelings and groupings by individual competition. (Dahrendorf, 1964, p. 262)

Dahrendorf on the one hand emphasizes, to some extent contradictorily, that class in post war Europe is no longer a matter of the antagonism of a small ruling group and a large mass of powerless subjects, and on the other hand concludes that after the landowning class as well as the classic capitalist class had lost their ruling positions a new minority, consisting of the top bureaucrats and administrators, was emerging and dominating the general value system.

This strong thesis of a new class, which still is a minority, but nevertheless ruling by generalizing its values all over Western Europe, is in the end, however, toned down by the author, when he declares class to be only one of several possible distinctions within Europe:

> ... class is clearly only one of many vantage points from which to survey the scene of European society. In some European countries, conflict between town and country, North and South, Flamands and Walloons, Protestant and Roman Catholics is far more important than that between people of different class positions. In all countries of Europe such other lines of cleavage cut across those of class and serve to complicate further a picture which is in any case more complex than our historical consciousness would have it. (Dahrendorf, 1964, p. 266)

In our day, we are quite familiar with the enduring influence or rather a re-emergence of regional aspects as well as ascriptive elements within the social structure. But for a while these forms of differentiation were considered secondary. Our next example represents such a significant reduction of complexity.

Proletarianization - Hagelstange

The 'miracles' mentioned by Dahrendorf did not occur without contradictions. Class struggles reflecting a class society of the 'old order' continued. This found its echoes in the social sciences. As a result of the fundamental critique of so-called bourgeois sociology, and as a result of a proper and very careful and thorough-going 'reconstruction' of Marx's original theory of capitalist society, quite a few sociologists in the 1970s were not only debating class society in general, but also undertaking empirical research about the existing class structure in their countries. (Projekt Klassenanalyse 1973, 1974, IMSF 1973, Beckenbach et al. 1973 and 1975, Poulantzas 1974, Wright 1978, Bischoff et al. 1982, Erbslöh et al. 1987)

There was competition and debate also among these 'Neo-Marxist' groups. In West Germany, there were two empirical studies of importance, one by the Frankfurt Institute of Marxist Studies and Research (IMSF 1973), the other by the

West Berlin Project of Class Analysis (Projekt Klassenanalyse 1973) - both gathering their findings from the 1970 official statistics. Both studies showed similarities in the distinctions between classes. They distinguished a working class, middle classes and a capitalist class. But they also showed considerable differences as to the exact distinctions and boundaries of these classes as well as to the fractions within the classes. Thus the proportions of the main classes, the quantitative distribution of the West German population differ very much - in one case (IMSF) more than 75 per cent belong to the working class and 22 per cent to the middle classes, in the other case (Projekt Klassenanalyse) only 65 per cent are classified as working class and nearly 32 per cent as members of the middle classes. The reason for different classification of the same statistical data can be found in the theoretical differences between the two analyses. In short, the question was how far one could rely on the distinctions Marx had made in 'Capital', and whether the theory of 'State Monopoly Capitalism' in the tradition of Marxism-Leninism did or did not provide good reasons for a modification.

Hagelstange has been engaged in these debates. His research is part of an international project stimulated by Erik Olin Wright (Erbslöh et al. 1988, Hagelstange 1988). In its theoretical part, Hagelstange (1988) lays out the Marxian assumptions of the fundamental conflict of capitalist society and the development of the class structure. Following the immanent logic of Marx's critique of political economy, the class concept of Hagelstange starts from the central dichotomy between capitalists and workers (productive as well as commercial wage labour, occupied by productive and commercial capital, respectively). From these classes he distinguishes the jobless, because in his opinion they are in terms of specific economic form, a distinct class. Two further class positions are made up by those wage labourers who are either 'non-market oriented' or 'market-oriented, but not profit-oriented', both situated outside the direct relationship between capital and labour. Apart from these groups in the workforce, there are those who are situated in positions belonging to non-capitalist forms of production, for example self-employed artisans and peasants with no or only few wage labourers.

The next step was to look at developments over time. According to the proletarianization thesis, there must be a historical trend of more and more parts of the active population losing their own means of production and thus becoming dependent on the purchasing of their labour power as a commodity. This assumption was confirmed by the results of all empirical analyses concerning developments in the United States of America and in the European Community between 1960 and 1982. Compared with this general trend, there are variations between some of the individual countries. France, which like Germany is very near to the average, has a much lower proportion of wage labourers in the state sector than Denmark which has much the same distribution as Ireland (Hagelstange, 1988, pp. 218, 263).

In the period between 1960 and 1982, the process of proletarianization continued in all countries and in all main branches of production, with the exception of the

United Kingdom where this process had almost come to an end. This general trend has been slowing down since the middle of the 1970s due to slower economic growth. The proportion of the self-employed workforce has become smaller everywhere. Between countries, however, there exist wide variations as to the sectors of the economy where the self-employed still remain a strong group, although there seems to be evidence of a change in this development. Toivonen (1989) shows a new rise of self-employment beginning in the early 1980s, and again there are significant variations between European countries.

According to Hagelstange's findings, the decline in self-employment was going hand in hand with a shift between economic sectors. In all countries, the primary sector (agriculture) was continuously diminishing while the tertiary sector (public and private services) was expanding. The share of non-market oriented wage labour was growing in nearly all countries, as a result of the expansion of employment in the welfare state. The proportion of unemployed people was also growing, especially from the middle of the 1970s when the rate of economic growth began to slow down.

From the data collected by the international project of class analysis, we can see that in the early 1960s, the European countries started with broad variations in their class structures. Since then they have become more and more similar in their structure, especially during those periods of rapid economic growth. However, the various branches are still taking a special position within different societies. When comparing European developments with those of the USA and of Canada, Hagelstange argues that the levelling out differences between the various countries is not primarily a consequence of the institutional preconditions of the European Community but rather a consequence of general modernization processes. (Hagelstange, 1988, p. 208)

It seems to Hagelstange that most of the assumptions of a Marxian analysis of modern class structure and its dynamics are confirmed. However, one has to bear in mind that his empirical study was restricted to class positions. Thus it shows a structure of relative positions, but there are no indications about the character of class relationships, nor about the conflicts due to class antagonism (for relation to economic business cycles of strike activity, see Erbslöh et al. 1988). Nor are we informed about the non-active population, or about the distribution of income by gainful employment and by transfers of money and services in a welfare state (this was done by Bischoff et al. 1982, Herkommer 1983). And there is no information about the consistency of class positions within the private household. Nothing is said about the relationship between class and gender, nor about the national or ethnic composition of the workforce.

Nevertheless, from these investigations into relative class positions we can gain a considerable knowledge about the general trends as well as variations between countries of the European Community. We shall see whether our third example, the most recent one, will provide us with more details and with more complexity.

Pluralization and individualization - Hradil

The article on 'Social Structure and Social Change' (Hradil 1992) contains both more and less of the sort of class analysis we have just referred to. There are more data in it about important issues such as the development of European population and demographic changes; family, household and biography; level of welfare and social inequality; work and education. For example, all over Europe there is a similar trend of a growing proportion of young people participating in education, although there also remain significant differences between European countries. But there is no attempt at an interpretation of the data within class theory. This neglect has to do with the conceptual approach of the author. (Hradil 1987, Berger and Hradil 1990)

Hradil distinguishes between 'classic' industrial societies and 'advanced' industrial societies. In societies of the first type, the percentage of those who have to work under the control of an employer is rising. Employment becomes more and more a key determinant of one's existence; it is the very centre of people's biographies. The centre of paid work lies in the industrial production of goods, while agriculture is losing its former relative importance. There are trends towards the standardization of working hours and working conditions and towards mass production and standard biographies.

In advanced industrial societies, Hradil claims, there are no principal changes in these trends, but nevertheless significant shifts. An increasing number of women participate in paid employment, with a very high proportion in part-time work. Women's share in overall part-time working is 90 per cent in Germany and in Belgium, 87 per cent in the UK, 83 per cent in France and 64 per cent in Greece (European Centre 1993). (See also Ryan in this volume). The tertiary sector is growing, while the primary and secondary sectors are declining. Occupation loses its key importance for individuals' lives, and the normality or standards of working hours, biography etc. are eroding, while flexibility becomes the norm.

This process of 'modernization' towards the 'advanced society' is proceeding all over Europe. All national societies within the Common Market are experiencing similar changes in their social structure due to the same trend of modernization. National, religious and regional differences are secondary to this trend. Most of the major differences between countries are caused by delays in the phases of modernization, as individual countries start from different levels of development and as they are not all developing at the same speed. This may widen the gap in wealth between European nations instead of diminishing it. Apparently, there exists a different degree of inequality within the countries, too. The data (Hradil, 1992, p. 84, table 2) show 'tolerable' inequality according to the standards of the World Bank only in the Scandinavian countries and in the Netherlands, while the most unequal distribution of income within the European Community exists in France.

While there is delay in modernization among all Mediterranean countries compared with the rest of the European Union, in general the common trend is towards the full realization of a classic industrial society, and from this, European countries are beginning, some earlier some later, to reach the next phase, which is a pluralization of the social structure. For these two reasons, delay and pluralization, homogeneity cannot be expected within Europe.

As in our other two examples, this interpretation of the empirical data is closely linked with the author's theoretical approach. In a recent article, Hradil (1993) draws an enlightening sketch of the theoretical debate that has been taking place in Germany in the last few years.

> Within the German discussion, the structural models 'class society' and 'stratified society' have retreated from their previous position of dominance into a defensive one. Their conflict has turned into a coalition. Today both of them are confronted by an abundance of new approaches... Silently the class concept has also moved closer to a 'stratumlike', more or less vertically graded concept of occupational groups. Already in the 1970s, the differentiation of occupational structures forced Marxist class studies in West Germany to take account of the 'middle classes' and 'middle strata'. Modern Marxist class schemes are more and more differentiated, especially with respect to the power and living conditions of the 'middle classes'. (e. g. Wright 1985). (Hradil, 1993, p. 669)

In the eyes of Hradil, interpretations based on class and stratification no longer seem to mirror reality. Therefore he favours concentrating on the 'new' dimensions of inequality - between men and women, between age groups or birth-cohorts, between residential regions and nationality. By the combination and accumulation of advantageous and disadvantageous conditions of living, he is able to take so-called 'problem groups', like the poor, the long-term unemployed, the asylum seekers, the homeless, drug addicts, handicapped, and older people with inadequate support (mainly women), into account.

> Accordingly, the most problematic inequalities are no longer to be found among wage earners, such as between an impoverished working class and a small favoured and predominant bourgeoisie, as in early industrial society, also no longer between an unqualified, poorly remunerated lower class of manual 'blue collar' workers and the middle class of qualified, better paid 'white collar' employees and officials, as in developed industrial societies, but between the wage-earning majority of the population and very heterogeneous problem groups, standing on the fringe of, or outside gainful employment. (Hradil, 1993, p. 680)

In addition to 'horizontal' cleavages of the sort we have already learned about from Dahrendorf, Hradil pays attention to those processes which have lead to individualized and pluralized forms of life. Like most of the sociologists recently doing social research on the structures of inequality, Hradil suggests that we should no longer look for the causes of social advantage and disadvantage exclusively within the economic sector, but wants to include cultural patterns which appear to be not directly linked with class or stratum positions. The key notions for this are socio-cultural milieus, way of life (*Lebensführung*) and lifestyle.

As to the findings of these studies, Hradil speaks of a threefold plurality within West German society.

> Firstly, people think and act in general more independently of external social determinants and of stratification and class membership in particular than had been previously assumed... Secondly, the empirical studies show a greater differentiation in the manifestations of modes of life, i.e., smaller socio-cultural groupings and more diversified ways of life than usual class and stratification patterns... Thirdly, empirical research has also shown that belonging to milieus and life-style groupings is nowadays an important determinant for everyday action... Electoral decisions, consumer behaviour, political participation, etc. are shaped nowadays, to a considerable extent, by an individual's mode of life and not so much by her or his conditions of life. (Hradil, 1993, pp. 682-4)

Hradil's conclusions could easily be generalised for all 'advanced' industrial societies. In his eyes, in advanced European countries we are living in a 'plurally differentiated affluent society' which is based on three essential factors. First, it is 'criss-crossed by multidimensional inequalities'. Second, 'the inequality structure appears to have many and diverse styles of behaviour superimposed'. Third, historically living standards are quite high, but the social structure is not characterised by levelling out but by pluralization: 'Varied and inconstant positions of social inequality, as well as of heterogeneous social movements, milieus and life styles, partly independent of 'objective' inequalities', are juxtaposed. But neither pluralization nor 'the concentration of the population in middle class positions' have prevented polarization. (Hradil, 1993, pp. 685, 686)

Does Hradil bring us back to Dahrendorf? Some aspects seem to point to this assumption. Both social scientists explicitly apply a non-Marxist view, which lays stress on sociological theory as opposed to political economy, and identifies a variety of cleavages instead of one central antagonism. But there are clear differences. Hradil focuses on inequalities, not the difference between ruling groups and the ruled majority as Dahrendorf does. He does not mention power and conflict, neither economic, nor political, and he seems to prefer a descriptive rather than an explanatory approach. What we should ask is, whether the obvious variety of groupings and inequalities in living conditions, milieus and lifestyles necessarily excludes a concept of social class. Can the approach of Hagelstange conceiving of

European society as a class society be brought together with the empirical findings of differentiation, pluralization and individualization?

Class, social class and lifestyles

The empirical data collected by Hradil as well as by others (like Erikson and Goldthorpe 1992, Blossfeld et al. 1993, Crompton 1993, Noll 1993) seems to provide evidence of a correlation between class structure and the social chances of individuals. Correlations between class position and income, education, conditions of work and conditions of living are evident. Noll and Habich (1990, p. 178) draw upon data which relate class position with income and working conditions (variety of work, control, qualification, and stress at work) from the West German Socio-Economic Panel 1984-1986, and show that class position is not only related to a wide range of gross earnings, but also to the sort of work, task autonomy and the degree and kind of stress at work.

Therefore one could argue, like Koch (1994), that there is no one factor which influences social chances in everyday life in a similar way to class position. 'The empirical findings do not prove the thesis of disjunction of class position and the way of living.' (Koch, 1994, p. 190.) To demonstrate this, he used the classifications which were provided by explicitly non-Marxist sociologists and researchers (e. g. Strasser and Goldthorpe (eds.) 1985, see also Winter 1990).

Koch has also discussed the debate among Marxists to which we have referred. After thoroughly dealing with the weaknesses and advantages of the most influential class analyses (theoretical and empirical), namely by the Projekt Klassenanalyse (1973), by Poulantzas (1974), by Wright (1985, 1989) and others, he proposes a model of his own. (Koch, 1994, p. 117) It reveals on a first level the underlying class antagonism in capitalism as constituted by the social forms of production and of property. On a second level there are five social classes, capitalists and petite bourgeoisie as owners of the means of production on the one hand, intelligentsia, middle class and working class as derived from the social form of wage labour on the other hand. These distinctions take into account the number of employed (in the first two classes), and a combination of the level of education and the position in the work process (in the case of the three other classes). The third level is made up by fractions within the social classes based on occupation and economic sector, as well as levels of qualification and control over working life.

When explaining his model, Koch refers to an important distinction which most non-Marxist sociologists disregard - the distinction between classes 'on paper' (Bourdieu 1985, 1987), or economically defined classes as an abstraction, and the concrete structure of social classes. This, of course, is to adapt Marx's procedure correctly, which is a very deliberate 'reductionism'. In order to find the hidden kernel of social totality and of its differentiation on the 'surface' of society, and in order to explain the typical dynamics of modern development as well as social conflicts and crises, Marx undertook an analysis of the elementary forms of social production and social relations. On the fundamentals of the labour theory of value, he theorised the forms of production and of distribution in capitalist society as a historical formation.

In our view, this should be the theoretical starting point for any empirical investigation into the real distribution of wealth and resources, and into the social chances of individuals in a given (capitalist) society. In order to describe the complexity of differentiated modern capitalism, it is necessary, however, also to take into account the special nature of the political system (the kind of welfare state) as well as regional and other specifications due to national history, and it is necessary to include the relationship between class and gender. (Herkommer and Mühlhaus 1992)

In fact, at least three aspects of historical change within the capitalist formation must be placed on top of the agenda if class analysis is to remain useful in explaining European developments. First, there are the effects of transfers in a welfare state society (Bischoff et al. 1982). Do they change the relative positions of the traditional classes? Are there emerging 'welfare support classes' (Alber 1984), and if so, is there a significant influence of the type of welfare state on the forms of closure as Esping-Andersen (1990, 1993) has pointed out? Is there emerging a new service proletariat, and - caused by increasing mass unemployment (Kronauer 1993) - a new ('under') class of the poor? (Katz 1993, Devine and Wright 1993, Andersen and Larsen 1995). Second, there are the effects of the feminization of gainful occupation, especially in the service sector. Will the sexual division of labour as known in the 'Fordist' regime of accumulation, be replaced by a new 'gender-divided stratification order with a male-dominated Fordist hierarchy, and a female-biased post-industrial hierarchy', as Esping-Andersen is suggesting? Or will there be less discrimination and a completely new social fabric which avoids gender segregation of labour markets and the increasing feminization of part-time and precarious work? What influence will trade unions have on these issues? (Therborn 1995). Third, there is the process of individualization and its assumed impact on eroding class structures. Can the obvious trends towards individualism and pluralized forms of everyday life serve as an argument against class concepts? Have milieus and lifestyles replaced social classes? Or, is it possible to link together the fundamentals of economic classes (as an underlying structure) with the structures of social classes and lifestyles, thus not only describing but also explaining the reasons for multi-dimensional social inequalities?

As for the relationship between lifestyle and class position, we can refer to the pioneering research by Bourdieu (1979) who has studied the strategies of pretension in France in the 1960s. In the meantime, there have been a number of studies into milieus and lifestyles in other countries (Klocke 1993). The most recent one has projected the social milieus of Germany onto the French landscape of class positions and lifestyles as portrayed by Bourdieu (Vester et al., 1993, pp. 40, 41). From this we can see a striking convergence of the German milieus and the French lifestyles.

Bourdieu's map consists of a 'space of social positions' made up by the volume of capital (high or low) and by the kind of capital (economic or cultural), and of a 'space of lifestyles' indicated by habits of cultural consumption and symbolic expression in everyday-life. A third dimension is a temporal one: intra- and inter-generational upward or downward mobility of the various occupational groups (Bourdieu 1979).

Table 1.1
Percentage changes in the social milieu in the German population
(according to Vester et al. 1993)

Milieu	1982	1991
Conservative upper	9	8
Alternative	4	2
Technocratic-liberal	9	9
Hedonistic	10	13
Upward oriented	20	24
Petite-bourgeois	28	22
New working class	0	5
Traditional working class	9	5
Workers without tradition	9	12

The results of both studies underline that there is no direct determination of lifestyle, expressed in different social milieus, by economic class position. Since there are nevertheless striking 'probabilities', the relationship seems to be one of 'relative autonomy'. This underlines our thesis, that plurality of lifestyles and an ever growing degree of individualization is not inconsistent with an analysis of the capitalist economy as containing an underlying fundamental class dichotomy. It rather is a consequence of the 'great civilizing influence of capital'. (Marx, 1953, p. 313)

However, stress must be laid upon the contradictions of this civilizing effect. Even those who do pronounce the disappearance of classes do not hesitate to admit a further polarization in the structure of social inequalities. The same is true for the contradictions of individualization. The effect of individualization is ambivalent because individuals have much more freedom of choice, because the ties of traditional institutions have been loosened. Constraints of the family as well as those exercised by religious and local communities have weakened. And, along with more money and more time to spend, wage labourers and employees have gained a wider space for the development and satisfaction of their personal needs. Thus they are, for the first time in history, 'personal individuals' alongside their position of 'class individuals'. They are, to some extent, indeed beyond status and class.

But within the capitalist formation of society this change towards more personal autonomy is accompanied by the experience of growing personal risks. As soon as the smooth reproduction of a prosperous welfare society is threatened by economic crises, followed by mass unemployment and diminishing social welfare policies, it becomes obvious that those traditional ties and social networks are lacking. Instead of an identity of autonomous persons the individuals experience the other side of the individualization coin, i. e. atomization. Class solidarity when needed most is no longer available and cannot easily be restored by new issues of a communitarian kind. The future potential of solidarity in an individualized society (Hondrich and Koch-Arzberger 1992) can only be developed by more and not less state welfare.

There is a strong theoretical argument and enough empirical evidence to interpret the changes in the social structure in Europe in terms of class analysis. Roughly summing up our thesis, we should have to start by investigating the primary inequalities in income and resources between the economic classes of (industrial) capital and (productive) labour, and then take into account the redistribution within these classes (shares of commercial capital etc.; non-productive labour, services etc.) as well as the redistribution of income by the state (transfer payments, pensions). The next steps would distinguish the levels of control and qualification and the cleavages caused by gender, ethnicity and nationality as well as regional features of historical development. On the grounds of this 'space of social positions' structured by the unequal distribution of resources, one could begin with investigations into the symbolic dimension, expressed in lifestyles.

Conclusion

In this chapter we have examined recent changes in class composition in Europe. We started with observations by Dahrendorf who as early as in the 1960s indicated both the general trends in Europe towards the 'service class society' and significant variations due to national, regional and cultural distinctions. Thus we demonstrated that the idea of other lines of cleavage cutting across those of class is one of the major issues of post war sociology.

A second part of the chapter dealt with the remarkable renaissance of Marxist thought within the social sciences in the 1970s. Class theory and class analysis became the prominent strategies of a critical sociology emphasizing proletarianization of the work force rather than workers' embourgeoisement. The results of some of the relevant studies like those of Hagelstange and Wright show similarities as well as distinctions between the countries of Europe due to their economic development. Comparing European countries with North America one can see that the tendencies of levelling out the differences between the countries is not primarily a consequence of the institutional preconditions of the European

Community but rather one of general modernization processes taking place in all capitalist societies.

The third part summarized those investigations in the social structure which were done in the 1980s and which can be understood both as a reaction to Neo-Marxist class analysis and as an expression of the far reaching changes after a long period of prosperity and social welfare. On the one hand, new identities stimulated by the processes of individualization and by a pluralization of lifestyles and, on the other hand, new gaps within societies and between some of the European countries, make for a picture of variety and heterogeneity, including new forms of polarization and cleavages in all advanced societies. We discussed the thesis of a general trend towards societies criss-crossed by multidimensional inequalities and demonstrated that there is no one factor which like class position influences the social chances of individuals in modern capitalist society.

We ended up by summarizing the major intermediating effects, among which, the kind and amount of welfare state transfers, the feminization of parts of the labour market, and the linkages between class position and symbolically signalised spaces of distinction and lifestyles, are the most prominent. Our main thesis is that the plurality of lifestyles and an ever growing degree of individualization is not contradictory to an analysis of the capitalist economy as containing an underlying fundamental class dichotomy. Therefore, we argued, the topics of traditional class formation and new group identities must not be dealt with separately from the contradictions and conflicts within advanced capitalist society.

2 Gender, individualism and social change

Jenny Ryan

Introduction

Within current concerns to map out the changing patterns of culture and of social relations in Europe, there is a growing interest in exploring how accepted definitions of gender roles are being challenged by changing labour market conditions and by the restructuring of family and household forms. In particular it is changes in the family that excite the most commentary in which, depending on the political persuasion of the commentator, the consequences of a growing diversity of family patterns are interpreted either in negative or positive terms. Hence, on one reading, the traditional family and its values are held to be in decline; with the breakdown of the family symptomatic of the moral and social disorder through which both social and individual ills of modern society are to be understood (Dennis and Erdos 1993, Davies 1993). In this argument it is both society and (individual) men, women and children who are depicted as the casualties of social changes undermining the institution of the family and the organization of personal life. In place of the stable framework that the 'traditional' family, and its values, provided we are invited to digest the prospect of an untrammelled explosion of lifestyle decisions and choices about marriage, parenting, family life. In the process of pursuing their self interests, men and women (but especially women) are held to undermine the social values upon which the stability of society is based. From this viewpoint the family is no longer central to the social order but rather a source of social disorder.

In this paper the wider corollaries of this argument will not be focused upon. No attempt will be made to explore issues of criminality, delinquency or any other such indicators of social malaise. Instead the focus is upon examining the claims being made about the breakdown of the family and the reorganization of gender roles. In the process of examining these issues another reading of the changes taking place is being suggested. They present new opportunities for women to take charge of their personal lives in ways that could not have been anticipated by earlier generations. Whether this is emancipatory either for them, for their children and for society is conditioned by ways in which these opportunities are still crucially structured by the gender inequalities in the labour market and within household organization.

The first question to be explored then is that of how far equality between the sexes is being fostered by changes in ideas and values underpinning contemporary family/household structures and patterns of parenting. How far does the formation of different family/household structures impact on the life choices open to women? Are there significant changes in how both men and women are integrating parenting within their lifestyles and life choices?

The second question to be explored focuses upon how the restructuring of the labour force impacts upon the ways in which the priorities of family life and paid work are adjusted to each other. Do the different life choices open to women and men in adjusting these priorities still reflect the determining influence of the private sphere for women and that of the public sphere for men? Or can it be argued that changes in how women relate to both the family and work suggest significant advances towards greater gender equality in making choices about how to combine family life and work (paid and unpaid)?

The empirical exploration of these questions furnishes material through which to assess arguments about the impact of institutional and cultural change on both the individual and society, but most crucially upon women. Within the perspectives that have developed in the post 1960s wave of feminisms is a recognition that the ways in which women are subordinate to men in society have changed (Walby 1990). The opportunities and experiences of contemporary women are interwoven in the changes in the family, in the labour market and in the climate of enhanced life choices with which this paper is concerned. Through this lens lifestyle choices for women are not some unfortunate outcome of a society breaking down into excessive individualism, but a significant way in which the battle for greater equality for women is being waged. The extent to which the battle is being won will be a theme of the analysis which follows.

The discussion is mounted within a Western European context with statistical data being drawn upon from a variety of sources. This broad task has to be sensitive also to the significance of local variation and local patterns within Europe (Harding, Phillips and Fogarty 1986, Vianello and Siemienska 1990, Boh, Bak and Clason 1990, Glasner 1992). One instance of the complexity of responses across Europe within a common experience is that of local variations in the labour market positions of women. The emergence of more and more women into the labour market has been evident across European societies in the post war period, but the pattern of labour market participation shows significant variations in how women in different European societies work part-time or full-time after marriage and child bearing. Similarly whilst there is an overall increase in the rate of divorce across

Europe, divorce statistics demonstrate the degree of local variations in divorce and remarriage patterns between societies. It is clear therefore in exploring any movement towards greater gender equality that the uneven development of any changes taking place must be recognized. The analysis must be sensitive to the impact of local historical experience and material/cultural factors that condition the patterns of family/household formation and the patterns of women's work.

Marriage, divorce and domestic organization

The analysis begins with examination of statistical evidence about patterns of domestic organization. Despite continuities in women's experiences of caring roles it can nevertheless be argued that there have been important changes in the household and family conditions within which this caring work is performed.[1] This is revealed in an analysis of changing patterns of household formation.

Comparative data across Europe and the USA documents the trends in patterns of marriage, divorce and parenting, and about how people feel about the changes taking place.[2] Since 1960 the marriage rate across the European Union has been declining from 7.8 marriages per thousand of the population in 1960 to 5.9 per thousand in 1989 (Statistical Office of the European Communities 1992). The lowest rate is recorded for France at four per thousand in the period 1986-88. Accompanying the decline in marriage rate has been an increase in the ages at which men and women marry for the first time. The earlier trend in the 1960s and 1970s towards a lower age at first marriage reversed in the 1980s. In 1988, across the European Union the average age at first marriage was 27.3 years for men and 24.9 years for women. In 1960, the corresponding ages were 26.9 and 24.1 respectively. Denmark is the country where the age at first marriage is highest - 29.8 years for men and 27.4 years for women. Greece and the United Kingdom have the lowest ages at first marriage, 25.8 years for men in the United Kingdom and 23.5 years for women in Greece (Statistical Office of the European Communities 1992).

As will be discussed later this overall trend has to be understood in the context of how far commitment to marriage as an institution, and the age at which this commitment is being made, is coexistent with patterns of cohabitation. Age at first marriage in itself does not tell us anything about the effect of this new pattern of family formation, or about how far cohabitation or marriage are seen either as alternative types of family pattern of a long duration or as stages in the lifecourse. With this qualification then it can be seen, however, that at the same time as age at marriage is increasing, and the marriage rate is decreasing, a significant shift is taking place in the divorce rate across Europe.

The divorce rate has increased from 0.4 per 1,000 population in 1960 to 1.6 per 1,000 in 1989. Denmark has the highest recorded rate at three divorces per 1,000 population. The United Kingdom closely follows with a divorce rate of 2.9 per

1,000 population making it the European State (on available data) with the second highest rate of divorce. The member states with the lowest recorded divorce rates in 1989 were Italy and Greece with a rate of 0.5 and Spain with a rate of 0.6 (Statistical Office of the European Communities 1992) The Republic of Ireland is the only member state where divorce was not possible, although the position has been changed by the referendum of 1995.

If we relate this statistical picture on divorce to comparative social attitude data we can explore the changes in social attitudes towards the family and marriage which may help account for rising divorce rates. Whether such data indicates that there is a decline in what are often termed 'traditional' family values and/or how the status of marriage has changed for people in Europe is more problematical. It should be remembered that what are defined as traditional family values are of very recent, post second world war, origin. They reached their height of dissemination in the 1950s and early 1960s and have been declining ever since. Hence populist concerns such as that expressed in one recent tabloid press article in Britain claiming that 'women are shunning marriage and motherhood'[3] should be interpreted with great caution. There is little evidence to suggest that this is so, or that it is in any case a historically significant contemporary shift. What is significant is that there are marked changes in women's attitudes towards what is a successful marriage, and upon their preference for divorce rather than a bad marriage. A recent analysis of International Social Survey Data looked at the responses of men and women to questions in the following areas of the organization of the private sphere: desirability of marriage; attitudes towards cohabitation (living together outside marriage); the purpose of marriage; the value placed on children; the acceptability of divorce; and the acceptability of lone parent family arrangements (Scott, Braun and Alwin 1993). The data analysed compared the social attitudes of men and women in Britain, USA, Republic of Ireland and Germany.[4]

The analysis affirms that, despite some difference in attitude between the four countries, there is a general rejection, by both men and women, of the notion that 'a bad marriage is better than no marriage at all'. (Scott, Braun and Alwin, 1993, p. 29). In a further study Elchardus and Heyvaert (1991) found this readiness to accept divorce was accompanied by a positive attitude in women to the prospect of living alone. The data from the Scott, Braun and Alwin study also shows that women are more sceptical about marital happiness. Women are less convinced than men that marriage brings happiness, and they are more favourably disposed towards divorce, as an escape route from an unhappy marriage, than are men. In terms of cross cultural comparisons they also note that, of the four countries compared, West German and British women and men are the least convinced of the likelihood of marital happiness. Women, and men, in these two societies are also reported as being most in favour of cohabiting before marriage.

The age factor makes itself most felt in terms of whom is most and least likely to hold this view. In Britain only 17 per cent of women and men born in the period

1950-70 felt that people should marry before living together compared to 64 per cent (men) and 61 per cent (women) born before 1930 who held this opinion. A similar age difference in opinion is found in West Germany, the proportions being 23 per cent and 21 per cent for the men and women born between 1950 and 1970, and 59 per cent, 54 per cent for the pre-1930 generation.

In Britain, this belief in cohabiting before marriage does not mean, as for example is suggested for the Netherlands and Scandinavia, that cohabitation is seen as an alternative to marriage.[5] Rather it appears that, whilst young British women and men are realistic about the need for the experience of cohabitation before commitment to marriage, marriage is still a popular institution. Boh argues that, despite the increasing evidence of cohabitation as 'trial marriage', there is little evidence that 'at least for the time being cohabitation will replace marriage' (Boh, Bak and Clason, 1990, p. 279). At the same time, the high divorce rate in Britain suggests that fundamental changes are taking place in how women and men position themselves within marriage. In particular, it is women who are now prepared to end marriages that do not work. Any links between the effect of cohabitation before marriage, attitudes to marriage and divorce rates have to be interpreted with caution. The preparedness to seek divorce may be the result of it being easier to obtain because of financial support for legal costs incurred. It may also be that what is being experienced in Britain, in terms of increased divorce, may mean that Britain is at the forefront of a more widespread movement which other advanced societies will experience at a later stage.

Nevertheless some interesting comparisons in relating these factors can be drawn. If we compare the British data to that for West Germany we find that men and women in both societies are sceptical about marriage and take a relaxed attitude towards cohabitation as a preliminary stage before marriage. Yet the divorce rate for West Germany is much lower than that found in Britain. Clearly, as one would anticipate, other social factors must be brought in to explain the difference in divorce rate between the two societies. An interesting response from the West Germans interviewed about the reasons for marriage may be suggestive of why the divorce rate in West Germany is not amongst the highest. 34 per cent of women respondents and 30 per cent of men in West Germany gave the main advantage of marriage as 'financial security' (Scott, Braun and Alwin, 1993, p. 29). The authors concluded from this that the existing tax policy in West Germany favouring married couples is an incentive to stay married. Such effects of changes in tax policies upon the marriage institution have yet to be thoroughly investigated empirically. Until such data is available caution must be expressed in making the connection between taxation policies and the stability of marriage. Hence recent changes in tax policy in Britain, with the increasing attention to the separate taxation status of men and women, on divorce rate cannot yet be reliably evaluated. This is despite the populist rhetoric that it is getting both easier, and more profitable, for individuals to divorce and hence the stability of marriage is undermined.

The examples given above raise questions about the extent to which state policy can be said to influence the organization of the private sphere in terms of providing incentives or disincentives for people to marry and/or maintain stable domestic relationships.[6]

This influence has to be weighed against other factors which shape perceptions about the desirability of either marriage or cohabitation. Social attitude data from the Netherlands and from Belgium suggests that women and men in those societies do not see cohabiting as a preliminary to marriage, rather it is accepted as an alternative to marriage (Harding, Phillips and Foggarty 1986, Elchardus and Heyvaert 1991). Whilst the institution of marriage may be viewed differently in these European societies this may not necessarily be associated with other differences in attitude and behaviour. For example the extent to which children are borne outside of marriage is not correspondingly higher in the Netherlands than in other societies where more supportive attitudes towards the marital status hold.

Whilst there has been across Europe a steady increase in births recorded outside of marriage, the highest rates are to be found in Denmark, France and Britain (Statistical Office of the European Communities 1992). Sweden may be the exceptional case where both cohabitation and high birth rate outside marriage occurs.[7] Perhaps not surprisingly in terms of the influence of both religious factors and levels of economic development, the lowest rates of births outside marriage are found in Italy and Greece. It is to aspects of continuity and change in the organization of parenting functions inside and outside marriage that we now turn.

Household composition and single parenting patterns in Europe

Trends indicate that households are not only becoming smaller in size but also changing in their social composition. The average number of persons per household across the European Union in 1986 is described as 2.7 persons. Belgium, France, the Netherlands and the United Kingdom record average household size at this European level. The Southern European member states - Greece, Portugal, Italy, and Spain all record average household sizes of 3 persons and above, as does Ireland which shares with Spain the highest average household sizes at 3.5 (Ireland) and 3.6 (Spain) persons per household (Statistical Office of the European Communities 1992). Differences such as these reflect a number of cultural and social factors through which different religious values and social attitudes towards parenting and the extended family/kinship patterns impact on the size of the nuclear family.

Caution must be exercised when interpreting these statistics in terms of social trends. Underlying demographic changes will also impact differentially in terms of the relative decline in fertility between different societies. It is not however so much the size of the household, as changes in its composition that has attracted widespread debate. This has centred critically upon the rise of single parent households, the majority of which are headed by women. Britain is reportedly at the top of a table which indicates the percentage of women aged 20-39 heading single parent households. Ten per cent of women in that age group are so positioned in Britain compared to eight per cent of West German women, seven per cent of Belgium women and six per cent of French women. By contrast, and with interesting reflections on the attitudes to cohabiting outside marriage described earlier, only 4.5 per cent of Dutch women in the same age group head single parent households.

As could be expected, the countries with the lowest percentages of single parent female headed households, are Greece, Spain and Italy, all of whom have proportions of below three per cent. Given the influence of religion, and the absence of the right to divorce, the six per cent reported for Ireland is anomalous and requires further explanation. Reports quoted by Boh similarly estimate that in Finland, Sweden and the (old) German Democratic Republic, the rates of female single parent headed families is 15 per cent, 12 per cent and 12 per cent respectively. [8]

How significant are these statistics in the context of available evidence about social attitudes to parenting responsibilities? Is the increase in the numbers of single parented households indicative of a fundamental change in attachment to 'traditional' family values in Europe? Recent comparative data on social attitudes towards parenting suggests that the great majority of Europeans (including 84 per cent of those actually married) feel that a child needs two parents in the home (Harding, Phillips and Foggarty, 1986, p. 117). Italy, Spain, West Germany, Belgium and France report highest support for this opinion with proportions of 80 per cent and over. By contrast only 55 per cent of Danes, 67 per cent of Britons and 69 per cent of Irish respondents (men and women) in the same survey felt that a child needed two parents in the home. The same study however reports a growing tolerance amongst people, under thirty five years old, towards the idea of a woman choosing to have a child without a stable relationship with a man. France and Denmark stand out as countries showing the most approval for this behaviour, in the former case this is consistent with the earlier reported statistic that France has the lowest marriage rate across Europe.

In Denmark there is a consistency in the attitudes towards the two questions. Danish people show both least support for the statement on dual parenting and most support for the positive extreme of single parenting (Harding, Phillips, Foggarty, 1986, p. 121). Ireland exhibits the lowest approval across Europe for consciously motivated single parenting but is not amongst the highest rate of support for dual parenting. These attitudes have to be understood in the context of statistics which demonstrate that Ireland has an illegitimacy rate of approximately 19 per cent (of live births) and a single parenthood rate of six per cent (of women aged 20-39 who head single parent households). In the light of these statistics and in the absence of any legal rights to divorce, it is not surprising that the Irish have been ambivalent on the question of appropriate patterns of parenting.

In comparison with other Europeans the Dutch appear, from available data, to fall squarely in between both extremes of support or disapproval for parenting behaviour different to the two parent family household. 74 per cent of Dutch respondents to Harding's survey felt that a child needed two parents and 31 per cent felt approval for the positive single parenting by women. Both percentages fall in the middle of the range in relation to the other European societies being compared.

A more detailed analysis is required of how these attitudes to parenting are located within a wider spectrum of opinions and values as to what makes for successful marriage, the rules for sexual behaviour in marriage and opinions about the raising of children. Notwithstanding this, and in an exploratory way, certain general conclusions can be drawn from the analysis so far. According to Harding 'three-quarters of all Europeans, and four out of five of those actually married, do not believe that marriage is an outdated institution (Harding, Phillips and Fogarty, 1986, p. 116). What has changed significantly is how marriage fits into the expectations people have of satisfactory long term relationships, and the willingness of women especially to end unsuccessful marriages. The tolerance for single parenting is also growing although within a cultural context which, whilst the stigma attached is declining, there is still a widespread believe in dual parenting. This may help account for the growing practice of second marriages and the establishment of much more differentiated household units, inside and outside marriage. In such households the children of previous relationships are integrated within new partnerships. The sharing of the responsibilities for custody between both parents suggests that the boundaries of the family unit may shift both in a temporal and spatial sense. Although these new forms of family have yet to be researched it is likely that the establishment of new forms of parenting around weekly, weekend or longer time routines has the effect of expanding or contracting what at any point in time constitutes the household for daily purposes of living. The statistical measure of single parent headed households will not capture the dynamics or diversity of these new family forms. It is clear that the concept of the family as a static, bounded unit of a nucleus of relationships becomes redundant in depicting these relationships.

It is in this sense perhaps that Rapoport is suggesting that this diversity of family forms, in which the conventional nuclear family is only one variant, is increasingly characterizing the new patterning of parenting and family life (Rapoport, 1990, p. 62). In her analysis each particular family form is seen as providing the structure for a lifestyle. It is in this contemporary recognition that the form the family takes becomes more a matter of individual choice than a prescribed constraint that the most profound implications for both society and the individual are suggested. This use of the concept of lifestyle to describe the family is not one that trivializes, or suggests instability, in the denigrating way in which the term lifestyle is often used. The radical consequences of what is happening to family if it becomes a matter of lifestyle choice have not gone unrecognized by critics from the right, such as Davies:

Marriage is now the great romantic act: everything ventured upon one great gesture of individualism....The logic of this drive to individualise the marriage decision is of course the drive to individualise the marriage relationship itself, with both spousal and parental responsibilities being increasingly regarded as matters of taste and fashion rather than of permanent social commitment. (Davies, 1993, p. 100)

What is implied here is that somehow lifestyle choices are not only more trivial, producing less stable motivations to marriage, but that they are evidence of a moral and social decline in society. One cannot escape the conclusion that Davies directs this interpretation particularly at the culpability of women for this decline, since evidence suggests that it is women more than men who are currently questioning the marital status and seeking divorce. What is conveniently ignored is that in the past decisions about whether to marry, or stay in marriages, were often conditioned for women by economic necessity and legal restriction.

The durability of marriages in the past, therefore, is not necessarily evidence that they were rooted in more meaningful heterosexual relationships than those presently experienced. Such evidence, as the history of marriage suggests, cannot therefore be taken to infer, in itself, that changes in how and why individuals form heterosexual unions of different forms can be held responsible for present social ills. Social and economic circumstances mediate the effects of current movements in the formation and dissolution of partnerships and marriages. After all, it is not middle class couples splitting up that Davies, and Dennis and Erdos focus upon in their theses about the deleterious impact of 'lifestyle families'. It seems that family as lifestyle is an acceptable social change if applied to the middle classes but helps create an urban underclass if applied to the working class, as seen for example in the work of Murray recently applied to the British experience (Murray 1990).

This undertone of moralizing about what is essentially a social class rather than a gender phenomenon is absent in another contemporary commentator on social change - Ulrich Beck. Beck is also alluding to what he sees as a revolutionary change when he discusses the basis of gender relations in the 'risk society' (Beck 1992). For Beck, the crumbling structure of the private sphere, with particular reference to the family, is significant for the breakdown of the feudal relations of gender that he claims have been the constant source of tension within modern society. At the heart of modern society, he claims, in which achievement of the individual is central, there has also been a counter-modern tendency in which gender relations are ascribed i.e. immutable and beyond individual control. In the 'risk society', that is advanced societies of today, this feudal order is dissolving with the transformation of institutions, like the family. As far as gender relations are concerned, this creates the possibility not only for women to move outside ascribed roles and behaviour, but for both men and women to construct and combine their biographies in different ways over their life course. It is this possibility of a continual process of transformation and change that the concept of 'family as lifestyle' explores in ways which suggest more fluidity and movement than more conventional analyses of the family.

Rapoport also cautions the need to understand the wider social trends which are responsible for variations in the creation of different family/household forms, and how women are positioned within them. For example, it is through the construction of women by the state, and the operations of the market, that the freedom to pursue differentiated lifestyles, forms of parenting and family life is constrained. Nevertheless the contemporary opportunity for women, albeit often in conditions of poverty and deprivation, to exercize more choice over their private lives cannot be denied. The principle of the right to choose now covers not only the control over reproduction but other conditions of family life

How this diversity model of different family forms should therefore inform the practices of social policy towards the family and women is a key issue for Rapoport (1990). But what is clear is that whilst the organization of the private sphere of the family is becoming increasingly complex and differentiated, this does not necessarily imply a significant fragmentation of its effects on the gender inequalities experienced by women. In Beck's terms what has been extended are the conditions of personal risk which may be born differentially by men and women. If, as could be anticipated, gender ideologies about the proper roles of men and women are not transformed to the same rate or degree, then structural, institutional changes in the family are likely to carry more risks for women than for men. The stigmatizing of the single mother in the social mythology of the aetiology of criminality and deviance is ample demonstration of this risk. Whether or not changes in the form of the family emancipate or further impoverish women will, to a large extent, be influenced by the role that state welfare policies play in constructing women, and in supporting and/or policing these new family forms. How far they become valued as positive alternatives to the nuclear family will depend upon how they are constructed in ideological terms in both popular and official discourses.

In this period of change certain social patterns do appear to remain constant across Europe, although with local variations. These relate to the sexual division of labour in the home which, despite the increasing rate of female participation in the labour market, still centrally locates women at the heart of household work and child care and marginalize men in both these areas. This continues to crucially determine the different gendered ways in which women and men participate in the labour market.

The restructuring of the labour market and domestic organization

In relating changes in labour market participation to changes in the family/household system, a central question becomes that of how far the changes in the private sphere described above are impacting upon the involvement of women in the public sphere of paid work. Again it is Beck (1992) for whom contemporary changes in attitudes are highlighting crucial questions about the contradictions between the organization of market societies and private life.

> Thought through to its ultimate consequence, the market model of modernity implies a society without families and children. Everyone must be independent, free for the demands of the market in order to guarantee his/her economic existence. The market subject is ultimately the single individual 'unhindered' by a relationship, marriage or family. Correspondingly the ultimate market society is a childless society - unless children grow up with mobile, single fathers and mothers. (Beck, 1992, p. 115)

Clearly such a society is a theoretical abstraction only. Were Beck to relate this model to a real society it would be possible to analyse how social class and gender differences mediate the tensions of relating the market to the family. In the absence however of such an empirical focus, Beck still wants to argue for the revolutionary impact of contemporary experience which is, in some revelationary fashion, 'bursting open these contradictions' and 'promoting a new kind of consciousness which can find no amelioration to the problems in institutional terms' (Beck, 1992, p. 116). Put in simpler language, Beck is claiming that because increasingly the pressures on individuals to realize themselves is not being matched by changes in social institutions themselves (like the family and work organizations) then more strain is taken in the investments placed in personal relationships (especially in the family). This investment carries a high risk premium at the level of such relationships, as couples try to resolve the contradictions between the market and the requirements of private life. New pressures and problems for bonds of intimacy are at the core of conflict and tension.

A major criticism that can be levelled at Beck is that he does not explore what happens to the institution of the family itself in the process. Consequently he has little to say about the structural and power dimensions of gender relations and ideology within which the personal is framed. It can be argued though that it is precisely the continued gendered nature of both the market and the private within which the roots of personal experience are located, and thus the effects of these new conditions of personal risk are felt. It is important to recognize these material and ideological historical realities. This criticism of Beck can be explored if we turn to an analysis of the relationship between labour market participation and family life in different societies.

According to 1983 survey data, 28 per cent of both women and men across Europe preferred the 'traditional' pattern of wives running the home and the husband only having a paid job outside the home. The same study also reported that there was 66 per cent support for families where the wife has a job outside the home. The conclusion was drawn that, whilst the traditional patterns had lost ground, the general achievement of a full symmetricality (equal involvement of women and men in work/home) is still a long way off (Harding, Phillips and Foggarty, 1986, p. 130). Nevertheless, one of the most distinctive changes in labour market participation in Europe has been the increased proportions of married women working outside the home.

Boh characterizes the differences in female labour market participation within Europe in terms of low, medium and high employment patterns (Boh, Bak and Clason, 1990, p. 270). Among the countries demonstrating low participation, the Netherlands is held to be different from the others because of its high proportion of part-time women employees compared to the low proportion of part-time women workers in Belgium, for example. Italy and West Germany are also characterized as falling in the low participation category. The medium employment pattern appears in Finland, France, Hungary and Slovenia where in each case the employment rate of women is higher than 40 per cent and of married women between 35-65. All of these countries have low part-time rates of employment of women.

Great Britain, Norway and Sweden have a pattern of female employment which falls between the low and medium types. Boh calls this pattern the 'high part-time pattern'. Its main feature is that whilst having employment rates for women of over 40 per cent, this is made up largely of part-time workers. If we compare the pattern of female employment in Britain with that of the Netherlands, a key difference is that whilst both exhibit high rates of part-time employment of women, this represents a much lower volume of women in absolute terms in the Netherlands than in Britain. The Netherlands has a low participation rate - high part-time rate, whilst Britain has a medium participation - high part-time rate. Given a much higher divorce rate and proportion of single parent households in Britain than the Netherlands, is it the case that more women in Britain need to work to support their families than is the case in the Netherlands? Is it this interaction of household form and work patterns that explains the difference rather than the need of the economy for female labour itself?

The contrast however must also be approached historically. One distinctive feature of recent employment history is the different impact of the second world war on women's participation in the economy in Britain and the Netherlands. According to Clason, (Boh, Bak and Clason 1990) the war did not lead to a large scale take over of jobs by women in the Netherlands, as it did in Britain. This was attributed to women withdrawing from the labour market in order to ensure that men did not have to take forced employment abroad, a move supported by the women's movement in the Netherlands as 'patriotic'. Clason argues that it has taken a long time for this tendency to change and that it accounts for the low increase in female employment. Equally, however, as Boh indicates, to explain the difference in pattern of female employment a much broader analysis of factors is necessary.

The employment of women does not necessarily depend only on economic factors but is related to employment policies, prevailing family ideologies, political practices, historical traditions and cultural values and norms. (Boh, Bak and Clason, 1990, p. 27)

Taking this perspective the fact that western Europe does not exhibit any cases of Boh's third category of high employment participation is understandable. This pattern, characteristic of socialist command economies (Poland, the old USSR and GDR), describes a very high participation of women in the labour market. There is however growing evidence of the impact for women's employment and for domestic organization of, amongst other factors, the growing problems of unemployment in these countries (Watson, 1993, p. 475).

Part-time work, gendered job segregation and domestic organization

Increased female participation in the labour market has grown in parallel with part-time work especially amongst married women. In 1989, 36 per cent of married women worked part-time (Commission of the European Communities 1989). The expansion of this kind of employment within the service sectors of advanced economies in Europe confirms the continuity of gender segregation in labour markets. This suggests a pattern of work for women in which flexibilization is accompanied by uncertain hours of employment, short notice of work schedules and job insecurity, all factors indicative of a weak labour market position (Elchardus and Heyvaert 1991).

Women accounted for approximately 45 per cent of all workers in the service sector in 1989 (Statistical Office of the European Communities 1992). Glasner suggests that work in the service industries, primarily located at the low pay, low skill end of the sector, accounts for 75 per cent of employed women in Europe (Glasner 1992). She goes on to argue that evidence suggests a correlation between high participation rates of women in the labour market and high degrees of gendered job segregation. Countries with the highest female participation rate also exhibit the strongest degrees of occupational segregation by gender (Glasner, 1992, p. 88).

In accounting for the employment patterns of women workers, there is obviously a need to disentangle the effects of government policies, equal pay and equal conditions of work legislation and economic/political factors from personal factors such as how women and men make lifestyle choices within different family formations. Caution has also to be shown in interpreting the pattern of participation since similar overall patterns may obscure different varieties of actual experience.[9]

The conventional way to account for the different employment profile of women compared to men is to regard them effectively as a different labour force. The theoretical construction of women as a 'reserve army of labour' brought into the labour market and dispensed with as economic conditions dictate has been widely used for this purpose (Braverman 1974, Beechey 1978, Bruegal 1979). This kind of analysis suggests a marginal role for women in the public sphere of paid work which, whilst useful for accounting for the pattern of women's employment in the past, may not be so relevant in the changed contemporary conditions. Given the overall economic restructuring which has characterized the advanced European economies, the growth of flexible work patterns, casualization and feminization have profound gender implications for the employment of women that are now being realized.

The work experience of women is central to these processes of change rather than marginal to them. The way women combine new and differentiated work patterns with changes in the organization of parenting and the family indicates the need to look afresh at the conventional divide drawn between the public and the private spheres. Both spheres are changing, both are in a different relationship to each other. The way in which women mediate the boundaries of the two spheres in their everyday lives is a crucial dimension of these changes.

Labour market participation is being integrated in different patterns with forms of parenting and family. For example, it can be tentatively suggested that the pattern exhibited in Denmark and in the United Kingdom shares certain similar features but also differences. Both countries have amongst the highest percentages of births outside marriage, and in the case of the United Kingdom one of the highest rates of female headed single parenting. In parallel with these features both countries are at the top of tables for the percentage of women working with high participation rates for married women. The juxtaposition of part -time female employment and single parenting in the United Kingdom could be suggestive of one kind of accommodation of the public and private. In fact, however, female heads of households of single parent families do not have high rates of labour market participation in that country; rather it is married women who largely make up the profile of female part -time working. Similarly in Denmark the pattern may be one where such an integration reflects the fit between dual parenting demands and employment. By contrast in the Netherlands, with an illegitimacy rate below the European average and a low percentage of female headed single parent households, there is also a relatively low female labour market participation, albeit one where part-time work predominates. This is suggestive of an accommodation in which part-time work is located within a dual parenting function but at a much lesser rate of labour market participation by women. Again, no direct causal connection is being suggested by drawing these tentative parallels. Rather the purpose is to reveal the complexities within which the relationship of the public and the private spheres must be viewed. The wider context must also be recognized of the effect of state intervention in the lifestyle choices made by men and women in regard to the family form and employment pattern they adopt. As Cernigoj-Sadar indicates:

Paid work and family life are becoming parallel life priorities for which people may have different motivations. It is difficult to determine which motive predominates because the prevailing state ideology, the economic situation of the family and individual motivation are often intertwined. However both spheres of life are strongly inter-related from a subjective point of view, no matter to what extent paid work and family are formally segregated and evaluated. Men's and women's experiences of the paid work/ family interactions may inhibit or enhance their attitudes towards changes of family patterns. (Cernigoj-Sadar, 1990, p. 142)

She goes on to argue that studies of the roles of men and women in paid work and the family confirm that the family has a constraining influence for women in the sphere of paid work, whilst the reverse is true for men. Paid work strongly limits the participation of men in family life. This somewhat commonplace observation is held to be associated with accounts of the stress experienced at the psychological level by women in relation to distress, low career aspirations and commitment in addition to an assumed lower achievement motivation amongst women. At the same time women are cited as experiencing paid work as a source of satisfaction in terms of social relationships with other workers, and as seeking this kind of job satisfaction compared to the different motivations of men. Men, it is argued look to paid work to furnish new skills and knowledge.

This kind of analysis can be contrasted to that of Curtice (1993) who draws attention to what he terms the 'part time paradox' in relation to job satisfaction. The paradox refers to the attitudes of women to their low paid, often low skilled and precarious employment prospects. Recent data, Curtice suggests, demonstrates that women report higher level of job satisfaction than men. Across Europe, he argues, not only do part-time women workers express job satisfaction but that, even if a comparison is made between full-time women and men, women still have a higher rate of satisfaction than men. Sources of job satisfaction for both sets of women are very similar, and do not appear to be related to levels of pay or flexibility of working hours. Conventional explanations of women workers being less committed or motivated than male workers are rejected by Curtice who finds no significant gender differences in this respect in his data. Neither do part-time female workers appear to be less committed than their full-time equivalent.

The explanation for the phenomena, he suggests, is that whilst the economic circumstances of part-time work are disadvantageous there are real psychological compensations to this kind of work (Curtice, 1993, p. 114). Part-time workers refer to lower levels of stress and the relative ease of combining work with their other parallel life choices/commitments. Unlike earlier studies of the expectations and motivations of women workers, Curtice is not suggesting that women define themselves as marginal to the work place. Rather it is implied that women are resolving the demands of both spheres as a matter of personal and subjective life choices. In line with the arguments developed earlier it can be suggested that what we may be observing in these adjustments is a transformation of individual interests, as defined through choices about family commitments and employment, within structures of work organization that are not being transformed at the same rate. It may be a case, as Beck (1992, p. 104) argues of 'consciousness running ahead of conditions'. Despite the evidence he sees of a crumbling away of the old structures of the private sphere, he argues that the organization of work is not being altered to the same degree. But although not by design, it could be argued that it is in the casualization and feminization of the labour market that this cultural change is being exploited in the interests of capital, without any reference to intervention which would make this process more beneficial for both women, men and their families.

Patriarchy, individualism and gender inequality

The aim of the foregoing analysis of change across Europe has been to raise questions concerning how far gender inequalities continue to shape the life experiences of women in the ways domestic organization and work are structured. This analysis suggests that significant differences between women and men still exist in how they combine these priorities in their lifestyles and lifestyle choices. Reference has been made to the variations between European states in the relationship between the restructuring of the labour market and domestic organization. What emerges however is a picture in which it has been demonstrated that women's experiences of both work and the family have changed in significant ways. Yet this does not signify that in the process much advance has been made towards greater gender equality. The ability of women to set up households independent of men is still at the risk of financial insecurity and/or dependence on the state. The participation of women in the labour market is still under conditions of gender segregation in terms of the kinds of employment, its pay and conditions. So how best can the changes that have taken place be understood?

The most common tool of analysis of gender inequalities, that of patriarchy, distinguishes between separate spheres of activity for women and men constructed in ideologies of the public and the private (Hearn 1992, Walby 1990). This dichotomy between the public and the private has been variously employed to characterize both gendered participation in society and the structure of power relations. In the emergence of modern industrial society, a social order stabilized in which the proper place of women was located in the private sphere of the hearth and home, and of men in the public sphere of employment and politics. In the modern capitalist industrial society the organization of the family and of paid work became increasingly separate. Structural differentiation went hand in hand with the construction of new meanings which made life understandable. Central amongst these was the notion of the individual exercizing free and independent will within society through the application of reason.

36

This concept of the individual, which became enshrined in law and politics was deeply gendered in that it was most properly applied to men and characterized by their capacity for reason and rationality. The nature of women rendered them less complete, or flawed, as individuals in that they were identified with the sensual as opposed to the rational, with the natural processes of biological reproduction as compared to the identification of men with production. A concept of individualism flourished in the emergence of modern society which was closely identified with the reformation of the conditions of patriarchy. This took the form of the ideology of separate spheres. The relationship between the increasingly gendered participation in the structures of family and paid work, and the growth of gendered construction of notions of the individual was a strong one. For Walby, the conditions of 'private patriarchy' were established in which the state acted only to reinforce the dominance of women by men in the family through control of reproduction, property and in the last resort physical violence (Walby 1990). At the same time, the same construction of the rational (male) individual legitimated the dominance of men in the public sphere and the exclusion of women from it.

The conditions of private patriarchy, rooted in the family, and the ideology of individualism can be seen as mutually constitutive. They drew upon each other for support in the growth of modern society. The separate spheres of activity for men and women was built upon a whole repertoire and reservoir of cultural meanings about sexual difference and sexuality. Individuality was constructed through the meanings expressed in gender difference. As subjects, women were constructed through their position as Other in relation to men. Thus individuality for both women and men expressed itself in a core sense of who one was, unified and centred through the meanings given to femininity and masculinity.

If we explore the changes that are currently taking place in modern societies, then changes in the family can be assessed in terms of their impact on this construction of individualism. Is it being maintained or disrupted by the changes in family formation that have been discussed? Are the changes themselves to be seen as the result of a new kind of individualism emerging in advanced modern societies? The latter thesis is expressed in terms of subjectivity becoming decentred with the fragmentation of any unified sense of who one is, and with the idea that individuals can adopt a multiplicity of identities (Kellner 1992, Mort 1988, Rutherford 1990). Central to the thesis is the notion of reflexivity, that is the ability of individuals in making sense of their experience to self-consciously reflect upon themselves and their environment (Giddens 1991, Featherstone 1991, Beck 1992, Lash and Urry 1994). It is living with the personal insecurity that comes from this reflexivity that gives modern existence its particular edge.

In relation to the analysis of the social changes discussed in this paper, this personal insecurity is witnessed in the conditions of personal risk relating to decisions about whether to break up old and form new family relations and household forms, whether and how to combine the priorities of work and family and so forth. For Lash and Friedmann (1992) this risk further centres upon the identity choices that individuals are required to make, an experience which for Kellner becomes the natural state of contemporary life. He argues:

> In contemporary society it may be more 'natural' to change identities, to switch with the changing winds of fashion.....one can always change one's life, that identity can always be reconstructed, that one is free to change and produce oneself as one chooses. (Kellner, 1992, p. 154)

What was problematical, that is the anxieties of maintaining stable identity, become less so for the (post) modern self which, in Kellner's terms becomes 'more multiple, transitory and open' (Kellner, 1992, p. 158).

This thesis then is about the growth of a new kind of individualism. One in which the individual is more capable of reflection, can emancipate (him)self, and above all which is based upon widened and enhanced opportunities for choice in identities and lifestyles. This is expressed through the notion that we can be whosoever we choose, and can do whatsoever we like in our pursuit of lifestyle interests. What this analysis of contemporary life experience ignores, however, is issues of inequality in the chances to exercize this new freedom. The evidence presented in this paper, does suggest that there is an opening up of new life spaces and life choices for women. It suggests that gender relations take on new dimensions, for both men and women, through changes in cultural expectations in marriage and parenting, and in women's participation in the labour market. But any judgement about how extensive is the freedom enjoyed by women, compared to men, in this emancipation from constraints on personal choice, has to be a guarded one.

The analysis has suggested women are taking advantage of removing themselves from untenable marriages, single parent households are becoming more significant (but only as one amongst many diverse forms of family life) and women are more able to chose how to juggle paid work and domestic responsibilities. Gradually, within different class based experiences and different national patterns and priorities, women's dual roles as workers and mothers are being recognized. Yet, at the same time, the position of women in the labour market remains segregated into part-time, low paid and feminized jobs. For many, perhaps most, women the risk of setting up independent households, of finding ways of parenting outside marriage, is still one of financial penury and state dependency. The conditions of risk in generating a new self and a new lifestyle remain conditioned by gender inequalities albeit rooted in different power relations and structures of patriarchy.

Two questions remain therefore. The first is that of whether the new individualism emerging is as gendered as was the old form? The second is how widespread is the consciousness of new opportunities for change, both in terms of the attitudes of men and women and in relation to other social groups differentiated by class, race and ethnicity? If it is still the case that the awareness of opportunities is still mediated by these differences in experience then this would suggest a deepening of inequalities rather than their erosion. It was pointed out earlier that, on one reading, the impact on society of the changes taking place are seen as catastrophic for moral and social order. Even if this analysis is accepted, the explanation of why this should be so lies in why the problems emerge when women exercize the same rights to choose as men. By this reckoning the right for women to be individual is still couched within a culture, and power relations, which denies them the full value of both the rights and responsibilities of independence. Not surprisingly therefore both women and society suffer in the process.

Notes

1   Demographic trends suggest that the caring roles of women can be expected to increase, despite falling birth rates, due to responsibilities for an expanding generation of the aged. Across nation states there is a reliance on the unpaid, and poorly supported, work of women to meet this need, resulting in new conditions of poverty and dependence for middle aged and young elderly women. (See, amongst others, discussions in Fincher 1993, Stevenson 1994, Glendinning and Millar 1992, Finch and Groves 1983.)

2   The measurement of these trends is usually made by calculating the rate of change in the particular feature being described per thousand population. Caution has to be expressed in the use of such statistical measures because of the problems of lack of sensitivity to underlying demographic changes that they exhibit.

3   The Daily Mail, a British daily tabloid newspaper, ran the story under the headline 'The Singles Market: A career is the thing as women shun marriage all over Europe'. As analysed in the text, this moral panic has little substance in the evidence available.

4   The authors indicate that whilst datasets are also available for Austria, Italy, Hungary and the Netherlands this comparative data has not yet been incorporated into the analysis.

5   Stephen Harding refers to a personal communication with a Professor R. de Moor in which he claims that in the Netherlands and Scandinavia cohabiting is more widely accepted as an alternative to marriage than elsewhere in Europe (Harding, Phillips and Foggarty 1986). Similar conclusions are drawn by Boh (Boh, Bak and Clason 1990).

6   A recent observation, expressed by my colleague Mark Elchardus, makes the point that in another society, Belgium, changes in the tax laws do not appear to have influenced divorce trends. Empirical research needs to be undertaken to test out hypotheses regarding the relationship of tax laws to marriage and divorce decision-making by couples.

7   The main source of data upon which this analysis draws is that of the official statistical abstracts produced by the Bureau of the European Union. The latest edition 'Europe in Figures' uses data from 1989. (Statistical Office of the European Communities 1992). Caution must be exercised in interpreting these statistics and drawing conclusions from them. Definitional problems concerning the classification of, for example, married couples differentially including consensual unions in addition to legalized unions, is indicative of the need for this caution in making comparisons over time and across societies. The extent of self reporting of marital status is a critical issues in different data sets. Hence Sorrentino points out that, since 1980, Swedish household statistics have classified all cohabiting couples together whereas earlier censuses classified married couples in a separate category. Similar problems emerge with the classification of families with children and with single parent households. Estimates of the numbers of single parent families may be inadequate because of a widespread practice of excluding in this classification single parent families who are part of larger households (Sorrentino 1990).

8   However whilst not based on comparable data other sources indicate that Sweden in 1980 experienced a very high rate of births to unmarried mothers as a percentage of all births i.e. 37.5 per cent of all births were in this category compared to percentages of under ten per cent elsewhere (UN Demographic Yearbook 1969 projecting to 1980 quoted in Boh, Bak and Clason, 1990, p. 292).

9   Glasner points out for example that in Britain and France similar rates of the participation of women in the formal economy are accounted for in very different terms. In Britain, by part-time work and interrupted career employment, in France by continuity and work patterns not dissimilar to French male workers (Dex and Shaw 1986).

3 Class, cultural re-alignment and the rise of the populist Right

Mark Elchardus

Introduction

Over the last 10 years Europeans have witnessed the growth of many extreme right-wing parties. The Italian MSI (Italian Social Movement, now NA, National Alliance), the French FN (National Front), the Flemish *Vlaams Blok* (VB, Flemish Bloc), the Spanish AP (Popular Alliance, now PP, Popular Party), the Austrian FPÖ (Austrian Liberal Party), the Danish FRP (Progress Party) and others have had noticeable electoral successes. Prior to 1960 only two European right-wing parties had gained access to Parliament (the Italian MSI and the German NPD, National Socialist Party). Today such parties are present in the parliaments of most European states. In the 1995 French municipal elections, the National Front got a majority in two cities: Orange (more than 20,000 inhabitants) and Toulon (more than 100,000 inhabitants).

While electoral changes in post-war Europe tended to occur within ideological blocs, with shifts from one conservative party to another conservative party, or from one progressive party to another party of the same ideological family (Mair 1989), the new or newly successful right-wing parties attract voters from other ideological blocs and from a broad range of social strata (Ignazi 1992). As a matter of fact, the new extreme Right seems to be particularly attractive to working class and former leftist voters (for the Netherlands: Voerman and Lucardie, 1992, p. 49, for Germany: Minkenberg 1992, p. 73, Mayer and Perrineau, 1992, p. 129). In the recent French presidential election about 18 per cent of the people who voted for Jean Marie Le Pen (National Front), could on the basis of their attitudes and political positions be classified as Left or extreme Left (Jaffré, 1995, p. 15).

In this paper I search for an explanation of both the rise of a new extreme Right and of its ability to break through the partitions of the old ideological blocs and to attract many working class people, even when they have not relinquished their leftist positions. In dealing with these questions, I start from observations, concepts, and explanatory theories, that have been developed in the course of studying different European and North American societies. I shall, however, confront these concepts and theories with a more in-depth analysis of political developments in one particular Western society, Flanders. The purpose of doing so is twofold, to decipher a local political situation in the light of concepts and generalizations that have been elaborated elsewhere, and to test, at the same time, and hopefully refine theories that aspire to be valid for highly industrialised or post-industrial societies in general.

The apparent decline of class based voting

The 'unfreezing' of the ideological blocs and the ensuing possibility for new parties to grow by attracting voters from different ideological families, has been related to the alleged decline of class based politics. At the beginning of the 1960s, Lipset (1963, originally 1960) observed that voting patterns in the industrialised countries were strongly class based. Working class people and lower income groups predominantly voted for parties of the Left, the middle classes and higher income groups predominantly for parties of the Right. On the basis of voters' studies, many authors have, since then, claimed that class based voting has almost uniformly declined in all industrialised societies (see, Inglehart 1984, Dalton 1988, Minkenberg and Inglehart 1989, Minkenberg 1992).

This development has been explained in terms of different changes in the structural characteristics of the working class and the labour market. The latter has become more diversified and differentiated, an evolution that is supposed to lead to greater cultural differentiation (Offe, 1985, p. 164) and to an increased heterogeneity of the working class (Jahn, 1989, pp. 157-8). This growing heterogeneity is said to have led to the 'extinction of the regular' (Streeck 1987), eroding the basis of both large scale working class organizations and class politics, premised upon the homogeneity of that class.

One form of differentiation of the labour market has received special attention. The expansion of the non-profit service sector has been related to the rise of a new class of highly trained people. These people, a fair number of them of working class origin, are said to be less interested in the old Left/Right cleavage and to be frustrated by a combination of relatively high educational achievement with relatively low income (Flanagan 1987). This idea has given rise to a whole series of theories about the 'new class'. Daniel Bell (1986, originally 1976), one of its earliest observers, sees this class as carrying largely antinomian, anti-institutional, anti-establishment feelings and attitudes. Even when it is not viewed as antinomian, the new class is considered as the principal carrier of the new attitudes and values that are transforming contemporary culture and politics. It is expected to stimulate the search for political innovation, outside of the old class based patterns, and their corresponding ideological blocs.

Class based politics have also been said to lose their relevance because they are related to issues of distribution and allocation. The very success of the welfare state, the post-war economic growth, and the rise in the standard of living, that in many countries was gained by increasing the labour force participation of women, is supposed to have reduced the salience of allocative and distributive issues. This proposition is, in fact, part of the so called Inglehart thesis that posits a shift from materialistic concerns with economic growth, (low) inflation, employment, and law and order, towards post-materialistic concerns with participation, personal expression, ecology, and self-realization (e.g. Inglehart 1977, 1987, 1989, Inglehart and Flanagan 1987). The 'new class' of highly educated young people employed in the service sector, is viewed as the privileged carrier of these 'new' values.

The rise of the welfare state has also been related to tensions within working class movements because its regulatory and bureaucratic impact on daily life (the 'colonization of the life world') is said to clash with the emancipatory aspect of those movements, splitting them internally between authoritarian and libertarian segments. The very success of the welfare state also implies that the relationship between the redistributive policies, typical of working class parties, and large segments of the population, has changed. While solidarity used to signal policies that were likely to benefit a large majority, they are today often perceived as a call for more taxes and solidarity with a minority that is, moreover, often ethnically separate. In this sense the ideological basis of the policies of the working class parties has at least partly shifted from a theory based on self-interest and class interest to an orientation based on values, moral appeal, and global societal projects or, as Gordon Brown and Tony Wright (1995) put it in the title of their anthology of socialism, to 'Values, Visions and Voices'.

In short, over the three decades running from 1960 to 1990, many voters' studies as well as various theoretical arguments have conspired to strengthen the view that class based politics and class based voting has become problematic and has, in fact, strongly declined. The results of the 1991 Parliamentary Elections in Flanders seem to bear out the thesis that class based politics has completely disappeared. The ideological blocs of the Left, the Centre and the Right, obtain well nigh identical percentages of the votes in each class. We shall later see that such a result does not, in fact, support the thesis of a decline of class based voting. Yet, precisely such observations have been extensively used to support the thesis that social class was becoming politically irrelevant.

About cleavages and alignments

To appreciate the importance attached to the perceived decline of class based voting, one should bear in mind the important role the concept of societal cleavage plays in political and electoral analysis. This concept was popularised by Lipset and Rokkan (1967), and fits into the more general frame of Parsonian modernization theory (1971). In this perspective the rise of modern society is considered as a process that consists of a series of profound, and conflicting, transformations or 'revolutions'. These result in stable conflict axes or cleavages that partition society and yield the structure for the organization of its political space and parties. The process of secularization and the conflict between Church and State, for instance, can be translated into a relatively stable cleavage between confessional and non-confessional political parties. The dynamics of capitalism and the growth of the labour market has in many countries resulted in the conflict between workers and employers, and can give rise to a relatively stable cleavage between parties of the Left and parties of the Right. The process of inclusion can give rise to conflicts between various ethnic groups and to enduring political cleavages between organised ethnic or ethno-linguistic groups. The political cleavage theory tends to view democratic politics as organised around such relatively stable cleavages or conflict axes, in the sense that political parties establish privileged and relatively stable relationships with one or more of the population segments that result from the way in which the cleavages partition society.

The Belgian political system has predominantly been viewed as divided or structured by three cleavages: an ethno-linguistic one, separating Flemish and French speaking populations; a religious cleavage, separating catholics from atheists or secular humanists; and a class cleavage politically expressed in the Left/Right conflict axis. The ethno-linguistic cleavage has lost much of its salience because Belgium has become a federal state in which the French and Flemish 'Communities' have taken over many prerogatives. These Communities are largely homogeneous in terms of the old ethno-linguistic divide. Due to secularization, the conflict between the different religious or philosophical groups has become less salient. In a country where the working class was organised in a catholic and a non-catholic, socialist union, this has led to a loosening of the relationship between religious affiliation, union membership and party preference (Billiet, 1993, p. 117). This, in turn, has increased voter volatility, in other words, people are more likely to change their party preference from one election to the next. This development has also been observed in other European countries (Dalton 1988, Mair 1989) and is considered as conducive to political change (Ignazi 1992).

One should keep in mind that the political cleavages are a theoretical construct. They can clarify voting patterns, but will rarely completely predict them, because all cleavages are not equally salient for all voters, voting is not completely determined by the cleavages, and the party system is rarely a perfect reflection of the cleavages, but a contingent adaptation to them. Yet, the cleavage model is not merely an academic tool to understand politics. It is also an important conceptual element of the ideologies and the culture of both politicians and voters, and it is embedded in their affinities and life styles. Political commentators and politicians have observed that due to the various developments that have been sketched, the stable conflict lines that structured the political space in which they operate, have lost much of their relevance. That development has made a once familiar political landscape look chaotic, fluid, unpredictable and unsurveyable. The alleged decline of class based voting and the concomitant loss of relevance of the Left/Right-divide and the other cleavages, have stimulated fundamental questions concerning the relationship between politics and the symbols, beliefs and values that constitute contemporary culture.

It is useful to briefly recall and refine the crucial concept of alignment. When using the concept, one assumes that most people do not have well thought out ideologies. People can hold collections of opinions that, to an ideologist or a philosopher who tries to think in a consistent way, may appear highly inconsistent, even monstrous (Maffesoli 1985). A measure of inconsistency and looseness is held to be typical for the way the majority of people hold ideas, beliefs, and values about most subjects. Yet, at the same time, one can observe that different forces - culture centres - are working in society to create seemingly consistent alignments of values, attitudes, behaviour patterns, memberships, life styles, etc. Through the actions of those forces - media concerns, voluntary organizations, social movements - some alignments can become so clearly crystallised that they can be expressed in a single binary choice: for or against abortion; for or against euthanasia; for or against, to use an older example, the 8-hour-working-day; for or against the right to strike, etc. When the movements promoting a certain alignment have been highly successful, people can express a whole way and a whole conception of life in a single choice, and people can be channelled towards a way of life through such a specific choice. Interpreting recent conflicts in the United States, Hunter (1990) suggests that in the areas of reproduction, family, art, law, and education, one can witness the emergence of a more encompassing cleavage between a libertarian and a traditionalist or essentialist position on ethical issues. He views this libertarian/authoritarian cleavage as signalling new 'culture wars'.

The ideologists that work out and rationalise such alignments, tend to think that the alignments themselves have an inherent, compelling logic - that the attitudes, values and behaviour patterns that have been aligned, do in some sense necessarily or 'naturally' fit together. As sociologists observing alignments, we should be sceptical of such claims and sensitive to both the internal logic and the creativity and contingency involved. If we look, for instance, at the precursors of the Greens - what the Germans call the *Lebensreform* movement - we see that they created an alignment of elements like: a preference for small scale enterprises, vegetarianism, resistance to vivisection, clothes of cotton and wool, nudism, rejection of industrialization and of other aspects of modernity, fear of professionalization

(Sprondel 1986). It does not seem to me that these items are related in a compelling way. In a culture that has not experienced *Lebensreform* movements, the enumeration just given might sound quite unexpected, even absurd. Alignments and the classifications they entail are not so much logical as socio-logical. They are to a large extent social constructions, pieces of art in fact, produced by social and cultural movements. Once such a symbolic alignment exists, it can become an element in a politically relevant alignment of values, ideas, attitudes, practices, organizations, associations, and voters. It is clear that the elaboration of a new or renewed alignment is a major cultural innovation, influencing the beliefs, values, symbols and practices of people, and apt to lead to the rise of new parties and a rearrangement of political space.

Using the concept of 'alignment', the reactions to the observed changes in the role of the familiar political cleavages can be grouped into two kinds of theories, the theory of postmodern politics and the theory of re-alignment.

Political postmodernism versus re-alignment theory

The political postmodernity thesis considers the apparently chaotic, fluid, unpredictable and unsurveyable character of the contemporary political landscape, as the crucial, defining characteristics of the new politics. It holds that the phenomenon of alignment itself depends on specific conditions and therefore belongs to a specific historical period, modernity, that is now closing. The adherents of this view emphasise developments such as the end of the 'grand narratives' and 'individualization' (Gibbins 1989).

Applied to politics this implies that a relatively stable alignment of values, practices, and membership in voluntary organizations, has become impossible in the postmodern world, because people will behave more like consumers and hop from one life style to another, from one set of values to another, from one political issue to another. 'Postmodernism does not recognise a gradual change in value priorities in the contemporary world, but *a turmoil of values and preferences...*' (Gibbins, 1989, p. 18, my emphasis). The possibility of new cleavages or alignments arising is rejected because

> ...in a pluralist consumer culture where traditional family structures are eroding, young people's value orientations are also pluralist, too diverse to be contained inside a materialist/post-materialist value conception (Reimer, 1989, p. 123).

A similar thesis was used by Hellemans (1990) to interpret post-war developments in the relationship between social movements and politics in Flanders. One of the aspects of successful alignment is that it can create ways of thinking, life styles and supporting organizations, with effects on different aspects of life (family, eating habits, dress, leisure, law, politics, work). Such encompassing alignments have become improbable, even impossible according to Hellemans:

> ...the disintegrating wave [of de-alignment] has consigned to the past the large totalizing movements, which strove with some success for the unity of the individual, the organization and the movement (and the society). And because the extreme contrasts have fallen away, contemporary society is more than ever covered by a veil of 'unsurveyability' (Hellemans, 1990, p. 271)[1].

According to the postmodernity thesis, politics will become less a matter of parties that exist by virtue of a relatively stable alignment, more a matter of short lived movements addressing various issues and entering into momentary coalitions. One of the institutional implications of this thesis is that democracy can be strengthened and adapted to contemporary culture, not by the consolidation of party based politics, but by frequent referenda and the introduction of such innovations as televoting.

Opposed to this interpretation of recent political and cultural developments and their institutional implications, is the re-alignment thesis. According to the latter, which will be elaborated in the next section, stable alignments are still possible and relevant. The present turbulence of the political landscape is ascribed, not to the disappearance of stable alignments, but to fundamental processes of de- and re-alignment, based on the decline of some, and the growing salience of other, issues and conflict axes. According to the political postmodernity thesis 'old politics' is politics structured by relatively stable cleavages and alignments, 'new politics' is a politics forever faced with new value orientations and short lived, shifting issues. According to the re-alignment thesis, 'old politics' is politics structured by the sedimented conflicts of early modernity, 'new politics' is a politics structured by the conflicts of late modernity.

Empirically evaluating the relative merits of these two theories is difficult because of the low degree of theoretical adequacy and the exceptional vagueness of the political postmodernity thesis. In order to validate it, it is not sufficient to show that a specific cleavage or alignment is losing its salience and relevance, for such a development would be consistent with the de- and re-alignment thesis. The proponents of the political postmodernity theory should be able to empirically document the thesis that relatively stable alignment no longer occurs. If one takes 'turmoil of values and preferences' literally, then the postmodernity thesis would imply that values and preferences no longer coalesce into alignments at all. Such a thesis seems however at odds with the recent rise of nationalism and fundamentalism, and the observed persistence of working class cultures (De Witte 1990). The thesis is even contradicted by the very alignment that is taking place along the conflict axis between postmodern multiculturalists and their opponents (Aranowitz 1993). It is, of course, possible that the relationship between cultural centres, subcultures or alignments on the one hand, and individuals on the other, are becoming more changeable and short lived. It is not easy to historically substantiate even this moderate version of the postmodernity thesis. But even if its plausibility could be empirically established, it would not imply that relatively stable alignments have become impossible. It would only mean that such alignments would become less likely and probably less enduring. Such a state of affairs would however in no sense be inconsistent with re-alignment theories[2].

Given the vagueness of the concepts used in the postmodernity thesis and the impossibility of empirically evaluating its otherwise quite grandiose claims, one has to establish its plausibility, or lack of it, by elimination. The political postmodernity thesis gains plausibility to the extent that the re-alignment thesis becomes less plausible. I shall, therefore, focus on the latter and on the question whether we can: (1) observe an alignment of attitudes, that seems new and that (2) can be considered as a new political conflict axis or cleavage that (3) helps to explain the emergence of new political parties, particularly the new right-wing parties, and (4) accounts for the rearrangement of the political space and the ability of the new right-wing parties to attract voters from other ideological blocs.

A post-materialist re-alignment

In contrast to the political postmodernity thesis, the re-alignment thesis has a rich theoretical and empirical history. That thesis has, to a large extent, been, developed against the backdrop of the rise of the so called 'New Social Movements' (ecological, peace, feminist) and Green parties (e.g. Kitchelt 1989).

The Green Party in Flanders is called AGALEV, an acronym for *anders gaan leven* (let us live differently). The sociological profile of the members and voters of that party, corresponds quite well to what one would expect on the basis of the new class theory. They are young, highly educated, with (using Bourdieu's terminology) definitely more cultural than economic capital. They are also concentrated to some extent in the service sector, but much more striking is the fact that they come disproportionately from groups that are not active in the labour market - students, housewives and the unemployed (Deschouwer and Stouthuysen 1984, Swyngedouw 1992, Pelleriaux 1994). The first local electoral successes of AGALEV date from 1979. The party entered Parliament in 1981 with 3.9 per cent of the vote. From election to election, the Greens climbed up to 12.2 per cent in the 1989 European elections and then (to their own surprise) experienced their first major electoral set-back in 1991, when they lost more than four per cent and dropped to 7.9 per cent of the vote. In 1995, AGALEV suffered a further fall in support to 7.3 per cent.

During the eighties, the re-alignment thesis has predominantly been discussed as an explanation for the rise of the New Social Movements and the Greens. The members and the supporters of the Green parties often present themselves explicitly as the representatives of a new class, the pioneers of a newly emerging post-materialist value-orientation, and the carriers of a new ideology or totality (Gaia) that transcends the old political cleavages. Various descriptions of the newly emerging value alignment have been proposed. The dominant thesis is associated with Inglehart and can be summarised in three propositions.

First, common to most theories concerning the nature of the new cleavage, and at the core of the Inglehart thesis, is the hypothesis that a cleavage related to class position and expressing class conflict, is replaced by a cleavage expressing conflicts over values and ethics that are no longer class related. According to Inglehart this new cleavage concerns a conflict between materialist and post-materialist values. Other authors have proposed variations on this, without touching the core of the thesis - the idea that class conflict and the familiar Left/Right divide are being replaced by a conflict axis based more on general value orientations. Flanagan (1987), for instance, has proposed that besides the growing cultural difference between 'people emphasizing material values and people emphasizing post-material values, there is also a growing difference between people who are authoritarian and people who are libertarian in their attitudes.

Second, the rise of a new value alignment (materialist versus post-materialist orientations and, at least for some authors, libertarian versus authoritarian attitudes) is not only considered to signal the emergence of a new political cleavage. It is expected that it will gradually replace the old class based Left/Right cleavage (e.g. Schmitt 1989). According to Minkenberg and Inglehart (1989), this shift from 'old' to 'new politics' leads to a profound rearrangement of the political space. The new, highly trained middle or service class will become the carrier of the new, post-materialist Left. It will form a stable political alliance with the members of the marginal groups, with whom many of the new class members are professionally involved. This new political actor will be opposed by a neoconservative, materialist alliance of the 'old' Left working class and the 'old' Right middle class (Minkenberg and Inglehart, 1989, p. 90). According to this scenario both the political separation between the working and the middle class, and the old Left/Right cleavage will wither away. They will be replaced by a conflict between, on the one hand, the new middle class joined by the marginals, the students, the unemployed, and, on the other, the groups that oppose the post-materialist, libertarian values of these new professionals and their dependants. The new Left will, in other words, not simply stand alongside the old Left. It will be a party 'beyond the Left', replacing it (Kitchelt and Hellemans 1990).

Third, according to Schmitt (1989), Minkenberg and Inglehart (1989) and to some extent Minkenberg (1992), the new salient political cleavage concerns value orientations and is, if at all, only weakly related to class. This, together with the two previous propositions implies that class inequality becomes politically unimportant and that classes that in many respects appear as each other's opposites - on the one hand, the new, highly educated new middle class and the semi-literate very poor, and on the other, the working class and the old middle class - will be joined in the same political formations or stable alliances.

The rise of the populist Right

A striking feature of the re-alignment model proposed by Inglehart, is that it focuses almost exclusively on the rise of the post-materialist and libertarian positions. That is, of course, a consequence of the undue identification between the rise of the Greens and the political re-alignment, that was routinely made in the 1980s. That one-sidedness was corrected by the manifest, and rather unexpected recent electoral successes of the extreme right-wing parties. Unlike half a decade ago, one now tends to see the new, post-materialist parties as a new Left that stands opposed to the new extreme right-wing or populist right-wing parties, and not to all older working and middle class parties (Ignazi 1992).

The new right-wing party in Flanders, the *Vlaams Blok* (VB), was founded by people who had been involved in neofascist movements for a long time. It started to become successful in the middle of the 1980s. It obtained 1.8 per cent of the vote in the parliamentary elections of 1981 and then started climbing in the European and Parliamentary elections - 2.1 per cent in 1984, 2.2 per cent in 1985, 3 per cent in 1987, 6.6 per cent in 1989, and 10.4 per cent in 1991. One of the major reasons for considering the election of 1991 as a turning point was that this extremist right-wing party went over the 10 per cent cap in 1991, as well as getting 25 per cent of the vote in the major Flemish city of Antwerp, together with the high voter turn-over and the first major electoral set-back for the Greens (for an elaboration of this point, see Billiet, 1993, pp. 108-10). Albeit the *Vlaams Blok* showed a slowing of its progress after 1991, it still improved its electoral performance in the municipal elections of 1994 and in the parliamentary elections of 1995. In the city of Antwerp it obtained 28 per cent of the vote. In the parliamentary elections it got a little over 12 per cent.

Building on the explanations that have been proposed for the rise of the Green parties, which emphasised changes in the occupational structure and the rise of a new middle class, the rise of the new right-wing parties is, in journalistic circles, explained in terms of the globalization of the economy, the economic crisis which started in 1974, and high rates of unemployment (e.g. Swyngedouw 1992). According to this view, the new middle classes carry the Green parties and the left side of the new political cleavage, while the working class victims of globalization and the economic crisis carry right-wing populism and the right side of the new political conflict axis. The first sociological analyses of the electorate of the *Vlaams Blok* do not really support this thesis, but are rather consistent with the observations, made in other European countries, that show that new right-wing parties are able to attract people from different classes, strata and occupational groups (Ignazi 1992). The relationships between the standard sociological variables and the probability of a vote for the extreme Right, are not very strong. Young people, people with a relatively low degree of schooling, people without religious convictions and secular humanists, people who do not participate in associational life, have voted disproportionately for the *Vlaams Blok*, but otherwise the electorate of the party is quite evenly distributed among occupational and income categories. The extreme right-wing vote turns out to be less well explained by material or economic variables such as income, labour market situation and occupational prestige, than by variables more directly referring to socio-cultural factors, such as education, ethnocentrism, religion, individualism and feelings of anomie (Billiet 1993, Elchardus et al. 1993, Elchardus 1994a). This observation lends support to the thesis that the new political cleavage concerns primarily matters of value-orientation (see also Minkenberg, 1992, p. 64), and can probably in part be understood as a reaction against the value orientations carried by the new middle class (Minkenberg and Inglehart 1989, Ignazi 1992).

In empirically evaluating the re-alignment thesis I will focus on the three propositions outlined earlier, but will look at them against the background of the rise of both the Greens and the new right-wing parties. First, I try to answer the question whether one can, in the value-orientations of the Flemish electorate, identify a new alignment. I then turn to the question whether that alignment can be considered as a politically relevant cleavage or conflict axis, related to the rise of new parties and to a rearrangement of the political space. Next I tackle the question whether the new alignment does indeed replace the older Left/Right-cleavage. Finally I will again take up the question of class based voting, and look at the relationship between the new alignment and different indicators of class inequality.

The nature of the new value alignment

While there is broad agreement that the new cleavage has a strong cultural character, that it primarily concerns matters of ethics, morals and values, there is certainly no consensus that Inglehart's contrast between materialist and post-materialist values correctly captures the essence of the new alignment[3]. The salience of the cleavage between the materialist and the post-materialist positions seems in many ways to belong to the first half of the eighties, when the rise of the Green parties was the most visible political manifestation of the cultural change taking place. Today, after the emergence of populist right-wing parties in most European countries, many issues that can no longer be directly related to the distinction between materialist and post-materialist values or between libertarian and authoritarian attitudes, vie for a place on the political agendas.

In order to identify the components of an eventual new alignment, I look at the issues the Green parties and later the populist Right have put on the political agenda. The new alignment of attitudes and value orientations should certainly be related to these issues. If a new alignment exists, then it should certainly express itself in a coalescence of attitudes that predict relatively consistent positions on the political issues and conflict matters that the Greens and/or the populist Right have highlighted.

Many of the issues the Green parties have put on the political agenda, can indeed be interpreted in terms of post-materialist worries, an emphasis on participation (Schmitt 1989), and a somewhat utopian search for communal solidarity on the basis of a libertarian conception of individual freedom. The populist Right has not only reacted to those positions, as Minkenberg (1992), Minkenberg and Inglehart (1989) and Ignazi (1992) emphasise, but has put different issues on the political agenda as well (see various contributions in Ignazi and Ysmal 1992). The most important issue has been the presence of ethnic minorities, the so called 'migrants'. In Flanders it is this issue that has enabled the extreme Right to transform itself from an insignificant and nostalgic neofascist group into a significant populist right-wing party. The populist Right has further expressed worries about the decline of traditional values and virtues, about too much permissiveness and the decline of traditional forms of authority. It has emphasised crime and law and order issues. It has drawn attention to political corruption, and exploited the anti-political mood and feelings of political powerlessness and cynicism. In their economic programmes one finds a strong emphasis on laissez-faire or neo-liberal policies, and elements of Social Darwinism, linked to worries about profiteering in the welfare state, for which ethnic minorities are held particularly responsible[4]. The values that are pertinent for these various issues, or the discourses in which these issues are discussed, seem to involve value dimensions such as post-materialism versus materialism, libertarianism versus authoritarianism, ethnocentrism or racism versus tolerance, social solidarity versus utilitarian individualism or Social Darwinism, feelings of political efficacy versus feelings of political powerlessness or political cynicism, traditionalism versus modernism.

The Flemish Voters' Study of the 1991 General Election (Carton et. al. 1993) makes it possible to measure most of these value orientations[5].

1   *Individualism versus solidarity* Individualism is understood as the doctrine according to which each individual is allowed to pursue their interest or pleasure, without much regard for the implications of that attitude on others. This attitude also implies that everybody should care for themselves and that those unable to do so are failures (Social Darwinism).

2   *Authoritarianism versus democratic relationships* Authoritarianism stands for an emphasis on obedience, respect for authority in general and, to some extent a belief in the political benefits of a 'strong leader'.

3   *Ethnocentrism versus tolerance* Ethnocentrism stands for negative attitudes towards migrants and ethnic minorities that are perceived as different (in Flanders these are mainly people of Moroccan and Turkish origin). The scale used measures negative attitudes towards ethnic minorities, not just

racism. The proportion of people with racist attitudes is estimated at about 10 to 15 per cent. The negative attitudes of most people derive from the fear that migrants are taking their jobs, are destabilizing the social security system and are getting too much government attention (50 to 75 per cent of the electorate tends to hold such views).

4   *Political cynicism versus political efficacy* Political cynicism means that politics is regarded as inefficient, corrupt, useless, not worth the effort of voting.

5   *Materialism versus post-materialism*

Analysis of the relationship between these attitudes, shows that they are strongly interrelated. Empirically there is a clear alignment of attitudes in which utilitarian individualism, authoritarianism, ethnocentrism, political cynicism and materialism go together and are opposed to solidarity, non-authoritarianism, tolerance, belief in political efficacy and post-material values[6]. The materialism/post-materialism scale is somewhat less strongly related to this alignment of attitudes than the other value orientations, without however being distinct from it. With regard to the hypotheses concerning the new conflict axis, that have been reviewed, the empirically observed alignment suggests a few critical remarks.

First, although the conflict between materialists and post-materialists is relevant to and part of the new alignment, it is certainly not its dominant feature and can hardly be used to express its essence. The core of the new alignment is constituted by value orientations that are directly relevant to the issues of inclusion, authority and solidarity.

Second, the contrast between libertarianism and authoritarianism, seems equally ill suited to designate the new alignment. The very notion of libertarianism poses difficulties. Utilitarian individualism, which is obviously related to economic libertarianism, is strongly aligned with authoritarianism and opposed to the preference for democratic relationships.

The very existence of a strong re-alignment of value orientations that are relevant for the issues that have occupied an important place on the recent political agenda, throws doubt on the political postmodernity thesis. According to the latter, such an alignment is unlikely and, when it occurs, short lived. Whether the observed alignment is a stable phenomenon can of course not be decided on the basis of the present observations.

The new political cleavage

Alone, the existence of a new values alignment does not validate the re-alignment thesis, for the latter also implies that the new coalescence of orientations draws a new political conflict axis and leads to the rearrangement of political space. On the basis of the re-alignment thesis one would expect that the new parties that have emerged (the Greens and the populist Right) would occupy extreme, and opposed positions on the new cleavage.

The different political parties can be situated on the new cleavage by calculating the mean score of their electorate on that alignment. The latter is measured as an additive scale with scores ranging from 0 (new Left: pro solidarity, democratic relationships, tolerance, belief in political efficacy and post-material values) to 100 (new Right: utilitarian individualist, ethnocentric, authoritarian, politically cynical, materialist). In the elections of 1991 the electorate of the *Vlaams Blok* occupied on average the most right-wing position on that scale; the electorate of the Green party, AGALEV, the position most to the Left. People who do not vote or spoil their vote[7] have, in terms of the new alignment, the same profile as the electorate of the populist Right. This reveals an important electoral reservoir for the extreme Right. The parties which in Flanders are referred to as 'traditional' - the parties identified with what in terms of the re-alignment thesis is called 'old politics' - the christian democrats, the social democrats and the liberals, occupy Centre positions on the new alignment. The average score of their electorates corresponds almost perfectly to the average score of the electorate as a whole (see table 3.1).

Table 3.1
Average score on the new alignment - New Left versus New Right
(Elections of November 1991, n=2425)

Party[*]	mean	% votes
Greens (AGALEV)	39	7.4
Moderate nationalists (VU)	49	8.8
Social democrats (SP)	52	18.1
Christian democrats (CVP)	53	25.0
Conservative/neo-liberal (PVV-VLD)	53	17.6
Spoilt/not voting	58	8.2
Extreme right (Vlaams Blok)	58	9.7
All voters	52	99.6

[*]Very small parties and 'one-election parties' are not reported.

These observations clearly establish the political relevance of the new alignment. One can quite clearly distinguish the electorates of the parties of the 'new politics' (the Greens and the populist Right) from the parties of the 'old politics'. Yet, at the same time these observations strongly contradict the Inglehart thesis. In terms of the new alignment the new Left does not stand opposed to the old Left and Right parties (christian democrats, social democrats and liberals), but to the new populist Right and the people who refuse to vote. The traditional parties of the 'old politics' occupy Centre positions on the new cleavage, meaning that their electorates have either moderate positions in that respect or are heterogeneous in terms of the new alignment (which for many of them is simply not salient). The electorates have either moderate positions in that respect or are heterogeneous in terms of the new alignment (which for many of them is simply not salient). The 'beyond the old politics' view according to which the political space would be rearranged because the electorates of the old parties would form a neoconservative front against the rise of the new classes that carry new, post-material, libertarian values, does not seem to apply to the Flemish situation.

Minkenberg, trying to explain the rise of the New Right in Germany, comes to a similar conclusion. He strongly qualifies the thesis he had previously shared with Inglehart (Minkenberg and Inglehart 1989) and concludes that his new model

> [d]oes not suggest that the Old Politics dimensions disappears as a result of the new conflict axis, but that the ideological tension between Old Left and Old Right decreases in the face of polarization on the new conflict axis. (Minkenberg, 1992, pp. 61-2)

Neither his observations, nor the one reported here, support the claim about a lessening of the tension between old Left and old Right. They do however clearly indicate that the new alignment has not replaced the old one, but has established itself alongside the more familiar Left/Right divide.

The two Left/Right divides

The idea that one should view the political space as structured by two, rather than one Left/Right conflict axis is hardly new. Many sociologists credit Lipset for it. In the same book in which he emphasised the class based character of electoral politics, Lipset also noted that working class people tend to be less tolerant with regard to ethnic and cultural minorities. He referred to that phenomenon as 'working class authoritarianism', and explained it as a consequence of deprivation and socialization practices (Lipset 1959, 1963, chapter 4). Both that observation and its explanation have been called into question (e.g. Miller and Reissman 1961, Hamilton 1972, chapter 11). Yet, the existence of two distinct Left/Right cleavages has frequently been empirically substantiated, and the offered explanation has been refined by the work on class and occupational differences in socialization patterns of, most notably, Melvin Kohn and Carmi Schooler (e.g. Kohn 1977, Kohn and Schooler 1978). These observations have strengthened the idea that the working class, or at least a significant part of it, could be considered Left on economic issues, but Right or conservative in terms of their value orientations with regard to civil right issues[8]. Expressing that view, Topf (1989, p. 70) describes the working class as opting for both economic egalitarianism and moral traditionalism. That idea has led some authors to distinguish two Right/Left-cleavages: an economic Left and Right and a more cultural or ethical Conservative/Progressive cleavage. This model was, for instance, used by Felling conservatisms, and by Grunberg and Schweisguth (1990) in France to distinguish between different forms of liberalism.

The 1991 Voters' Study contains a number of questions which make it possible to measure the respondents' position on the 'old', familiar Left/Right-cleavage: 'the trade unions have to adopt a much harder line if they are to promote worker's interest'; 'workers still have to struggle for an equal position in society'; 'the differences between classes ought to be smaller than they are at present'; 'the difference between the high and the low incomes has to be reduced'; 'the government must intervene to reduce the difference between the incomes'[9]. The positions people take on these issues can be considered as part of a single value alignment[10]. This alignment distinguishes the so called 'old' Left from the 'old' Right. The first consist of people who think that social and economic inequality is too great, that unions should be combative and important social actors, and that politics and the government should be used to reduce inequality, the latter comprises the people who want to reduce the role of unions, believe that there is enough equality, that the 'verdict' of the market should be respected, and that politics and the government should not be used for redistribution. The average score of the various electorates on this 'old' Left/Right-cleavage is given in table 3.2. The alignment is measured as an additive scale going from 0 (old Left) to 100 (old Right).

Table 3.2
Average score on the old Left/Right alignment
(Elections of November 1991, n=2425)

Party	mean	% votes
Social democrats (SP)	28	18.1
Spoilt/not voting	31	8.2
Greens (AGALEV)	32	7.4
Extreme right (Vlaams Blok)	34	9.7
Christian democrats (CVP)	35	25.0
Moderate nationalists (VU)	38	8.8
Conservative/neo-liberal (PVV-VLD)	46	17.6
All voters	35	99.6

As one would expect, the social democratic party (SP) appears at the Left end, the conservative liberal or neo-liberal party (PVV-VLD) at the Right end of this alignment. The Centre is occupied by the electorate of the christian democratic party, which has the same average score as the electorate in general. The electorates of the new parties (the Greens and the populist Right) are Centre Left, the electorates of the moderate nationalists are Centre Right. The position of the populist Right's electorate is surprising and clearly indicates that 'populist Right' is a better label for the *Vlaams Blok* than 'extreme Right'. The electorate of the

Vlaams Blok is composed of two quite different groups. One of them is consistently extreme Right, with an extremely rightist position on both the old and the new Left/Right cleavage. The other, larger part of their electorate has an extreme rightist position on the new alignment, and a rather leftist position on the old Left/Right divide. There is in fact a difference between the *Vlaams Blok*'s official party position on economic policy, redistribution, and the unions, and the position of a large part of its electorate (De Witte 1994).

In terms of the new alignment, the extremities are formed by the Green party (AGALEV) and the populist right-wing *Vlaams Blok*; in terms of the old alignment the extremes are the social democratic party (SP) and the neo-liberal party (PVV-VLD). Of the people who in 1991 voted for AGALEV or *Vlaams Blok* one can, solely on the basis of their position on the new ideological alignment, predict in eight cases out of ten for which of the two parties they would opt. Their position on the old Left/Right alignment has no effect whatsoever on their choice. The reverse is true for the people who voted for the social democrats or the neo-liberals. The new alignment does not effect their vote, while their position on the old alignment allows one to correctly predict in seven out of ten cases for which of the two parties they voted[11]. The two alignments clearly constitute political cleavages. For the population as a whole, they are moreover nearly independent of each other[12]. For the population as a whole, the correlation coefficient between the two alignments is -0.11.

The rise of a new value alignment has obviously not led to the demise of the old Left/Right cleavage, as Inglehart and many other analysts of post-material values and the New Social Movements expected. There is clearly a new alignment, different from the old Left/Right alignment, but it exists alongside it. The labels 'old' and 'new' politics are therefore misleading. They have to be interpreted in the sense of 'more familiar' and 'of more recent salience' respectively. I now turn to the last aspect of the dominant re-alignment theory: the thesis that the new alignment can no longer be understood in terms of class position.

Social class and the new alignment

Whichever indicator one uses - occupational group, level of schooling or subjective class identification - the two Left/Right alignments turn out to be strongly related to social class. With the exception of subjective class identification which is more strongly related to the old Left/Right axis than to the new, the relationships are stronger between the new alignment and class than between the old one and class. The relationship between the level of education and the new alignment is extremely strong (*eta* = .50). Clearly, one cannot consider the rise of the new value alignment as indicative of a decline of the relevance of class and class inequality. The contrary seems to be the case.

Table 3.3

**Average score on the new and old Left/Right alignment by class
(Indicated by class identification, occupation and schooling)
(n=2668)**

Class	Old Left/Right	New Left/Right
OCCUPATIONAL GROUP		
Not employed	34	56
Unskilled worker	30	55
Other blue collar	35	54
Routine white collar	35	47
Middle management	40	45
Higher management*	46	39
Small self employed	48	54
eta	.24	.35
SCHOOLING		
Primary school	27	62
Lower secondary	32	56
Secondary vocational	34	55
Secondary general	40	48
Post secondary	43	42
eta	.33	.50
CLASS IDENTIFICATION		
Lower	27	58
Middle	36	52
Upper	44	48
eta	.37	.27

*Including independent entrepreneurs

The relationship between class and the alignments is as expected on the basis of the cleavage models derived from the working class authoritarianism thesis: the higher the occupational position, class identification or level of schooling, the more to the Left on the new alignment and to the Right on the old alignment. The small self employed, who are extremely conservative on both alignments, form the only exception to this surprisingly regular pattern.

Of the people who belong to the third of the population with the most leftist position on the old cleavage and to the third with the most rightist one on the new (17 per cent of the electorate), not less than 61 per cent identify themselves as lower class, and only 10 per cent as upper class, of these people, 52 per cent left school after primary level. Only three per cent continued training beyond secondary level. Of the people who belong to the one third of the population with the most rightist position on the old cleavage and to the one third with the most leftist position on the new one (12 per cent of the population), 58 per cent identify themselves as upper class, only 7 per cent as lower class. Only 5 per cent of them did not continue beyond primary school and 53 per cent went on to obtain a degree in post secondary and university education. The relationship between social class and the ideological cleavages can hardly be illustrated in a more striking way.

The strong relationships between class position and the two Left/Right cleavages, make it very unlikely that class based voting has in fact declined. The effect of class position on voting has been obscured because the distinction between the 'old' and the 'new' Left/Right cleavage has not been made. If one makes that distinction, the class based character of voting clearly appears. In the lower class, a leftist vote is in 85 per cent of the cases a vote for the social democratic party (the old Left), only in 15 per cent of the cases a vote for the Green party (the new Left). In the upper class these two parties divide the leftist votes equally, 50.4 per cent going to the socialists and 49.6 per cent to the Greens. In the upper class, a vote for the Right is in 86 per cent of cases a vote for the neo-liberal party (the old Right), in only 14 per cent of cases a vote for the populist Right (the new Right). In the lower class, the populist Right gets not less than 40 per cent of the rightist votes.

Taking stock of the findings reported in this paper, it is obvious that political postmodernity theory performs less well than the re-alignment theory. As far as the influence of class position on voting is concerned, the Flemish political system even seems to become more rigid, rather than more fluid. Yet most of the specific hypotheses of the dominant realignment theory must be rejected, when applied to Flanders and, I would suggest, to welfare states with a high level of educational development. The new alignment is not centred around a conflict between materialist and post-materialist values, but rather around conflicts about inclusion, authority, the sense of democratic politics, solidarity, morality and ethics. The new alignment that can be discerned does not replace the old alignment, but establishes itself alongside the older Left/Right divide. It is not less, but more strongly related to some indicators of class position than the older or more familiar Left/Right alignment. This implies that working class people and/or people with a low level of schooling are placed in a situation in which two distinct alignments of attitudes and orientations can influence their vote. If they give priority to issues concerning migrants, traditional values or law and order, or to feelings of political powerlessness or cynicism, they are apt to vote for parties taking a conservative or rightist position on those issues. If they give priority to issues of allocation, distribution, and social welfare policy, they are likely to vote for parties taking a leftist position on those issues. Since few socialist or social democratic parties have (as yet) combined leftist positions on issues of allocation and redistribution with rightist positions on immigration, integration, law and order and ethical issues, the working class vote has had a tendency to split, with the crossing of ideological blocs as a consequence. When a new populist right-wing party has emerged, as in Flanders and in France, this has resulted in a crossing from communist, socialist, and social democratic parties to the new extreme right-wing parties and in the success of these parties in the working class milieu. Where the electoral position of the extreme Right is complicated by the existence of a Westminster type two party system (as in Great Britain) or where its electoral space has been pre-empted by conservative parties taking rightist stands on the new alignment, this has resulted in a crossing over from working class, leftist votes to conservative or neo-conservative parties. The latter occurred in Britain in the 1979 election, when Thatcher promised to stop immigration, in Bavaria in 1981 and 1982 when the CSU (christian democrats) made 'foreigners' a target of their campaign, and most recently in the Netherlands, in the 1995 provincial elections, when the VVD (conservative liberal party) targeted immigrants and asylum seekers. The rise of the new alignment, and the recent success of the extreme Right, introduces a political pressure towards more conservative positions on inclusion, solidarity, relations of authority and ethical issues. Whether this results in the success of populist, extreme right-wing parties, depends on the response of the established parties. Yet it always threatens the electoral success of the older socialist or social democratic parties that are dependent on a working class electorate. In the next, concluding section, I formulate some hypotheses concerning the origins of the salience of the new alignment.

Toward a new cultural class strife

We saw that the older Left/Right-cleavage is more strongly related to (subjective) class identification than the new one. That suggests that people consider the old cleavage more as a political expression of class position than the new alignment. When considering more 'objective' indicators, such as occupation and schooling, class positions however turn out to be more strongly related to the new alignment than to the old one. The new alignment can therefore be considered as an expression of the class position that has been created by the educational and occupational changes of the post-war period. The strong relationship between occupational and educational inequalities on the one hand, the position on the new alignment on the other, indicates that the new alignment is becoming a cultural expression of the class differences that have arisen in post-war Europe. The two Left/Right-alignments should therefore also be regarded as two different cultural elaborations and interpretations of contemporary class conditions.

In discussing post-war changes in the class conditions attention has disproportionately been focused on the rise of the so called new middle class, based on the spectacular expansion of higher education and the equally spectacular expansion of employment in the service sectors. That however is only one side of the relevant developments. The educational expansion and the concomitant transformaticns of the occupational structure, hiring and selection processes and the increased efficiency and performance based on increased education, have also contributed to making the level of schooling a much more strongly discriminating characteristic in our society. The level and the kind of schooling one has been able to obtain, has very strong effects on both the kinds of occupations and the kind of cultural objects one can have access to. One of the unintended consequences of the educational expansion is a deepening of class inequalities between the highly educated and the others. This inequality has probably also hardened over time. The first waves of educational expansion gave working class youths from families in which conditions favoured educational achievement, despite a low level of schooling of the parents, a chance to be educationally and socially mobile. Today, as a consequence of the educational expansion, a low level of schooling of the parents is probably more strongly related to conditions unfavourable to educational achievement. There are also signs that intra-generational mobility has declined and that educational certification plays a more important role in the final allocation of occupational position (Gershuny 1994). Therefore, and because of early tracking in most educational systems, pupils know at an early age what their future, likely class position is going to be. Such developments increase the likelihood of the growth of a new sharp class divide, centred around the different life chances of people with low and high degrees of education.

In a society that has gone through its educational revolution, inequalities created by schooling do moreover no longer distinguish a small highly trained elite from the masses. They instead divide large classes whose inequalities in schooling imply a radically different relationship to both the economic and cultural processes of their societies. For the classes that have come out of these transformations, the labels 'working' and 'middle' class, although not wholly inappropriate, are much less telling than the labels that are gaining currency in everyday usage and which, so we found in in-depth interviews, are used by people to class themselves and each other as 'ordinary' versus 'educated' or 'learned'.

The relationship between the ordinary culture and the learned culture[13], has also been profoundly transformed. The relationship between the ordinary people and the cultural centres of society, can no longer be defined in terms of marginality or deprivation. The commercialization of cultural production and the mass media imply that the ordinary people constitute an important market of culture consumers. This increases the likelihood that a large part of the resources devoted to cultural production, will be geared towards their tastes. I propose to see the new alignment and the corresponding political cleavage as the cultural and political expression of a class struggle between the ordinary and learned people, in (knowledge or information) societies characterised by high levels of education, relatively open schooling, and a tight relationship between educational credentials and occupational position.

Because the new class cleavage is so strongly related to education, it can, even less than before, be understood in purely socio-economic terms. Feelings of cultural inequality and cultural identity will play an even more important role than before, creating a situation in which cultural dynamics can play a crucial role in the way that class position is translated into political action.

Notes

1   For other discussions concerning the applicability of the political postmodernity thesis in Flanders, see, Billiet, Swyngedouw and Carton 1993, Deschouwer 1993, Elchardus 1991a.

2   One specific development that is relatively well documented and that has already been referred to, is often mentioned in support of the political postmodernity thesis: the tendency for voters to become more 'volatile', less faithful to the political parties of their choice (Billiet, 1993, p. 102, Dalton 1988, Mair 1989, see also, Mair 1984, Reider 1989). Yet, all processes of de- and re-alignment will increase voter turn over, especially when they involve the rise of new political parties. The observed increase in voter turn-over can therefore not, at face value and in the short run, be taken as an indicator of voter 'volatility' or as an argument in favour of the postmodernity thesis.

3   For the discussion in Flanders, see Deschouwer 1993, Elchardus 1992, 1993, Hellemans 1993, Swyngedouw 1992.

4   The link that many European extreme right-wing parties, including the *Vlaams Blok*, have established between an emphasis on 'traditional values', ethnocentrism and neo-liberal economic policy, makes it plausible to describe them as 'neo-conservative' (e.g. Ignazi 1992). Yet it is more correct to emphasise the populist element of the new extreme Right because the electorate of these parties does not so much opt for neo-liberal policies as for a discourse stressing personal responsibility and a direct link between personal merit and reward.

5   Those scales are measured as additive scales as indicated in Billiet 1993, Billiet and De Witte 1993, except for utilitarian individualism which is based on a sum-score of items V27.1 to v27.4 inclusive (see Billiet 1993 and Carton et al. 1993). The Voters' Study does not allow for the measurement of 'traditionalism versus modernism', yet we would expect such a scale to be strongly related to the observed alignment.

6   A factor analysis yields only one factor with an eigenvalue greater than one (equal to 2.4). This factor explains about 49 per cent of the total variation (see table 3.2).

7   In Belgium there is an obligation to vote.

8   One finds a thorough review of the literature in De Witte 1990.

9   Questions V67.1 to V67.5 of the Voters' Study, scaled as Likert items (Carton et. al. 1993).

10   A factor analysis of the various items reveals only one factor with an eigenvalue greater than 1, which explains 49 per cent of the common variance. The factor loadings of the different items are almost equal. The additive form of the scale or alignment has a Crombach's alfa of .74.

11   These observations are based on discriminant analysis. The canonical correlation between the new alignment and the choice between AGALEV and *Vlaams Blok* is .60, Wilks lambda .64. Between the old alignment and the choice between SP and PVV-VLD, the canonical correlation is .46 and Wilks lambda .79.

12   Among the highly educated the two alignments tend to be positively related (with a correlation of about .2 for voters with a university degree). Among the people with a low degree of education, they tend be negatively related (a correlation tending towards .2).

13   It is obvious that I use the adjectives 'ordinary' and 'learned', not in any evaluative sense, but as sociological constructs that seem to correspond to the way people themselves make crucial class distinctions. I therefore use them without quotation marks.

4   Integration to disintegration? Nationalism and racism

Mike McGuinness

Introduction

The intention of this chapter is to look at the process of integration within the European Union. It will attempt to look at the extent to which it is possible to achieve a European identity without the process leading to disintegration. As we move closer to a more Europe focused structure, there is a counter development based on the reawakening of forms of national, ethnic, cultural and linguistic identity. Much of this is illustrated by the growing incidence of racist activity and more open expressions of nationalistic groups and parties. This is a growing picture across the whole of Europe including the European Union and the former states of East and Central Europe, where their new found independence after 40 years of central domination has changed perceptions and policies.

The 'demons of European history' threatening unification

Across Europe we are seeing clear signs of this 'disintegration' reflected in a number of activities causing some concern. First, there are growing numbers of attacks on, especially, 'visible' minorities and foreigners, that is, those who do not appear to belong, by whatever criteria. Second, there is the re-emergence of fascist and neo-nazi groups and parties, including paramilitary style organizations. Third, there is growing electoral support for such groups, e.g. in France, Italy and Austria, and a noticeable presence in the European Parliament after the 1994 elections. Fourth, there is growing nationalism linked to integration policies in the European Union and the re-emerged states of East and Central Europe. Fifth, there is growing intolerance towards refugees, asylum seekers and immigrants linked somewhat to the growth of 'Fortress Europe'. Sixth, there is an increase in official or governmental activity in this direction, a form of institutionalised racism and violence as has been suggested, for example, in France in recent years. Seventh there is increasing anti-Semitism. These activities are not just confined to those states with which we tended to associate it in the past e.g. France, Germany, Belgium, Italy and the United Kingdom. They are also to be found in what have been considered the more liberal states of Europe, namely the Netherlands and the countries of Scandinavia, especially Sweden. In this case the view of liberal democracies is being shattered and distorted. Bjorgo and Witte (1993, p. 1) go as far as to suggest that racist violence has reached alarming levels all over Europe although admitting that this is nothing new in European history. It is possible to suggest that all nation states have an element of ethnic exclusion, if not racism, and often chauvinistic ideologies. In the case of the European Union, there is an added element as many of the states have had a significant colonial past, and underpinning that colonialism is the idea of white superiority. Despite decolonization feelings of superiority, racism, jingoism, etc. often emerge at moments of stress or change, much as we are experiencing at the moment (Eatwell 1994).

The movement towards European Union after the signing of the Maastricht Treaty can lead towards two views. On the one hand, an optimistic view that Europe is eventually moving towards an integrated future building upon the developments started when the first six states came together in the 1950s. An integration built upon a social, economic and political union in the spirit of the Schuman declaration on 9 May 1950. A proposal ostensibly to place Franco-German coal and steel production under a common High Authority but with the intention that '...this proposal will build the first concrete foundation of a European federation...indispensable to the preservation of peace...' (reprinted in Pinder, 1991, p. 1). The fragmentation of Europe in the twentieth century, it was believed in the aftermath of the second world war, had led to the problems blighting the continent. The only way to secure a peaceful, stable and prosperous future was by tying together, and ultimately fully integrating the states of Europe into one regional bloc. This would be able to meet the threat of the Soviet Union, a threat now ostensibly disappeared, confront the economic challenge of the United States of America and Japan (and now South East Asia) (Andersen and Eliassen, 1994, p. 3), and tie Germany firmly into Europe.

On the other hand, there is a more pessimistic view which feels that as the image and the reality of integration have loomed into view a reaction to this programme has been created. Hunt (1993, p. 56) writes: 'Ironically, as the European Community moves towards political and economic unity .. racial intolerance and a misguided nationalism has become part and parcel political life'. Baimbridge, Burkitt and Macey (1994, p. 435) argue that racism in the European Union is extremely widespread and that 'It permeates every aspect of life both in its institutionalised form and, increasingly, in terms of the organised street violence that appears to have a transnational character'. Much of the pessimism expressed revolves around the idea that the intentions of integration have foundered on the nationalist leanings of the various populations, which are retreating into a more narrowly defined identity. This concept of nationalism, if indeed it is this, is leading to a growth of racial tension, xenophobia and disharmony.

Reports and committees of the European Parliament make clear the concern of European institutions. Their first action in this area was the Evrigenis Report of 1985 (officially the Report on the Findings of the Committee of Enquiry into Racism and Fascism in Europe) and the 1986 Joint Declaration against Racism and Xenophobia signed by all member states which makes it incumbent on institutions and individual states to combat all forms of intolerance, hostility and use of force against persons or groups on grounds of racial, religious, cultural, social or national differences. These actions reflected the views of the Parliament that there was an increase in racism in Europe with a concomitant rise in extreme right wing groups. In 1991, the European Parliament produced the Report of the Findings of the Committee of Inquiry on Racism and Xenophobia giving a comprehensive analysis of the situation in Europe generally and not just in the European Union. This reflected the feeling that there was an increase in racism in Europe.

At the Corfu Summit in July 1994, as the result of a Franco-German initiative, a Consultative Committee on Racism and Xenophobia was set up and this had its first meeting in September 1994. This represents recognition at the highest level of the political importance of this issue and the burgeoning danger of racism and xenophobia, although it has limited terms of reference which will restrict its work, and it is in danger of becoming little more than a public relations exercise (Ford, 1994). It produced its first report in November 1994 and presented a rather gloomy picture of the situation in the European Union, expressing concern and fear about displays of racism which are increasing in number and seriousness. Under the chairmanship of Jean Kahn it has made a number of recommendations designed to develop awareness and understanding, and to provide a code of ethics, to develop education programmes in schools, information and access to a European Ombudsman for national and foreign nationalities. Glyn Ford, the European Parliament's representative on the committee, was supportive of the measures but did not want it to be an excuse for the Commission to avoid using those powers it already possessed (John Carvel, Guardian, 17 November 1994). The Report was delivered to the Cannes Summit in May 1995 and called for common legislation to stop discrimination in employment, and to make incitement to racial hatred an explicit criminal offence in member countries. It has been suggested that the heads of government will find it hard to ignore the demand that race relations should become part of the Maastricht Treaty review in 1996.

As indicated earlier, these developments are not just confined to the member states of the European Union and can be identified in all states of Western, Central and Eastern Europe. The collapse of the Berlin wall has revived many of the old tensions held back by the more centralised regimes that had existed previously. Equally this must be linked to national disintegration and a push for recognition of the nation state (an attempt at defining this concept will form part of the discussions within this chapter). The disintegration of the Soviet Union, the collapse of Yugoslavia and the conflicts which followed and ethnic awakening across the breadth of Europe has opened what George Bush described as a 'Pandora's Box of ancient ethnic hatred' (Hunt, 1993, p. 52), or as Verdery (1993, p. 179) says there is a view, especially in the US, that the end of Communism took the lid off ancient hatreds that party rule had suppressed. Whether this is the correct interpretation is open to debate. But the evidence in East and Central Europe is one of national conflict with separatism in Slovenia, Croatia, Slovakia, and the Baltic and other Soviet Republics; bloodshed between Romania's Hungarians and Romanians, and between Bulgaria's Turks and Bulgarians; attacks on gypsies in the Czech Republic and Slovakia, Hungary, Romania, Poland and Bulgaria; and widespread anti-Semitism. At the very least the collapse of ostensible supranational communist authority has prompted what Pearson (1992, p. 500) called an 'unconscionable - and probably internecine - struggle for nationhood...'.

This process has been clearly evident in Western Europe for some time, sometimes with the complicity of national governments (e.g. regional autonomy in Spain, the creation of a federal state in Belgium between the Flemish and Walloon sections of the population). There has been a growing national awareness sometimes reflected either in electoral representation at Parliamentary level (e.g. the Scottish National Party and *Plaid Cymru* in the United Kingdom, *Vlaams Blok* in Belgium, MSI in Italy), or in the development of directly nationalistic and racist parties with varying degrees of success in most European states (e.g. *Front National* in France, the British National Party in the United Kingdom, the FPO in Austria, CEDADE in Portugal, SD in Sweden). More recently, the ascendancy of both the *Lega Nord* (Northern League) and the *Alleanza Nazionale* (incorporating the neo-fascist MSI) was evident in the 1994 elections in Italy, which brought them into government in alliance with Berlusconi's *Forza Italia*, and has created fear and concern both inside and outside the state. There has been a profound change here with the main parties, which had occupied government and shaped the rules of Italian politics since the creation of the Italian Republic in 1946, suffering disastrous losses in all areas. Gallagher (1994, p. 456) feels that the ending of the cold war in the late 1980s destabilised Italian politics with one of the features being an anti centralist movement as illustrated by the creation of *Lega Nord*. This was linked to the great economic and social change which had taken place in the 1980s unbalancing the stability of the state which had been based on economic development and cultural standardization. Another element of this is the almost racist North - South divide emerging in the debate. Italy may be a specialised case but some of the tendencies developing here are being reflected in many of the other states of the European Union and beyond.

Marquand (1994) has a strong interpretation of this situation feeling that Europeans have been cocooned by the cosiness of the Community and have forgotten what history was like before the Rome Treaty, suggesting that: 'If present trends are allowed to continue we may be brutally reminded, with what consequences we cannot imagine.' He refers to the demons of European history, (chauvinism, xenophobia, irredentism, racism and scapegoating) being on the march in the former Soviet bloc but still present in 'Community Europe'. Indeed, he feels that if anyone puts a match to it then the entire Community system may be destroyed (Marquand, 1994, p. 17). This view is endorsed by Macey (1992, p. 147) when she argues that there is considerable evidence that the traditional 'isms' of intolerance in Europe - fascism, racism, anti-Semitism and neo-Nazism - have expanded to encompass nationalism, chauvinism, extremism, xenophobia and religious bigotry. Writers like Eatwell (1994, p. 313) see this as a major factor and refer to it as a 'notable revival', a view backed up by the European Parliament's statement that since they adopted their joint declaration against racism and xenophobia in June 1986, they see 'an enormous mass of evidence pointing to the growing strength of racism and xenophobia'. Eatwell (1994, pp. 313-7) identifies voting, violence and propaganda as three areas where one can identify this growth. An earlier assessment came out of the European Parliament's concerns by Ford (1992, p. x), who noted that in the period after the European Parliament's report and presentation: '.. Europe witnessed a series of incidents of the kind to which the report sought seriously to give attention and which .. I believe we ignore at our peril'.

It is not my intention to concentrate wholly on the issues of racism and fascism, indeed it is unlikely that we will see the re-emergence of the overtly fascist mass paramilitary units of the inter-war type (Eatwell, 1994, p. 343). However, I believe that these issues are inextricably linked to the rise of nationalism, the increase of racially motivated incidents, anti-Semitism, etc. which are a result of the move towards integration. This is not to ignore that there is, and always will be, a debate as to the relationship between these factors. Betz (1993) feels that the period following the second world war gave the liberal democracies of western Europe a remarkable degree of social and political stability and economic growth which eroded support for extremist solutions on both the left and the right. But this does not seem to have lasted long with the climate changing from the late 1960s with disenchantment

> ... with the major social and political institutions and profound distrust in their workings, the weakening and decomposition of electoral alignments and increased political fragmentation and electoral volatility (Betz, 1993, p. 413).

There has been much recent debate as to the extent of this process and where it has been most significant. Good examples of this are the studies of the new right in Germany by Minkenberg (1992) and the examination of extremism in Germany by Roberts (1994). There are those like Dogan (1994, p. 281) who feel conversely that there has been a decline of nationalism within Western Europe and that we have reached what he calls a 'postnationalistic phase'. A further backing for this idea is the process of 'denationalization' by Pearson (1992) which he describes as a 'nationalism ripe for supersession'. Indeed, he quotes Hobsbawm who argued in 1985 that nationalism was no longer a 'major vector of historical development' retreating before the new 'supranational restructuring of the globe' (Hobsbawm, 1990, p. 181-2). It is debatable how many people would agree with these ideas in the light of the evidence but Dogan is right in stating that the debate about nationalism is confusing because scholars assign different meanings to the word. In this context, it is important to spend some time considering some definitions of some of the concepts already alluded to and then to return to the main debate.

Features of nationalism

Berger (1994, p. 55) and Smith (1979, p. vii & 1995, p. 1) feel there is a new/old spectre haunting Europe and that is the spectre of nationalism. According to Smith (1979, p. 1), 'Of all the visions and faiths that compete for men's loyalties in the modern world, the most widespread and persistent is the national ideal'. On the other hand, nation, nationality and nationalism have all proved notoriously difficult to define, let alone analyse. Seton-Watson (1977, p. 5) writes 'I am driven to the conclusion that no scientific definition of the nation can be devised; yet the phenomenon has existed and exists' but it is not just something which exists but it has been seen as an ideology with a future. Schopflin (1991, p. 51) feels that it is 'one of the great puzzles of the twentieth century', a concept which has been written off repeatedly by people on all sides of the political spectrum yet survives, with good reasons. The essence of his argument is that nationalism and nationhood operate on their own criteria and impose their own rationality upon events.

Verdery (1993, p. 179) argues that a 'striking concomitant of the end of communist party rule was the sudden appearance of national movements and national sentiments'. Haas (1993) argues that national identities are chosen, not genetically implanted, and are subject to change, as with Schopflin (1991); nationalism is a form of rationality, an effort to impose coherence on societies undergoing modernization. Alternatively, Anderson (1983) feels that there are three paradoxes associated with this idea: first, the objective modernity of nations to the historian's eye versus the subjective antiquity in eyes of the nationalists; second, the formal universality of nationality as a socio-cultural concept (in the modern world everyone can, should, will have a nationality as he/she has gender) versus the irremediable particularity of its concrete manifestations (i.e. nationality is unique); and third, the political power of nationalisms versus their philosophical poverty and even incoherence. Anderson states that nationalism has never produced great thinkers unlike other 'isms'. Is it therefore an emotive concept which cannot be defined but only felt?

Further confusions revolve around the concepts of nation and state and in this context it has implication for the development of integration in the European

Union. One is concerned to see how far it is possible to create an identity within Europe and whether the processes of integration, the 'deepening' of the Union, are the best method or are counter productive. Europhiles, according to Smith (1995, pp. 121-3), argue that Europe must be created as a federal, and even a unitary, state thereby ending the thousand years of 'internecine European strife and the wars of nationalism'. It is only by uniting in this way that Europe will be restored to its position as a great power in the world and become prosperous within a single market. Eurosceptics, on the other hand, feel that European unity was fuelled by the Cold War and now the reasons for its existence are no longer necessary because of the collapse of the Berlin Wall. Further, it will tend to benefit the larger, more powerful, states over the smaller and weaker ones, possibly allowing for German economic and political domination of the Union, and it will harm the developing (third) world economically. A pessimistic view considers the chance of European unification at anything but the most superficial (and bureaucratic) level to be fairly remote. Smith (1995, pp. 126-33) goes further by suggesting that the pessimists view the rising tide of ethnic nationalism as being something which would postpone the European project even more.

Mann (1993, p. 115) suggests that some people feel that we have reached the old age of the nation state and that since 1945 its sovereignty has been overtaken by transnational power networks, especially those of global capitalism and postmodern culture. The national state is threatened by external forces as its role as the primary economic, political and cultural actor has been thrown into doubt and is perhaps being replaced by a supra- or super-nationalism (Smith, 1995). But the nation state is generally resilient and not in decline anywhere, in some ways it is still maturing (Mann 1993).

Pearson (1992, p. 499) quotes Ernest Gellner's view in 'Nations and Nationalism' that there is an interpretation which suggests that nationalism is primarily a principle which holds that the political and national unit should be congruent. Some changes taking place in Europe at the moment revolve around this interpretation. Nowhere is this more apparent than in the former Soviet Union where the break-up into the fifteen republics as states has led to further dealignment as nations look for the sum of their parts. The dispute between Armenia and Azerbaijan over the enclave of Nagorno-Karabk, the war in Georgia, and the emergent nations in Russia, e.g. Chechenia, are only a few examples. Across the world this process is being repeated.

A state can be defined as a legal and political organization with the power to require obedience and loyalty from its citizens. A nation can be defined as a community of people whose members are bound together by a sense of solidarity, a common culture, and a national consciousness. Verdery (1993, p. 180) sees it as a name for the relationship which links a state (actual or potential) with its subjects and has historically had a relationship of two kinds: a citizenship relationship where the nation is the collective sovereign emanating from common political participation; and an ethnicity relationship where the nation comprises all those of supposedly common language, history or broader cultural identity.

Haas (1993, pp. 521-4) adds to this the ideas of status as a shaper of identity, i.e. the process of status deprivation and the desire to retrieve this status, and of culture as a shaper of identity, i.e. in this instance a system of ideas and signs and associations and ways of behaving and communicating. This one can include language in this definition as this links them to people who are not necessarily part of the face to face groups or closely related kin. It is not uncommon for these concepts to be confused and develop into what one can describe as a national ideal. A belief that all of those who shared a common history and culture should be autonomous, united and distinct in their recognised homelands. The period after the end of the second world war proved somewhat lean in the pursuit of the nation-state with a western European movement towards federalism and in East and Central Europe ambitious strategies designed for the assimilation of individual nationalities (Pearson, 1992). Nationalism was seen as a scapegoat for the outbreak of both wars and as something to be contained. Various stratagems to accommodate national sentiments were developed: the compromise of federalism; consociationalism linked to the idea of a multinational government; and multiculturalism as benign state intercession into a pluralistic society.

The nationalism which emerges from this is one which has its members striving for territorial autonomy, unity or independence and Keating (1990, p. 174) argues that the growth of minority nationalism has been one of the features of post-war western European politics, confounding the predictions of integration theory. It demands several elements - a vision, a culture, a solidarity, a policy and an identity. It is identity which Haas (1993, pp. 508, 513-5) sees as being important for the process of nation and nation building and he goes as far as to suggest that we can treat nationalism as rationalization. A more provocative reference can be made to the interpretation put forward by Stalin in 'Marxism and the National Question' in 1913. He suggested, rather simply, that a nation must have four characteristics: a common language; a common territory; a common economic life; a common mental make up (Seton-Watson, pp. 3-4). Ironically this description appears to make it easier to look at the question of integration and identity within the European Union. How far is it possible to create a supranational state from twelve, sixteen or more individual states, who in turn may have a multinational dimension?

Integration and the European Union

As we move further into the debate about integration and the 'deepening' of the European Union the appeal of nationalism seems to grow stronger. Zetterholm (1994, p. 1) suggests that faith is expressed in higher levels of integration, certainly at a political and economic level, but one wonders how effective this can be, bearing in mind, the differences in mentality, traditions, ways of life and social institutions between the states. He expresses a pessimism about the future of European integration drawing attention to its cultural diversity. This is not to say that cultural diversity is a problem, indeed the European Union has done much to support and preserve the differences of language and culture throughout the member states.

There is confusion about the term 'integration', especially from a British political perspective, where this is usually taken to mean an integration of national economies. George (1991, p. 1) suggests for many Europeans outside Britain this is only one aspect of a wider process that will eventually involve the integration of national political systems. In trying to arrive at a definition of 'integration', Laffan (1992, pp. 1-15) saw it as a process for the creation of political communities and transforming previously separate units into components of a coherent system. In moving towards a more formally integrated structure it has created, despite the relatively low level of integration, a reaction. How far is it possible to create a European identity which can be transformed into a European nationalism? Despite the movements towards economic integration, both official and unofficial, the political dimension is the most problematic. Pinder (1994, p. 506) points out that during the 1994 European election campaign most elections were fought on national policies rather than in a European context. They were more about national rather than European issues, in particular the government's general performance. Indeed the only campaigns on European issues seem to have come from the anti Maastricht parties in Germany, Britain, Denmark and France. The European parliamentary elections can be seen as 'second-order' elections and as long as the national party arena remained pre-eminent in the minds of parties and voters, European parliamentary elections must be seen as events dependent on a national political agenda (Reif and Schmitt 1980).

Haas (1993, p. 518) suggests that the only way to achieve an authentic nationalism or identity is where state-building proceeds the growth of nationalism, i.e. where the state 'built the nation'. If there is to be any way forward for the European Union, then it may be necessary to attempt to forge an identity amongst the diverse nations making up the Union at the moment. But he also argues that multicultural settings are inhospitable to the establishment of nation states. The idea of a European identity replacing loyalty to separate nation states may seem fanciful and is strongly resisted. Even the development of multiple loyalties 'in which the mental maps of European citizens would add an additional dimension to those national and regional loyalties they already possessed ...' has also not been realised (Wallace, 1990, p. 17). The concept of European citizenship promoted in the Maastricht Treaty suggests the creation of such an additional loyalty. However, Grahl and Teague (1994, p. 379) suggest that the future for European integration revolves around the economic content of the Union. This will determine whether people in member states feel a real sense of belonging, and come to view European Union institutions as relevant to their lives. This may be optimistic. It seems more likely that the 'citizens' of the Union are unaware generally of the benefits of their citizenship and the creation of an identity will take some time. A contrary development seems to have taken place with the creation of a 'local' identity perceiving threats from outside the Union and the inequalities develop between regions of Europe.

The growth of racism and barriers to integration

Nationalism has often been confused with racism. Generally, nationalism may be associated with racism and a rejection of multiculturalism (Haas, 1993). Nationalism fuses a theory of society and politics with a prescription for action and change. It is a struggle for self generation requiring cohesion and autonomy. And, it develops deep bonds of emotional solidarity. The national question may involve the development of genetic explanations which emphasise physical differences. This ethnocentrism, i.e. the tendency to analyse and assess aspects of other cultures by use of one's own culture as a frame of reference (Roberts and Edwards, 1991, p. 45), is closely allied to nationalism especially where an ethnic group can be classified as a social group whose members claim a common history and culture and possess feelings of mutual solidarity marking them off from other groups. Ethnocentrism involves a belief by the members of a community in their centrality, rightness and superiority and a corresponding denial of value to other communities. Haas (1993, pp. 524-5) refers to the idea of ethnonationalism in the same sense and feels that concept has been finding favour, especially in those states where there had been a growing dissatisfaction with what had been perceived of as highly successful nation states. It has within it a reasoned and instrumental response to a perceived discrimination felt by the group and to back this up he uses the example of the situation of the Flemish people in Belgium. In recent times the growth of ethnocentrism has been encouraged by the decline and restructuring of economies during the 1980s which has led to a more inward looking focus, and a reaction to the continuing levels of immigration linked to that decline.

There are significant barriers to the process of integration within the European Union, and there is a fertile territory for those who wish to develop policies which have racist or xenophobic overtones. At this stage I will deal with three interlocking issues: Sovereignty; Citizenship; Border policies and the impact of enlargement. Behind each of them is the issue of internal and external migration and its place in an integrated union and the past and future reactions of member states.

Sovereignty

Sovereignty has come to dominate our understanding of national and international life with a history which parallels the evolution of the modern state (Camilleri and

Falk, 1992, p. 11). Within a Europe that is in a 'state of flux', it is evident from the political landscape of the early 1990s that the debate is about how far sovereignty is a relevant category for 'understanding and action in the contemporary European world' (Hedetoft, 1994, p. 15). The debate about accountability and the 'loss of sovereignty' has become even more pronounced since the adoption of the Single European Act and the Single Market, which has led to an expansion in the activities of the Community/Union (Bogdanor and Woodcock, 1991, p. 481). Sovereignty is generally meant to denote the condition of political autonomy which a state enjoys when it is recognised by other states as the sole source of legitimate exercise of power within its territory (Roberts and Edwards, 1991, pp. 134-5). It is at this point where the relationship between the concept and the nature of integration clashes. How far are the states of the European Union prepared to give up the full national sovereignty which has been theirs since their states were created? Mrs Thatcher articulated this when she said that working more closely together 'does not require power to be centralised in Brussels', and criticizing the tendency to create 'an identikit European personality' (Laffan 1992). This is not confined to the United Kingdom. De Gaulle precipitated the 'empty chair crisis' in 1965 by withdrawing France from the deliberations of the Council of Ministers over a policy which implied a diminution of national sovereignty (Laffan, 1992, p. 51).

More recently the ratification of the Maastricht Treaty in various member states and the referenda on membership of the Union have been less than overwhelming and may show a difference of opinion between the governors and the governed. Conventionally the process of integration is conceived of as being driven by elite actions, but public support for the integration process is becoming increasingly important. It is clear that however incisive the leaderships and secure the institutions, people will not forge any genuine European unity without movement away from national sentiment and attitudes towards a commitment to a European identity (Smith, 1995, p. 123). Eichenberg and Dalton (1993, p. 508) argue that elites must 'convince their domestic audiences that the benefits of further integration are worth the costs'. The Maastricht Treaty was supposed to capitalise on the 'triumph' of the Single European Market by opening the way to a political union that would complement the economic union. Support for further developments were not only supported by the governments of the EC member states but also the vast majority of organised political forces throughout the European Community (Franklin, Marsh and McLaren, 1994, p. 456). There was a feeling that there would be little difficulty with ratification but what emerged was an apparent wave of popular opposition which raised questions about the underpinnings of the European Union. Franklin, Marsh and McLaren (1994, p. 456) suggest three possible explanations for this. First, popular sentiment on Europe was by no means as positive as had been believed. Second, voters changed their minds during the campaigns because they did not like what they heard about the Maastricht Treaty. Third, the Maastricht results can be best understood in terms of domestic party competition.

The Maastricht referenda held in Denmark and France in 1992 and 1993 are clear examples of this. In Denmark they had two referenda, the first rejected Maastricht by 1.4 per cent and the second, nearly twelve months later, ratified it by a margin of 13.4 per cent. The Danish electorate were offered two chances before agreeing. In France the referendum showed similar hesitancy and only ratified the Treaty by a majority of 2.1 per cent. It is this process of the 'little yes' which concerns many commentators and does not instil confidence in the long term ability of the European Union to move towards a more integrated system. As Woollacott (Guardian, 19 October 1994) said the era of the 'little yes' probably began with the Maastricht referendum in France. The phrase, he feels, was coined to describe the lukewarm endorsement by a narrow majority of a policy, a leader or a government.

Germany was the last of the member states to ratify the Treaty. The President did not sign pending the outcome of twenty complaints made to the Federal Constitutional Court that ratification was in breach of the Basic Law (Constitution). In October 1993 it was declared to be in conformity with the Basic Law and signed by the President. However, although the Court found that the objections were inadmissible and unfounded, the ruling gave interpretations of the Treaty which were expected to influence the future development of the European Union. German sovereignty was not deemed to have been impinged since the Union was described as a confederation or association of states rather than a European State. The judges felt that there was sufficient democratic control over the development of the Union but warned that an overpreponderance of tasks and responsibilities at the European level would weaken democracy at a state level. It is the latter part of the ruling which is of most interest. On the one hand it endorses the Maastricht Treaty but on the other hand there is a reference to the preservation of German sovereignty.

The question of sovereignty was an element in the accession referenda held in the European Economic Area / European Free Trade Association states. In Austria the vote was relatively decisive in favour of entry, but in both Finland and Sweden, although in favour, they were close. This is another example of the 'little yes' which seems to be developing and makes the longer term issue of integration less than conclusive. The result of the referendum in Norway in November 1994 did nothing to support the view of integration. Fears about loss of sovereignty and the need to retain Norwegian identity were as important as the economic issues surrounding fish and agriculture. The 'no' vote was more decisive than the 'little yes' coming from many of the new and old states. The possibility of governments without mandates just at a time when critical decisions in both national and European policy ought to be being made may yet create paralysis.

Citizenship is an issue which has emerged in recent times as the borders between states begin to fall but it must be clearly distinguished from nationality. Citizenship has assumed ideological as well as political significance and is at the root of a great deal of conflict and discrimination against black and ethnic minority peoples. When people are denied the citizenship of a country in which they have lived and worked for many years they face the daily experience of marginalization and insecurity. The possession of citizenship will take on greater importance as the Union develops as there is a tension between the European Union's commitment to human rights, and its concern to protect its own citizens relative to non-EU nationals. Citizens of the European Union have certain rights and/or obligations derived from their citizenship. Both the Maastricht Treaty 1991 and the Single European Act of 1986 promoted and developed the idea of a 'free' movement of goods, capital, services and, importantly, persons. King (1993, p. 183) argues this is a movement for some, whilst restricting 'outsiders'. An immediate effect of this is on the position of residents within member states who are not citizens of one of the member states. Free movement of citizens within the EU for all citizens of member states is an important issue of democracy and of human rights for the minorities who are not citizens of member states. The freedom may be at the expense of third country nationals who then face threats to their right of entry, mobility within the Community and access to jobs, benefits and general security of life. The abolition or relaxation of internal frontiers has created increasingly strict external controls, through the Schengen Agreement 1989 (Baimbridge, Burkitt and Macey 1994). In some ways this might be a blueprint for 'Fortress Europe'. There is an attempt to harmonise national policies on visas, immigration and asylum laws, as well as co-ordinated crime prevention and search operations (Bjorgo and Witte, 1993, p. 2). Further controls on immigration have developed within nearly all of the states within the European Union and it is seen by many that it is the visible minorities who are disproportionately targeted for exclusion. The racialization of the public discourse has consequences for those visible minorities born in Western Europe and has helped to create the climate of racism in Europe (Baimbridge, Burkitt and Macey, 1994). Macey (1992, p. 140) identifies three categories of minorities within the European Union, firstly, citizens of a member state who share, in theory, the same rights as other European citizens; secondly, migrants from one EU country to another EU country who are protected by EU law; and thirdly, third country nationals who are 'highly vulnerable', having no rights or protections under EU law. It is the last of these who cause most concern, especially those identifiable minorities who are highly visible in terms of skin colour. The origins of such minority populations are related to Europe's history of colonization and have produced different populations within the member states. The continuum ranges from full citizenship carrying civil, political and social rights, as in the United Kingdom, to guestworkers with few, if any, rights, as in Germany.

The issue of citizenship has assumed ideological as well as political significance and is at the root of a great deal of conflict and discrimination against black and ethnic minority people in Western Europe. When people are denied the citizenship of a country in which they have lived and worked for many years they face the daily experience of marginalization and insecurity (Baimbridge, Burkitt and Macey, 1994, p. 425). The possession of citizenship will take on greater importance over the next few years as there is a tension between the European Union's commitment to human rights per se and its concern to protect its own citizens relative to non-EU nationals. In general terms the impact of the free movement of persons has somewhat been reduced by three conditions (see Phillip, 1994, p. 169 and Carter, French and Salt, 1993):

1   In the early years the European Union was essentially the preserve of similarly developed high income and high welfare providing states (apart from Italy) in which there seemed little to attract cross border movement.
2   There has been surprisingly little mobility of persons within the states, and a large majority of those who have moved are non-EU nationals.
3   Control over the granting of nationality and citizenship of a member state remains in the hands of member states even though citizenship of a member state confers economic and social rights exercisable in all European Union states.

Border policies and the impact of enlargement

The development of a European Union concept of territoriality, a process of integration which has become more holistic, with internal and external policies intended to transform the spatial reference of the populations of the nation states towards the European system boundaries (Magone 1994), has major implications. In attempting to remove the psychological barriers between member states in terms of boundaries, it appears to be creating different outcomes to those intended; on the one hand, a reaction against this loss of identity, even when accepting some of the economic advantages going along with this, and on the other hand a reaction against immigration from outside the European Union. This has been referred to as 'Fortress Europe' and applies generally, including refugees, and raises the issue of how well the EU is dealing with the issue of immigration, with states concerns clashing with the need to harmonise. John Major's comment, during the European Summit meeting in Luxembourg in June 1991, that 'we must not be wide open to all-comers just because Rome, Paris or London are more attractive than Bombay or Algiers' (King, 1993) is typical of this approach. It is hardly surprising, therefore, that 'popular' responses to this issue are any less than those of our official representatives at national and European levels.

If third country nationals are refused entry by one EU member state this then becomes tantamount to refusal by all others. It is in the interests of individual member states to develop more restrictive immigration policies as failure to do so could result in one state, with the perceived most liberal immigration legislation, facing a potential inflow of third country nationals. There is also a compelling incentive for EU nations to prevent immigrants from entering their countries in order to avoid subsequent responsibility for them (Baimbridge, Burkitt and Macey, 1994, p. 429). The enlargement of the Union will not dilute the problem. All states have seen a growth in intolerance and the formation of extreme right wing groups. Expansion into the former states of East and Central Europe will not make things easier, there has been a growth in all of the elements in most of the states.

The reasons for the growth of a less tolerant response and the growth of parties and organizations on the far right and extremist end of the spectrum, even fascist, are relatively easy to identify. Macey (1992, pp. 147-9) shows that there has been a significant growth in intolerance in Western and Eastern Europe and this is being consolidated by the forging of international links between far right groups. Eatwell (1994, pp. 317-8) endorses this view and adds that the process of socio-economic change has also had an impact upon this growth.

From a Marxist perspective parallels have been seen between the 'capitalist' crisis of the post-1970s and that of the inter war years, but the major attention has been focused on unemployment and immigration. Most countries have seen a significant rise in the levels of unemployment, an issue focused upon by Jacques Delors as part of his social strategy, and some relationship has been found in, for example, the rise of the Northern League in Italy (Gallagher, 1994) and discontents in the former East Germany. The presence of immigrant communities has some connection, with a lot of the activity being concentrated in those parts where these groups are located (this includes refugees and asylum seekers). However, the links between the two elements and the growth of activity and organizations is not totally proved, but there is no doubt about the perception this produces within the wider population.

Conclusion

One of the concerns of this chapter has been a worry that the 1996 Intergovernmental Conference may produce less commitment to the dream of Schuman and others for an integrated Europe with peace and harmony as its basic themes. There is an accepted view that what has been produced is a significant period of peace with no physical conflict between nations in Europe, apart from the internal conflict in the former Yugoslavia. This is not to say, however, that there are no tensions existing between member states in the European Union or that there are no tensions within states. The myth of 'shared nationality' (Goodin, 1995, pp. 30-1) comes very strongly to the fore as we move closer to an integrated future, which can work at competing levels. Firstly, within states there are growing demands for the independence or recognition of nations or minorities, as with the Scottish National Party's call for independence in the European Union - a recognition that power, policy and decision making is moving away from the nation state towards a more concentrated and centralised Union. States like Germany and Spain have been able to structure a regional identity, although not necessarily stopping calls for independence, e.g. the Basque country. Belgium has recognised its divisions and created a federal structure, but others, like the United Kingdom, have been unable or unwilling to recognise this disintegration taking place. Secondly there is pressure to bring together states of Europe into a closer relationship with a European identity, although recognizing and acknowledging the cultural diversity of Europe. How far countries are prepared to give up their sovereignty to a supranational entity is at the heart of this. Both of these competing tensions have the ability to fuel the nationalistic and racialistic tendencies inherent in all societies. This includes the present and future states of the Union and as we approach the end of the millennium actions need to be taken to ensure a smooth and peaceful move into the next century.

Decisions will have to be taken as to the future developments within the Union and according to Andersen and Eliassen (1994, pp. 7-10) there are only three possible solutions: a federal Europe, around the idea of a United States of Europe; a Europe of States, where the member countries continue to play the main role; or a Europe with variable geometry, or a multi-speed option. Whatever the decision or the outcome of the political deliberations they all potentially have an impact on the issue of nationalism and all that attends it. The first model is somewhat utopian to be realised in the near future with cultural differences being too deep and national interests being too strong, and potentially getting stronger. The second model would go against the principle of integration, but it may be more realistic if one relates it to the organic growth of integration at certain levels, e.g. business, trade, commerce, industry. The third model has an image of drift and represents an untidy picture of development and integration with a two-speed or multi-speed Europe emerging, especially with enlargement. All, however, have elements of disintegration and it may be a question of how best to control the more negative aspects of development in Europe.

5   Lean production: Between myth and reality

Sebastian Herkommer

'The machine that changed the world'

Change or Die! The message of the MIT study published under this title (Womack et al. 1990) has become common knowledge. Any industrial nation or industry in the capitalist world would be threatened by relative ineffectiveness and by decline if it dared to neglect the principles of a new mode of production and enterprise which first proved successful in Japan and which is said to be responsible for the outstanding growth and strength of her economy. Although the investigations by the team of the Massachusetts Institute of Technology are concerned with automobile manufacturing only, the results could easily be generalized.

Comparing productivity, quality of the products and costs (money and time), the authors found remarkable differences between the leading industrial companies in Japan and their competitors in USA and in Europe, as well as between Japanese owned companies in USA or Britain (transplants) and home industries. In each aspect the East Asian manufacturers of motor cars were performing better.

The message says, consequently, there is a new 'one best way' of manufacturing complex mass products which allows one to reduce the costs of production and to improve the products according to the changing demands of consumers for growing variation in consumer goods, allowing for an expression of individuality. In short in contrast with the craft producer and the mass-producer:

> the lean-producer combines the advantages of craft and mass production, while avoiding the high cost of the former and the rigidity of the latter. Toward this end, lean producers employ teams of multiskilled workers at all levels of the organization and use highly flexible, increasingly automated machines to produce volumes of products in enormous variety. Lean production ... is 'lean' because it uses less of everything compared with mass production - half the

human effort in the factory, half the manufacturing space, half the investment of tools, half the engineering hours to develop a new product in half the time. Also, it requires keeping far less than half the needed inventory on site, results in many fewer defects, and produces a greater and ever growing variety of products.' (Womack et al., 1990, p. 13)

In fact, the lesson taught by their Japanese competitors was learned quickly by American and European managers. We can read about it every day - sharp cuts in employment, reduction of personnel not only on the shop floor but also in the (middle) ranks of management, especially those parts which belong to the traditional control system; establishment of team work, manufacturing islands and other organizational experiments which in Europe were already known from the Swedish Volvo company. In these days, there seems to be no firm, of at least moderate size, which would not try and change towards integrated or participative management and new concepts of work organization known as 'lean production'. In Germany the outstanding examples in the automobile industry are Volkswagen, Mercedes-Benz and Opel. The most recent case in Europe is the new plant of SEAT near Barcelona. But these are only the most popular examples, as a current research project of the Soziologisches Forschungsinstitut (SOFI) Göttingen shows, where a manufacturer of farming machines, a producer of special package and a firm of 'outsourcing' in the branch of software services are the subjects of intensive case studies (Dörre et al. 1993).

In order to improve the knowledge and to accelerate the acceptance of the new mode of management thousands of workshops on 'lean production' are organized by the big companies and by federations of employers, and more and more by the unions, too, because of their immediate concern with employment and working conditions.

Nevertheless, if we look at the discussions among industrial sociologists it seemed for a long time as if we could only choose between an interpretation of lean production as a fashion or as a myth. The myth was - Japan, the fashion, calling something qualitatively new which was in reality, old. To some extent this reaction is understandable. This sometimes Messianic message - Change or Die - has an apocalyptic sound. Yet, the 'Japanese threat' goes hand in hand with praising a model of harmonious working communities and autonomous work teams. It may seem to be just ideology, or merely propaganda.

Explicitly, the authors rejected the idea that their book was just another 'Japan' book. 'We pay little attention to the special features of Japanese society...This is not a book about what is wrong with Japan or with the rest of the world but about what is right with lean production' (Womack et al., 1990, p. 9). It is this explicit abstraction from the special cultural and political features of a given society, which is often criticised.

What is right with lean production?

If we try to answer the question, what is right with lean production?, it seems to be necessary to take a general standpoint as well as a comparative one. We should analyse the concept in the context of the wider structural changes that are taking place in all the metropolitan centres of the modern world, yet take on different forms of appearance due to the specific economic, political and cultural conditions in the different countries. There are general laws of economic development as well as contingent economic, political and cultural factors. There are certain 'necessities' the representatives of social institutions must not overlook if they want to be successful, and there is a need for creativity as well. In this sense we are dealing with structural change which can be influenced, and which takes place in the various political arenas and contested terrains of modern society: not only on the shop floor but in the entire field of industrial relations as well as in the fields of law and politics, culture and ideology.

The continuous structural change of industry, its technological equipment and organization, is normal in modern capitalism. More than that, it is the necessary consequence and condition of capital accumulation. We know about its contradictory forms, the civilizing effects as well as the risks and damage it produces. It can also be taken as given that this continuous change, steered by the laws of competition, is far from smooth or even. Embedded in the continuous flow of innovation there are periods of a more or less revolutionary character. Known as business or industrial cycles and long waves of innovation, we can distinguish epochs of accumulation regimes (Aglietta 1976). Economic crises and the shifts in the world leadership or supremacy in the world market are the landmarks in these periodical changes.

In the sense of a structure or an accumulation regime, consisting of dominant economic conditions and interrelated political and cultural elements, the epoch which is now ending has been defined as 'Fordism'. The period of mass production and mass consumption, the period of rising scientific management and deskilling as well as polarizing effects of technological improvements, has been broadly described, especially as far as its impact on industrial work is concerned. As Thompson summarizes:

[Science has] deepened the trend towards deskilling and task fragmentation, which is most commonly associated with the emergence of the assembly line... Indeed, for some writers ... assembly production is the characteristic form of mechanization. Palloix asserts that this development, labelled Fordism, innovated and extended Taylorism, the flow line principle allowing for greater mechanical control by management, while high day-wage rates regulated the supply and conditions of labour. The unskilled assembly worker is therefore seen as a central result of accelerated mechanization. (Thompson, 1983, p. 79)

Fordism, first developed in the USA in the 1920s, broadly introduced to Europe after World War II, has in our days reached its immanent borders. This is what studies like that of Piore and Sabel (1984) tell us. And this is what the MIT study also tells us. First, the 'Fordist' mode of production has become too expensive, because the time of the capital cycle as compared with new competing forms is very high. In other words, competing industrial companies are forced to reduce the periods in which the stock of capital is not used productively, whether in the process of production itself or in the process of circulation. Second, mass production fails to reach high standards of quality. This results in expensive repairs to products before they can leave the plant (costly inspection and repair, and rectification of defects). Third, traditional mass production turns out to be inflexible in responding to a quickly changing market and to the demands of consumers. Last, but not least, Fordism is lavish with the central productive force, labour power, which through the deskilling effects of the Taylor system is deprived of its potential creative and intellectual functions.

Much of the enthusiasm about Computer Integrated Manufacturing (CIM) in the 1980s can be understood as a response to the experience of the sharp and deadly competition taking place in terms of costs, quality and flexibility. But it turned out to be a partial answer. Modern information and communication technology, the basic technology of micro-electronics, is the irreplaceable prerequisite for any new concept of production. But, this can only be more effective within a new organization of science and technology on the one hand and of the labour process on the other.

The new quality of a 'post-Fordist' type of manufacturing lies in its systemic and integrated character. Much more than the mere mechanization and rationalization of single units, it is the integration of all parts of the enterprise and of all steps of market strategy, product development, engineering and design, components supply, and the complex labour process in the final assembly plant. And we should know that 'assembling the major components into a complete vehicle, the task of the final assembly plant, accounts for only 15 percent or so of the total manufacturing process.' (Womack et al., 1990, p. 58)

Integrated process management, simultaneous engineering, lean design, just-in-time supply of the components, systematic control and continuous improvement of the performance of labour in the last stage - the assembling of the end product, and, finally, the system of selling the cars are the main elements of the new production concept: 'It is critical to understand the mechanism of coordination necessary to bring all these steps into harmony and on a global scale, a mechanism we call the lean enterprise.' (Womack et al., 1990, p. 73)

The central elements of 'lean production' can be summarised as:

-   the organization of the manufacturing process around the ideal of zero-mistakes and zero-buffers (small stocks);

- team-work and intensified co-operation within a unit and between the units of the manufacturing process;
- activities which aim for continuous improvements in output through quality circles, a system which motivates employees to act creatively;
- a flow of information to employees from management in order to help them understand the entire process of manufacturing;
- more job control through worker participation, compared with Taylorism and Fordism. (Jürgens, 1992, pp. 32, 33, Jürgens et al. 1989)

In the lean-concept, the emphasis is laid on the human factor. With this emphasis laid upon labour process organization, people return to the centre of interest. They become essential in the measures taken to rationalize production. Although we should keep in mind that the degree of mechanization is not irrelevant to the productivity of lean production (flexible automation), there is broad consent as to the decisive elements which are seen in the organization of work and a reskilling of the workers - in as far as they are concerned with the central functions of lean manufacturing.

Yet another trait should be emphasized. As compared with Taylorism or the Fordist mode of production, the 'deep and far reaching change of organization philosophy', as one of the MIT authors put it in a propoganda campaign, demands much more co-operation between management and workforce:

> Asking the employee to invest more of his brain as well as his physical power, only works if the employee realises a reciprocal sentiment of responsibility and obligation. The secret key to a steadily growing effectiveness is not High Tech but the employee. Therefore, in the long run it will be decisive for the success of lean production to motivate the commitment of the employees and to invest into the personnel. (Jones, 1992, p. 20)

As much concern is dedicated to the key role of team work. The authors of the MIT study report on the first experiments in the Toyota factories in the late 40s.

> The first step was to group the workers into teams with a team leader rather than a foreman. The teams were given a set of assembly steps, their piece of the line, and told to work together on how best to perform the necessary operations. The team leader would do assembly tasks as well as coordinate the team, and, in particular, would fill in for any absent worker - concepts unheard of in mass-production plants. (Womack et al., 1990, p. 56)

Next the team was given 'the job of housekeeping, minor tool repair, and quality-checking. Finally, as the last step, after the teams were running smoothly, ... time was set aside periodically for the team to suggest ways collectively to improve the process.' (ibid.) These *kaizen*, later in the West called 'quality circles', worked in collaboration with the industrial engineers who were reduced to a much smaller number.

Closely linked with these changes was the system of problem-solving, the zero error-method. 'Production workers were taught to trace systematically every error back to its ultimate cause, then to devise a fix, so that it would never occur again.' (Womack et al., 1990, p. 57, see also p. 92) To summarise:

> So in the end, it is the dynamic work team that emerges as the heart of the lean factory. Building these efficient teams is not simple. First, workers need to be taught a wide variety of skills - in fact, all the jobs in their work group so that tasks can be rotated and workers can fill in for each other. Workers then need to acquire many additional skills: simple machine repair, quality-checking, housekeeping, and materials-ordering. Then they need encouragement to think actively, indeed proactively, so they can devise solutions before problems become serious. (Womack et al., 1990, p. 99)

Team work implies, it seems obvious, much more responsibility and more job control by production workers than Taylorism. The workers are conceived of as integrated into the processes of innovation and detecting defects, and this implies the necessity and opportunity for their upgrading and intellectual qualification.

The authors discuss the consequences when replying to the critique which charges lean production with inhumanity. Critics would suggest that the new concept would much better be labelled management by stress, because of the lack of any time-buffers.

> We agree that a properly organized lean-production system does indeed remove all slack - that's why it's lean. But it also provides workers with the skills they need to control their work environment and the continuing challenge of making the work go more smoothly. While the mass-production plant is often filled with mind-numbing stress, as workers struggle to assemble unmanufacturable products and have no way to improve their working environment, lean production offers a creative tension in which workers have many ways to address challenges. This creative tension involved in solving complex problems is precisely what has separated manual factory work from professional 'think' work in the age of mass production... What's more, we believe that ... by the end of the century we (can) expect that lean-assembly plants will be populated almost entirely by highly skilled problem solvers whose task will be to think continually of ways to make the system run more smoothly and productively. (Womack et al., 1990, p. 101)

Myth or reality? a critical evaluation of lean production

Contrary to the optimistic (if not euphoric) interpretation of the benefits of post-fordist production teams, Ulrich Jürgens, who has participated in comparative research in the international automobile industry (Jürgens et al. 1989), calls this an unbearable extenuation of reality. 'Automobile manufacturing in Japan is highly repetitive, often short-cycled and highly intensified work under very great stress - day after day, and during long working hours.' (Jürgens, 1992, p. 31) This is confirmed by another expert in East Asia industrial sociology: 'Lean production in Japan is not only based on a subtle system of coordination and organization of the chain of value production, but also on long working hours, low wages and bad working conditions.' (Altmann, 1992, p. 31)

A black and white picture with mind-numbing stress characterizing mass production, and creative tension representing lean production, is much too simple to portray reality. The reproach of these critical industrial sociologists is, that the MIT authors are far too imprecise when describing the Japanese organization of work - and thus are weaving a myth. To understand reality better, it seems to be important to analyse the same concepts in their specific cultural environment. This is what Jürgens et al. (1989) have done.

Team work in Japan is different from team work in Europe. When we think of group work, we think of task structuring, time sovereignty, the allowance of a certain latitude in work, discretion and room for maneouvre, partial autonomy etc. In short, group work is a result of the creative organization of work. The connotation of team work in Japan is more that of recruiting and socializing the plant workforce, the group is the unit where new workers are introduced to the factory, where they are qualified, where they are confronted with positive and with negative sanctions, mainly exercising social technologies to fit in with the firm, and which provides them with a social network at the same time.

Jürgens (1992) identifies three elements of what he calls 'Toyotism', and interprets them in a much more critical manner. First, just-in-time organization with its reduction of buffers 'leads to continuous chronic stress in the form of process pressure - one of the essential elements of group coherence.' (Jürgens, 1992, p. 28) Second, the hierarchical structure on Japanese shop floor results in no self-determination or self-organization in the sense of democratization. Third, the evaluation system of the workforce places importance on the workers' behaviour in the group, their loyalty towards work and firm, their participation in group life and innovation activities in problem solving.

In order to underline cultural distinctiveness, one can add the results of an examination of working time in Japan by Christoph Deutschmann:

A comparatively high level of annual and weekly working time reflects the weak boundary between work and leisure that characterizes Japanese employment. Through management-orchestrated peer-group pressure, male employees are prevailed upon not to take vacations and to accept endemic unscheduled overtime. Even the time nominally available for leisure is colonized by the corporation, especially in core sector firms. Male employees are expected to socialize with colleagues and bosses in order that the ethic of commitment that binds people together in their daily work is reinforced outside the sphere of work proper. (Hinrichs et al., 1991, p. 9)

This critique of a myth, which is created by imprecise definitions and undue generalizations, cannot, of course, wipe out the fact that some fundamental changes are going on in key industries and their work organization all over the world. Their revolutionary character lies in a specific change in the combination of the forces of production. As the capitalist mode of production is not questioned, the new concept of a lean plant represents a new type of rationalization within capitalist economy and within large scale machine production. While in earlier periods, the different elements or factors of production could easily be separated from one another, this separation becomes more and more obsolete when the two components, machinery and work organization, are dissolving into one another, and merging into one integrated complex economy of capital. By shifting intellectual power - control, responsibility and 'think work' - to the productive workers on the line ('those workers actually adding value to the car on the line', Womack et al., 1990, p. 99), the employee has to internalize the categories of value production. Housekeeping and zero-error; preventive providing for high quality; encouragement of proactive thinking as part of conditioning and qualifying for the new professional type of worker: these are thought to create a mentality of self control, or rather an intrinsically economic motivation without remaining merely instrumental.

The internalization of economic action and the consequent identification of one's own satisfaction with the success and effectiveness of the corporation are the most overt purposes of the new philosophy of organization. This goes much farther than Scientific Management and includes much more than the ideology of Human Relations does. As one of the top managers of the Volkswagen company put it: 'Our aim is to make our employees think as enterprises!' (Weißgerber, 1991, p. 32)

The religion of economic everyday life that Marx (1956, p. 838) wrote of, is so deeply rooted in the minds of workers that the ideological efforts of the new organizational philosophy might well be successful. However, the mystificated forms of bourgeois consciousness - liberté, egalité, fraternité, proprieté privée! - make up only one side of the workers' contradictory ideas and concepts. The other side is made up of 'wage slavery' - the experience of continued inequality, dependence and exclusion from productive property. (Herkommer and Bierbaum 1979)

Because of this, we cannot expect a smooth obeisance to the offers of the management. There is much evidence for assuming that workers will take it literally, when the other side speaks of the importance of 'reciprocal obligations'

(Womack et al., 1990, p. 103). Recent research findings underline considerable changes in value orientation. As a result of broader educational facilities and enlarging fields of participation in the wealth of our modern nations, it becomes more and more typical for younger workers - and particularly for women - to make greater demands about working conditions. The famous instrumentalism of the 'affluent worker' in the 1960s (Goldthorpe et al. 1968) has always been only half the truth. Today, the so called post-materialistic values of participation and self-determination, identity, personal autonomy and individual pursuit of happiness, are not confined to the sphere of non-work, but have become a measure to judge the sphere of work as well. This also means that the call for more information and participation goes farther than the immediate range of one's own work, and that obsolete structures of hierarchy should be cancelled and changed in favour of group work and (at least) partial group autonomy, including more possibilities for free discretion, codetermination, decision-making, and improved training on the job.

Reality is considerably lagging behind these needs. But at least for some parts of the workforce there seems to exist a potential within the changing conditions of work. In fact,

> the new concept of production meets to a great deal the explicit wants of the young skilled workers (*Facharbeiter*) for their professional qualification and extension of their own competence. When this new type of worker, the 'system regulator' (*Systemregulierer*), becomes an actor, just in the sense of the lean-production concept, he does not, as Womack et al. are insinuating, because of some 'spirit of reciprocal obligation'. Subjectively, from the point of view of the worker, the integration into the politics of shop-floor rationalization is less founded in a self-obligation in the interest of the firm or in his chances of job security, but is due to the special characteristics of the job a system regulator has to do and from a certain parallelism of interests which is mediated in the work situation. (Schumann et al., 1992, p. 21)

In this context, the creative impact of individual identification with the performance of the task has gained much attention. The tendency towards more 'normative subjectivity' on the job (Baethge 1991, Herkommer 1991) seems to be the result of two parallel forces working in the same direction, first the change in work and its progressive evolution in both, technological and organizational dimensions, the second the change in attitudes and values, and their progress in the dimensions of autonomy and communicative competence. 'From the self-made man to the man-made self' (Leinberger, Tucker, 1991, p. 226) expresses very well what is going on. The separation of instrumental orientation in professional life from an expressive private life is being eroding, and the desire for an integrated lifestyle which reconciles instrumentalism with expressivity is growing.

Both forces, those emerging from the changed conditions of work and those generated by a higher level of education, are emphasizing a greater demand for creativity, competence and flexibility. They are mutually reinforcing each other. As far as the big capitalist companies have to an increasing degree become dependent on the greater competence, creativity and motivation of the workforce, they have to make concessions to the workers, in order to be able to exploit the full potential of their skills and qualification. In other words, the externally generated needs for living more intrinsically, more communicatively and more expressively, will be internally confirmed and developed in the work situation. (Baethge 1991)

Risks and chances of the new mode of management

The structural and mental changes we are observing might well have an essential effect on the relations between employers and employees. The question is, however, whether the emergence of a lean enterprise (as the new organizational paradigm within capitalism) will be the end of class confrontation and class conflict. Will the shop floor lose its classic character of a contested terrain (Edwards 1979), will the old ideological dreams of social partnership come true as a new pragmatic co-management (Müller-Jentsch 1986)? The spectrum of answers in the recent debate among industrial sociologists reaches from the assumption of a New Deal between the classes including the prognosis of full democratization on the one hand to the thesis of perfecting management control and workers' alienation on the other hand. (Dörre et al., 1993, p. 16)

My own answer would try to be more differentiated and would start from the underlying contradictions, it would underline the risks and the chances, and it would emphasize the decisive role of power, the relative strength of capital and labour according to the economic and political as well as the organizational conditions of the participants in industrial relations.

First and on a very general level, I should say that the essential configuration is unchanged. Capital ownership implies a monopoly of decision as to investment, labour allocation and working conditions. In order to promote equality in the exchange relations and to struggle for fair wages, normal working times and human conditions on the job, the workers are dependent on collective action. Even in a democratic welfare state, where individual rights are politically guaranteed and social security belongs to the achieved human rights, the workers' associations, the unions, remain the fundamental precondition for the reproduction of the worker. The unions abolish competition among the individual workers in order to be competitive with capital. But they cannot abolish the asymmetry between capital and labour. These general traits have remained valid in the so-called industrial relations, as they are constitutive of a system of private ownership.

But second, if the type of accumulation regime changes from Fordism to something 'post-fordist', there will be likewise a change in the regulation of the relationship between capital and labour. Apart from the fact that employers could always rely on the silent pressure of economic necessity, they have always been, to some extent, dependent on the consent of their employees, also. 'Even in the nineteenth century, mechanisms for creating consent ran parallel with coercive measures connected with increasing the intensity to work.' (Thompson, 1983, p. 55) In a double sense free, the workers are not only free of property, but they are also free as persons who are able to dispose of the amount of their time, energy and skills. This is why control strategies in industrial organizations can not be confined to the crude methods of slavedrivers. This is true for the age of Manchester capitalism as well as for Taylorism. Now, in the foreshadowing epoch of a new mode of management, called lean production, motivation and good will, consent with the aims of the company, and participation in shop floor or management decisions have become much more important than at any time before. If it is true, that modern management is becoming more and more dependent on the creativity, on the intellectual power and on a mentality of economy and instrumental rationality incorporated in the worker, then it seems to be plausible to assume new chances for workers and improved bargaining power.

However, scepticism arises when we realize some of the empirical consequences that the new concepts of production already have had on the internal and external labour market. Externally, the reduction of the plant workforce has led to increasing numbers of jobless in the population and mass unemployment. There is a developing split between the core and the fringe workforce, between the 'winners' and the 'losers' of modernization. Growing disparities and segmentation mean that precarious conditions of reproduction and a high number of repetitive, unqualified tasks on the shop floor are the other side of the coin which the MIT propaganda campaign tries to hide away. The increasing cleavages of this sort may have a negative effect on the strength of the unions and shop floor workers' representatives. 'Any success in improving the working conditions in the core of 'lean production' leads to more social problems and contradictions in the marginal zones of the labour market and of society.' (Deppe, 1993, p. 32)

This may be the fundamental dilemma. On the one hand, if the unions remain in a ghetto of total refusal and ignore the modern concepts of production and enterprise, they lose their influence. On the other hand, if they give support to the cleaving of working and living conditions and are successful in taking part in the management practices of participation, job enrichment, reduction of hierarchy by teamwork, they gain support from qualified workers, while they lose support from the unqualified and marginalized ones.

I am not sure whether there is an unsurmountable obstacle. But it shows us the contradiction between the necessity of protective functions of the unions and their chances for creative participation. In order to overcome this dilemma, the unions have to come up with new answers to traditional questions on the shop floor (wages, evaluation of work, on the job training, co-determination), but they have also to include new functions in their programme. They cannot survive and they cannot fulfill their traditional and classic functions of protection, if they deny their social role of policy making. Protection from the inroads of capital and management decisions and creating humane conditions on the job and beyond affords participation in the politics of labour market, structural and regional economy, education, traffic, health, science and the new field of ecology. It affords, moreover, a creative role in the process of capital investment and economic development, rational planning and regulation, thus acting as a break on the uncontrolled working of the market economy.

Co-management cannot be confined to a single company or to the shop floor. If at all, it can only work for the best of the majority if it becomes an entirely social co-management, if it takes on - at the very centre of modern society - the quality of civil society. On the assumption, that the very centre remains constituted by the social form of work and the relations of production, a policy of reforming the crucial social relations and structures (including the conditions of everday life) cannot exclude changing the monopoly of decision-making about investing capital and labour as well as the way of using our natural resources.

If this change is the aim, the way to achieve it is 'antagonistic cooperation'. Although some participants in the debate would still argue that experience from the past shows that any class-collaborative policy of cooperation and any pact of 'solidarity' between the antagonistic social forces of capital and labour, run the risk of reducing union strength, there seems to be - even to them - no other alternative. To put it more positively, apart from the fact that there seems to be no other choice for the unions than creative participation in the modernization process, there exists considerable potential chances, too, which can be used in order to improve working and living conditions altogether. To avoid the illusions of the past, it is necessary to conceive the new model for a post-Fordist mode of production and regulation as a form of antagonistic cooperation. Its functioning depends on strong unions.

Trade unions can only keep (or get back) their strength if they succeed in combining collectivism and collective action with the needs of a highly differentiated and individualized workforce. This is why in my eyes the workers' organizations should become defenders or even promoters of the normative subjectivity, referred to earlier in this chapter. This is far from pleading for utilitarianism and ego-centred 'individualism' as the core values of our society. On the contrary, what we could call a highly differentiated and rich individuality can only grow out of social conditions in which the members of society are collectively and consciously participating.

But this leads us to yet another conclusion. The same changes which are responsible for the new functions of the unions and a modified union strategy also highlight new responsibilities for political institutions. Taking seriously the idea of a 'post-Fordist-Keynesian mode of regulation' (Streeck 1987) means that the functions of the state and of the public institutions, including the political parties and local as well as regional social movements, will not only expand but at the same time take on a new quality. As the economy and the state, and correspondingly the functions of the conflicting parties of capital and labour on the

6 Industrial conflict: A comparative analysis

Gerrit van Kooten

Introduction

In the last fifteen years, major social trends can be identified which have had a major impact on socio-economic relations in Europe. These trends are distinguished by administrative changes and economic changes. The administrative changes involve increasing decentralization, as central government withdraws and responsibilities are moved to a lower level. Sometimes, this brings about greater authority for local governments. Sometimes, it leads to the dominance of a less regulated market (Ferner and Hyman 1992). Decentralization is also related to increasing deregulation. Numerous social rules are recalibrated as the standard becomes the extent to which rules sustain and promote an efficient functioning of the market and autonomous social processes. Privatization follows from deregulation. Where possible, the performance of government tasks are being transferred from the semi-public sector to social organizations and/or the market. In addition, there is increasing criticism of corporatist decision making (Ferner and Hyman 1992). Of the three co-ordination mechanisms to be distinguished in pursuing socio-economic policy, namely the (welfare) state, corporatist arrangements and the free market, the market becomes most important. Finally, one may observe an Europeanization of policy. As the European Community takes more and more shape, there is a transfer of political and administrative decision making to Brussels (Nagelkerke 1994).

In addition to administrative changes there are economic changes, such as the internationalization and globalization of production and competition. Economic relations are, to an increasing degree, of a global character. Borders become less important as economic lines of demarcation. Companies strive for new markets throughout the world or leave for those areas where production and/or distribution costs are lowest (Nagelkerke 1994). This is both a consequence and an expression of increasing competition. The emphasis on free trade has liberalized markets. Worldwide, national protective policy is attacked. Internationalization of production and competition has set in motion a process in the direction of expansion and integration (Ferner and Hyman 1992). Indicative of this development is the increase in merger and concentration processes and the growth toward strategic alliances in the form of co-operation treaties and joint-ventures. Against the internationalization of production and competition there is an increasing individualization of needs. Consumers show less and less interest in group norms and stable spending behaviour (Nagelkerke 1994). Fast changing preferences, strongly distinguished in groups, prompt flexibility in the supply of goods and services. The production process must be organized flexibly and, commercially speaking, changing individual needs and preferences have to be anticipated.

Changes in systems of industrial relations can be summarized as follows. Economic standards have become more important for the organization of industrial relations than social standards (Baglioni 1990). National governments withdraw as a greater part of industrial relations becomes regulated by employers and employees without regulation by national government. Common promotion of interests by organizations becomes more difficult. Companies, each in their own competitive environment, have separate wishes, needs and preferences; employees develop more individual wishes and have different employment positions. Company interests as well as interests of employees are lumped together less easily.

In this chapter we will discuss the consequences of these developments for national systems of industrial relations. The central question in this respect is whether or not there will be a tendency towards either convergence or divergence. The question will be answered by focusing upon patterns of industrial conflict. There are at least two reasons to do so. First, since the second world war there have been marked differences in patterns of industrial conflict between nations as well as within nations over time. Second, some of the developments described above are central to explanatory models of industrial conflict.

Industrial conflict is variously shaped. Besides the well-known strike, a distinction may be made between, among other things demonstrations, working to rule, slow-downs and plant-occupations. Moreover sabotage and absenteeism are considered to be manifestations of conflict. Strikes, however, are the only form of conflict for which official records are kept. Therefore, a comparative analysis of industrial conflict is necessarily limited to differences in strike activity. In this chapter international variations in strike activity are described and, if possible, explained. Attention is focused on Germany, Sweden, the United Kingdom, France, Italy and the Netherlands. In order to compare these countries, the second part deals with indicators of strike activity. In the third part, two explanatory models of short term fluctuations in strike activity are examined. Subsequently two theoretical approaches to the variations in the level of national strike activity are discussed, namely Ross and Hartman's institutional model and the politico-economical approach by Hibbs. In the concluding section these theoretical approaches and the respective models are evaluated.

Industrial conflict

Conflict is intrinsic to industrial relations. Kerr enumerates four reasons. First, he points out that the wishes of the parties are more or less unlimited; in contrast to the available means. Almost by definition, the level of both wages and profits does not meet the expectations either of employees or employers. Second, systems of industrial relations generate positions of subordination, and conflicts of interest. Third, Kerr emphasizes the dynamic character of industrial societies. If parties are able to reach a mutually acceptable distribution of income and power, this distribution is immediately called into question due to external developments. For example, new rules, higher costs of raw materials or inflation may necessitate employers and employees to agreeing upon an alternative way of distribution. Fourth, the presence of conflict is one of the conditions for the parties to preserve their characteristic identities. The trade union which is always in agreement with the employer loses its raison d'être (Kerr 1954).

As to the contents, conflict between employers and employees may range from wages and other financial aspects to working hours, physical work load, employee participation, problems related to reorganisation, disturbed social relations and so on. Industrial conflict is an integral part of industrial relations. Both the manifestation and resolution of conflict, however, are multifold. Regarding the resolution of industrial conflict, a rough distinction can be made between on the one hand 'diplomatic' means, such as collective bargaining, and on the other hand more 'aggressive' means, such as strikes. As to manifestations of conflict, a relevant distinction is between 'individual' and 'collective' expressions of conflict. Sabotage, absenteeism and a high degree of turn-over are generally considered to be individual reactions to conflict situations. Combined with the above this results in four types of conflict, of which an example is given in the figure below.

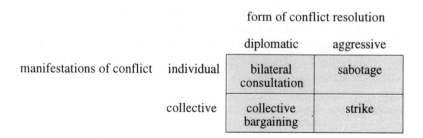

Figure 6.1 Four types of industrial conflict

It should be mentioned this distinction is purely analytical. 'Diplomatic' as well as 'aggressive' should rather be understood as the opposite ends of a continuum than as two values of a dichotomous variable. With respect to collective manifestations of industrial conflict, many other forms can be situated between collective bargaining and strikes, such as working to rule, slow downs and protest demonstrations. Furthermore, sabotage has individual as well as collective variants. Finally, some diplomatic and aggressive forms may not only be considered functional equivalents, but also may be found in combination. There are at least three logically possible relationships between the strike and collective bargaining. First, a strike and bargaining may take place simultaneously. In such cases, striking is mainly meant to put pressure on and thus to expedite the bargaining process. Second, a strike may follow bargaining to get it going again after an impasse. Third, a strike may precede bargaining. Then generally the aim is to make certain issues, until then unmentioned, the subject of serious bargaining.

The nature and the largely concealed character of individual manifestations make it extraordinarily difficult, if not impossible, to analyse these types of conflict from a comparative point of view. With respect to collective manifestations, bargaining is considered the way to resolve conflicts of interest between employers and employees. In the literature on industrial conflicts more aggressive forms are emphasized. The most visible, and thus the most well-known, example is the strike. As the strike is the only form for which official records are kept, international comparison of industrial conflict is often limited to differences in strike activity. There are, however, restrictions in this type of comparison.

First, the criteria for registration in official strike records differ from country to country. For example, in Germany and the United Kingdom a strike has to last at least one day and at least ten workers are to be involved, before the strike is officially recorded. In Italy and France, on the other hand, such criteria do not exist. Second, strikes don't form a homogeneous category. They differ not only in scale and duration, but also in point at issue, outcome, way of organising and strategy. One distinction in this respect is between the strike organised by a recognized trade union versus a so called wild-cat strike. Third, a strike aimed at the preservation of employment requires a completely different strategy from a strike for a wage raise. Or, in more general terms, defensive strikes, aimed at the preservation of existing conditions of employment are in more than one way incomparable with offensive strikes, aimed at the improvement of conditions of employment. Nevertheless, this distinction is hardly ever made in explanatory models of strike activity. The figures presented in the next part of this article should be interpreted with these restrictions in mind.

Strike activity

Comparative research generally deals with four dimensions of strike activity: frequency, average scale, average duration and volume. Frequency is the number of strikes during a certain period of time, usually a year. Scale is the number of employees involved and duration is expressed in the number of working days. Volume is represented by the total number of working days lost. To improve comparability, these dimensions are averaged over time. The following table shows these dimensions with respect to the countries under discussion for the periods 1972-81 and 1981-93.

Table 6.1
Indicators of strike activity
(1972-81/1981-93)

Country	frequency (100,000)		strikers per 1,000 employees		average duration in days		working days lost (per 1,000 employees)	
	'72-'81	'81-'93	'72-'81	'81-'93	'72-'81	'81-'93	'72-'81	'81-'93
Germany	-	-	7	12	4.4	2.0	31	24
Sweden	3	2	26	11	5.5	6.0	144	65
UK	10	3	68	33	7.8	5.7	531	202
France	19	13	85	8	2.2	10.5	187	52
Italy	22	7	741	260	1.9	1.3	1382	353
Netherlands	0.5	0.5	5	4	4.4	3.3	22	14

(source: Poole 1986, OECD 1995, ILO 1994)

Table 6.1 illustrates marked differences between as well as within countries from period to period. France and Italy, for example, have known the highest frequency of strikes during the seventies, while these countries were lagging behind in terms of average duration. In Italy, the average number of employees involved, however, was nine times higher than France. At the same time it can be concluded that strikes are rather rare and of a moderate duration in the Netherlands and Germany. The United Kingdom has been mainly characterized by the long duration of strikes. Sweden combines a low frequency with a relatively long duration. In the case of Sweden the figures are distorted by one very extensive strike in 1980.

It is worth remarking upon some of the differences between the two periods. There has been a decline in the number of strikes in the United Kingdom and in Italy, there has been a reduction in frequency by a third between the two periods. With respect to the number of employees involved and the average duration the greatest change took place in France where the number of employees involved decreased to a considerable extent, whereas the average duration increased. In the eighties, the averages for several countries are distorted by a number of exceptional years. As a consequence, the variation over time within countries is concealed. But, to gain an insight into the fluctuations in strike activity, the use of frequency as an indicator has a number of problems. The principal objection is that all strikes, regardless of scale or duration, are assigned the same weight. Knowles points to

97

this.

> What meaning can one attach to a change in the number of strikes when a one-day stoppage of ten clothing workers, a seven-month strike of a million miners, and a nine-day general strike of workers in all the main industries of the country each counts as one strike? (Knowles, 1954, p. 215)

By taking the total number of working days lost, the problem is overcome. This takes into account both scale and duration. In table 6.2 the total number of working days lost per thousand employees is given for the respective countries. In combination with table 6.1, table 6.2 indicates that on the whole the number of working days lost has decreased, especially in Italy. In that sense there is more or less a tendency towards convergence.

Table 6.2
Number of working days lost per 1000 employees
1984-93

Country	'84	'85	'86	'87	'88	'89	'90	'91	'92	'93
Germany	217	1	1	1	2	4	13	5	50	19
Sweden	7	117	160	3	181	92	178	5	6	44
UK	1135	264	79	143	145	156	73	27	19	23
France	65	42	50	46	59	42	24	21	14	20
Italy	426	187	274	224	159	213	243	121	111	-
Netherlands	6	18	8	10	2	4	34	16	14	7

Source: OECD (1995), pp. 36-69, ILO (1994), pp. 1074-91

Obviously, even in the short term, there are considerable differences in the level of strike activity in several countries. In the next part of this article, two approaches are dealt with, explaining short term fluctuations in strike activity. Later, two comparative approaches are reviewed.

Trend studies

In this part, the explanation of short term fluctuation in strike activity is central. In classic studies on this subject, strike activity is almost exclusively connected with economic variables. Through the years, there has been a development of better theoretical foundations as well as the use of more advanced statistical methods. This development culminated in the study of Ashenfelter and Johnson (1969). Their explanatory model may be considered as exemplary for what in this chapter - because of the emphasis on economic variables - is called the 'economic approach'. Partly in reaction to the economic approach, a 'political approach' has been

98

developed.

The economic approach: Ashenfelter and Johnson

In their explanatory model Ashenfelter and Johnson (1969) assume that in case of collective bargaining three instead of two parties are involved. In addition to management and union leaders, there are also union members. In this view, which is based on the ideas of Ross (1948), the goal of union leaders is twofold. On the one hand they strive for the continued existence and growth of the union as an institution. On the other hand, their personal political survival as union leaders plays a part. Both goals are mostly attained by fulfilling the expectations of their members. Besides, union leaders are generally more aware of the possibilities within negotiations than the rank and file and they do more than merely represent the members. If the members expected wage raise (the minimally acceptable wage claim) is much higher than the wage raise with which management will agree, union leaders will try to get the rank and file agree to less. If this fails, there are two alternatives. Either a contract is signed that lags behind the expectations of the members, or a strike is called. Choosing the first alternative implies that the members withhold their support from the contract. Discord within the union and decline of the electoral attraction of the union leaders may be the result. Therefore union leaders tend to prefer the second alternative, although it may be contrary to the interests of the members in the long term. Calling a strike creates at least the impression that the union leaders are acting as opponents of management, which favours their electoral position and in general closes ranks. As a result of the outbreak of the strike, the expectations of the rank and file are readjusted downwards, because of the impact of the resistance of the management and because of the loss of income which results from the strike. After some time the minimally acceptable wage raise will be down to such a level, that union leaders and management can enter into an agreement and the strike will be ended without endangering the position of the union leaders with the rank and file.

Ashenfelter and Johnson put forward the proposition that the chance of a strike increases the higher that the minimally acceptable wage raise is for the rank and file. Then the deciding factor, the size of the minimally acceptable wage raise is determined. According to Ashenfelter and Johnson, this involves three economic variables: unemployment, profits and past changes in real wages. The impact of these variables is as follows:

1 *Unemployment* The acceptable wage raise is assumed to be negatively related to the percentage unemployed. Three reasons for this are brought forward. First, at the time of minor unemployment the average employee is in a better position to obtain a better paid job. As the costs of moving for example can be considerable, she or he will initially try to improve his/her wage in his/her current position, what results in an increase in the

acceptable wage raise. Second, in case of a strained employment situation union leaders probably don't attempt to reduce the acceptable wage raise: in that situation the negative employment effects of a considerable wage raise are minor and there are huge funds to meet the loss of income of the strikers. Third, during a period of minor unemployment one's job opportunities are better, so the resistance against a more militant form of action is smaller.

2   *Recent profits of the company* In case of high profits employees will take the view that they deserve a considerable wage raise. In such a situation the union leaders are hardly motivated to induce the members to be satisfied with less.

3   *The average of changes of the real wages in the past* The level of wage raises in the past is assumed to have a conditioning effect on the expected outcomes of new wage bargaining.

At the opposite side of the negotiating table management has a choice between meeting the demands of the union, which correspond with those of the members, or 'accepting' a strike to bring about an agreement with a lower wage raise. According to Ashenfelter and Johnson, employers are more easily inclined to adopt an indulgent air at the moment that profits are high. Therefore, the ultimate effect of the variable 'profits' is the result of the impact on all parties. If the wage demand exceeds the offer of the employer, a strike will follow, with the result that as time passes the wage demand is readjusted downwards until it is equal to the offer of the employers. The model is represented in figure 6.2.

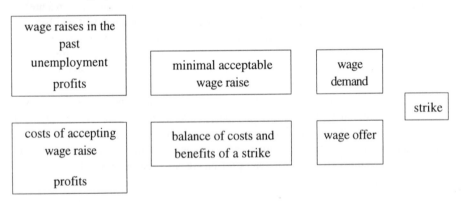

Figure 6.2 The Ashenfelter and Johnson model

In their model Ashenfelter and Johnson include three 'quarter dummies' to control for seasonal fluctuations in strike activity. With the help of this model almost 94 per cent of the variance of strike activity is explained. The explanatory value and the mathematical elegance of the model contributed to the fact that it - although sometimes in an adjusted form - is frequently imitated. Empirical tests through other studies are impressive. Nevertheless the model is criticised.

The criticisms of the model may be subdivided into two main points. The first point concerns the fact that the model is only adequate in explaining strikes that result from contract bargaining over wage raises. The model can not explain strikes that are taking place during a contract period. These strikes often concern conditions of employment other than wages and therefore are not necessarily related to the variables in the Ashenfelter and Johnson model. Nor do wildcat strikes fit into the model. A second criticism concerns the view that as time passes, only the wage demand of the employees is readjusted downwards. Several authors point out that during the strike employers make concessions.

A more general point of criticism that is more relevant within the scope of this chapter is the biased emphasis on economic variables. Ashenfelter and Johnson consider the strike as an outcome of the bargaining process. Therefore specifying economic conditions under which the outbreak of a strike is more or less probable is emphasized. The conversion of a potential conflict situation into an actual conflict is more or less taken for granted. The conversion of potential into actual conflict is defined as a problem by other authors, for example Shorter and Tilly (1974). As distinct from the economic approach the approach of Shorter and Tilly is referred to as political.

The political approach: Shorter and Tilly

In the political approach, industrial conflict is explicitly interpreted as a form of collective action. This starting point brings Shorter and Tilly to the expectation that the mobilization capacity or the organizational capacity of the unions, operationalized as the level of membership, is the most important predictor of fluctuations in strike activity. In their analysis of strike activity in France during the period 1830-1968 this argument is, broadly speaking, empirically subscribed.

'Political' variables, such as level of membership and occurrence of political crises, have a greater impact on developments in strike activity than economic variables, such as unemployment (Shorter and Tilly 1974).

According to Snyder (1975) this difference in explanatory value can be traced back to the 'institutional setting' of a system of industrial relations. In order to explain this, Snyder first makes four explicit assumptions that underlie the economic approach. In the first place, Snyder assumes that employers as well as union leaders and union members are rational decision makers. Their decisions are based on weighing the economic short term benefits of an agreement against the costs of a strike. In times of prosperity, the costs decrease for employees and increase for employers. Consequently, the bargaining position of employees and therefore fluctuations in strike activity are affected by changes in economic conditions. A second assumption is that the process of collective bargaining is institutionalized. Parties are willing to bargain and there is a contract between the parties based on past bargaining, the parties respect the contract's validity. As a result, strikes are a possible outcome of the bargaining process and occur when parties cannot reach an agreement on a new contract before the old contract expires. The third assumption is that the decision to strike is made by a trade union. The union is supported by the members and only members go on strike. Consequently, unions are a necessary precondition for strike activity on a large scale. The final assumption is that, apart from general trends, the level of membership does not fluctuate. Thus, changes in strike frequency and scale can not be explained by the level of membership. If level of membership and fluctuations in strike activity are connected, the relationship can be traced back to the impact of economic variables on both.

According to Snyder, the United States of America, France and Italy differ considerably with respect to the degree to which these assumptions are valid. The assumptions do not apply (to the same extent) to each of these countries because of a number of interrelated characteristics of the industrial relations: the degree of stability of union membership; the political power of labour nationally, and the degree to which collective bargaining is institutionalized.

Together, these characteristics determine the 'institutional setting' of industrial relations, which has consequences for the way in which fluctuations in strike activity can be explained. Snyder distinguishes two ideal types, represented in figure 6.3.

	Institutionalization of collective bargaining	
	high	low
Level and nature of union membership	great and stable	minor and fluctuating
Political position of labour	legitimate interest group, involved in decisions concerning allocation of means	not a legitimate interest group, playing no part in the allocation of means

Figure 6.3 Two ideal types of institutional setting

In the first type, the organizational power of the trade union movement is not problematic. Actions are primarily directed at economic goals and strikes fluctuate in relation to changes in the economic situation and wages.

In the second type, on the other hand, the organizational power is problematic. Actions are primarily political in nature and fluctuate in relation to changes in level of membership and political developments. Snyder tests the influence of the institutional setting by fluctuations in strike activity in the United States of America, France and Italy. A distinction is made between the periods before and after the second World War for each country. Snyder concludes from the test that to the extent that within a national system of industrial relations there is a shift in the direction of a higher and more stable level of membership, institutionalization of collective bargaining, and political integration of labour, strikes should be explained on economic rather than on political grounds.

International comparative studies

In comparative studies of strike activity a distinction can be made according to the nature of the explanatory variables. In this part Ross and Hartman's (1960) classic study of the institutional approach and Hibbs (1975) politico-economical approach are reviewed.

The institutional approach: Ross and Hartman

The study of Ross and Hartman contains the statistical analysis of official strike records for fifteen non-communist industrialized countries in the period 1900-1956. Ross and Hartman use two indicators to construct a typology of strike patterns. The first indicator, the so called 'membership involvement-ratio' is the number of employees in strikes as a percentage of the number of trade union members. The second indicator is the duration of strikes. Both indicators are averaged for three subsequent periods: 1900-29, 1930-47 and 1948-56. The last period is the starting point for their final classification of countries into variants. To do so, both indicators are assigned three values. Up to three per cent the membership involvement-ratio is considered 'minimal', from three to 20 per cent 'moderate', and above 20 per cent 'high'. Duration is labelled 'low' (less than five days), 'average' (between five and ten days) or 'high' (ten days or more).

Combination of the indicators results in the typology as shown in figure 6.4. As can be seen, Denmark, Germany, the Netherlands and, to a lesser degree, the United Kingdom are classified into the first North-European variant.

Ross and Hartman point to five variables, to explain differences in strike patterns. First, the organizational stability of the trade union movement - the longer the trade union movement exists and the less the number of members fluctuates, the less the strike activity. Second, the presence of leadership conflict within the trade union movement - the existence of rivalry within the leadership of trade unions is favourable to militant factions and thus intensifies strike activity. Third, the nature of the relationship between trade unions and employers - the more this relationship is institutionalized, the smaller the number of strikes. Fourth, the presence of a political party with broad political support among employees - if the wishes of employees are reinforced in the political arena, the number of conflicts in the industrial arena will go down. This effect is even stronger, if the party referred to has governmental responsibilities. And, fifth, the degree to which the government is actively intervening in the system of industrial relations - the higher this degree, the lower the level of industrial conflict.

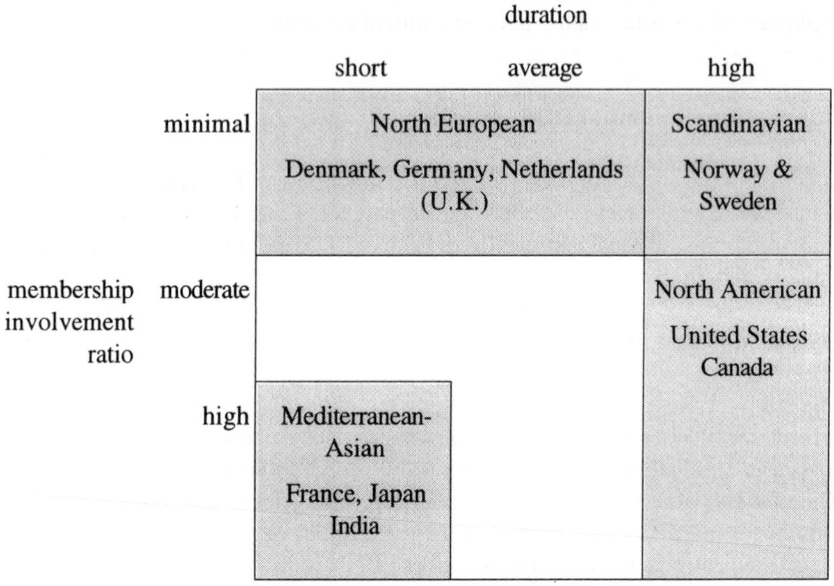

duration

	short	average	high
minimal	North European Denmark, Germany, Netherlands (U.K.)		Scandinavian Norway & Sweden
moderate			North American United States Canada
high	Mediterranean-Asian France, Japan India		

membership involvement ratio

Figure 6.4 The Ross and Hartman patterns

Countries in the North of Europe are characterised by the presence of a mature and stable trade union movement without leadership conflict. Collective bargaining is highly institutionalised and strong social democratic parties are established. Finally, these countries experience a fair degree of governmental intervention in the system of industrial relations. The relatively high level of industrial conflict in France is mainly explained by the instability of trade union membership and the internal frictions within the trade union movement. The same partition characterizes the left wing of the political spectrum. Apart from differences in strike patterns, Ross and Hartman conclude on the whole range a decline in strike activity in the long term. They give three reasons for this. First, on the side of the employers better social policies and more effective organizations have been developed. Second, governments have become ever more prominent players as employers, economic planners, providers of social security and supervisors of industrial relations. Third, in many countries the trade unions have traded the strike weapon for a broader political strategy. It is this thesis, well-known as 'the withering away of the strike', that is criticised on empirical grounds by, among others, Hibbs (1978).

The politico-economical approach: Hibbs

The main aim of Hibbs' study is to refute the thesis of 'the withering away of the strike', when long term developments are considered. To Hibbs, strikes are manifestations of the class conflict over the division of national income. He argues that changes in the level of industrial conflict are mainly explained by the degree to which political parties associated with the trade union movement have succeeded in socializing the eventual division of national income. Thereby the struggle is transferred from the market, with its allocation through collective bargaining and industrial conflict, to the political arena, where 'labour' and 'capital' dispute by means of political negotiations and the mobilisation of the electorate. In order to empirically support his thesis, Hibbs shows that only in countries where social democratic parties took part in government, the number of strikes has reduced to negligible levels. Hibbs adds to his argument that it is not the governmental power of such parties per se which is crucial, but the degree to which their policy influences the division of national income. Combining the degree of government intervention with the nature of this intervention results in the typology as shown in figure 6.5. Examples for cell I would be the United States and Canada. There, the national income is primarily allocated by means of collective bargaining between employers and employees. There is no decrease in strike activity.

In the countries in cell II, for example France and Italy, the allocation also takes place through industrial relations. In this case, however, it is accompanied by a high degree of government intervention in the market. The main consequence of this type of government intervention is the transition of the strike from an economic to a political phenomenon and a stabilisation of the level of strike activity. The third cell groups the countries where the allocation of national income is highly regulated through the political process. Countries in this category, such as Sweden, Germany and the Netherlands, witnessed a reduction in the level of industrial conflict.

degree of government intervention

		low	high
Political/economic goals	market conform	I	II
	market corrective	n/a	III

Figure 6.5 Government intervention and politico-economical goals

Conclusions

In this chapter, two approaches to the short term fluctuations in strike activity have been reviewed, namely the economic and the political approach. Besides, two cross sectional studies have been discussed. The study of Ross and Hartman is primarily aimed at the explanation of differences in strike activity between countries. At the same time they pay attention to the long term trend of strike activity. Explanatory variables with respect to international differences in strike patterns are the organizational stability of the trade union movement, the degree to which the relations between trade unions and employers are institutionalized, the presence of a political party with a broad political support among employees, and the degree to which the government is actively intervening in the system of industrial relations. The study of Ross and Hartman is classic in more than one way. Their empirical data covers the period up to 1956. This raises the question as to how far the explanations put forward are still valid nowadays. A retrospective view of table 6.1 shows that the established international differences in strike patterns were still present in the seventies. During the eighties in particular the position of Italy altered. However, even today both France and Italy are characterised by a large number of short strikes. Germany and the Netherlands still experience a few strikes of mainly average duration and the United Kingdom can be placed in an intermediate position.

On the whole there is some convergence. The validity of Ross and Hartman's explanatory variables has eroded however. In the Netherlands, for instance, the level of collective bargaining has been decentralized. This implies that government intervention has decreased. In the meanwhile, the United Kingdom has been confronted with tendencies in the opposite direction causing a decline in both the number of strikes and the number of employees involved. France, on the contrary, is still characterised by instability, internal divisions of the trade unions and therefore by the continuation of the original pattern of strikes.

All in all Ross and Hartman's thesis of 'the withering away of the strike' is no longer tenable for all the countries studied. Hibbs explains differences in long term developments of strike activity mainly in terms of the nature of government intervention in the system of industrial relations. Despite Hibbs' variegated conclusion, other authors, as Crouch and Pizzorno (1978) and Barkin (1983), point to a general resurgence of industrial conflict in Europe in the 1960s and 1970s. Table 6.1, however, indicates that during the 1980s strike activity has been decreasing. Thus, the observed long term development is dependent upon the period under study. That changes the subject of this chapter to differences between short term and long term developments.

With respect to the explanation of short term developments in strike activity two theoretical approaches are reviewed. These are indicated as the economic and the political approach respectively. According to the economic approach strike activity fluctuates in relation to cyclical developments. Labour market and business profits are especially important in this respect. In the political approach more politically tinted variables are emphasized, such as the level of membership and crises in the political system. Empirical research shows that the explanatory value of both approaches is dependent on the institutional setting of the system of industrial relations. If in the system there is a stable level of membership, institutionalization of collective bargaining and political integration of labour, then short term fluctuations in strike activity will be explained by economic rather than political factors. In this respect there is a distinction between France and Italy, where political factors are dominant, and the other West European countries. This explanatory model lost value in the 1980s. The frequency, scale and volume of strikes have decreased in France and Italy remarkably, although Italy may still be distinguished from the other countries with respect to strike volume. To explain the decrease in France one may point to government participation by the socialist party in the 1980s. Although this variable is of a political nature, strike activity in France and Italy as well is more and more sensitive to economic fluctuations. Developments within the European Union, as far as they affect the national systems of industrial relations, are mainly economic in nature, as described in the introductory part of this chapter. In combination with the conclusion reached above concerning the growing sensitivity of strike activity in France and Italy to economic variables, existing differences between national patterns of industrial conflict will decrease in significance in the future. Explanations of long term developments in strike activity, however, should be approached with caution. The trends to be explained turn out to be very sensitive to both the indicators used and the period under study. Besides, strikes are too easily considered a homogeneous category and trends unilinear and irreversible. Thus, patterns of industrial conflicts in the different countries of the European Community grow more alike, but in which direction is dependent on economic variables, especially the labour market.

Acknowledgements

This is a translated and revised version of 'De werkstaking in vergelijkend perspectief', chapter 4 by the same author in J. van Ruysseveldt et. al. (eds.) (1992) *Arbeidsverhoudingen in Europa*, Open Universiteit: Heerlen. I would like to thank my colleagues Bert Jetten and Sandra Groeneveld for their unselfish cooperation.

7   Schooling and social justice: Some current trends

Paul Littlewood and Ingrid Jönsson

Introduction

In this chapter our aim is to describe certain sets of features which characterize the education systems of a variety of European countries. The features we have chosen are those which have figured most prominently in recent debates and, in many cases, in policy changes. But we have also introduced two other dimensions into our analysis. We have located our account where appropriate in the context of key forces, economic, political and cultural, which have shaped the education systems we outline; and we have related our descriptions to some of the main ideals or principles of social justice brought into the debates and used to justify the policy changes.

By the late nineteenth century states throughout Europe had established systems of, at least in principle, free, compulsory elementary schooling for all the children of their respective citizens. The systems varied, as did the content of the education provided and the degree to which attendance was enforced; but what is remarkable is the degree of uniformity in the provision and in the timing of the introduction of this sort of formal instruction, closely related to the various interests and pressures characteristic of nineteenth century economic, political and cultural developments.

Generally there were three broad sets of inter-related forces behind these developments. First, there were changes in the nature of work, with in many areas rapid industrialization and the accompanying process of urbanization, the capitalization of industrial and agricultural production, and the growth in the demand for graded levels of literacy and numeracy in a rapidly diversifying workforce largely comprising employees dependent on wages and salaries. Second, there was the establishment and development of representative government by nation states and the concomitant elaboration of the political and juridical rights and duties of their citizens, requiring their willing support through the ballot box and the payment of taxes. And third, there was the expansion of the welfare role of the state as provider or at least facilitator of certain basic social services: primarily those of health, sanitation and hygiene, communication and transport and education.

National systems of schooling, in which all children were at least formally compelled to undergo basic technical and moral instruction under the aegis of the state, were established throughout Europe and were to continue to expand during the course of the next century. Today the right to a free education, as well as the obligation to undergo it, are so deeply embedded in popular consciousness that it is perhaps difficult to realise how historically recent the establishment of mass schooling actually was. But this right is being increasingly challenged by the demand to be able to choose where one's child may be educated, and by the expectation that parents should contribute directly towards the financial costs of their children's schooling. At the same time, most education systems developed discriminatory policies, restricting access and training, particularly at the higher levels of education, along the lines of social class and gender.

School systems exist, of course, in very changed material circumstances than those of a century ago, and have been in the process of undergoing continual reforms, in part as a consequence of these changes. The key changes have been economic, technological, political and cultural. Throughout Europe there have been changes in the nature and levels of employment, with a sustained shift from manual to non-manual work, the expansion of female labour, and increased levels of unemployment, particularly among young people and among certain minority ethnic groups. The trends towards European economic integration are affecting labour mobility and entrepreneurial collaboration and competition. The nature of work has also changed, with the continual introduction of new technologies and the concomitant demand for new skills. Politically, the process of European integration has been characterized by demands for - and against - greater standardization in a whole array of institutions, not least those of schools themselves. And culturally, there are countervailing tendencies towards and away from uniformity, involving fuller integration of disadvantaged social groups and strata, including the assimilation of minority ethnic groups and struggles over the preservation or dissolution of regional and national identities, and the emergence of a supra-national, European identity. These various forces have all influenced the elaboration of a host of policies designed to reform systems of formal education (Husén et al. 1992), and the degree to which the various ideals of social justice have been championed. While we are not directly concerned here with the levels of disparity in scholastic performance among different social groups and categories which is one of the major themes of comparative European education (Shavit and Blossfeld 1993), we are going to consider the systems and reforms which are both a product and a cause of some of these disparities. And the disparities themselves can be closely linked to the elaboration of certain ideals which tend to predominate in debates about education.

More or less since its establishment in the last century, compulsory schooling in Europe has been an arena in which competing forces have sought to champion different and often conflicting ideals of social justice. The ideals with which we are primarily concerned are on the one hand, the broadly egalitarian ideal of equality of opportunity and access to schooling, and on the other, the more libertarian ideal of freedom of choice in the selection of one of several forms of differentiated schooling. (For a discussion of these and other ideals in the context of schooling, see for example Lauder and Brown 1988, Hargreaves and Reynolds 1989, Jones 1989, Knight 1990, Paquette 1991.) In practice, however, these two ideals are not so easily separable. For example, the notion of equal opportunity contains within it the meritocratic and arguably libertarian notion of the opportunity to become unequal and, at least in principle, freedom of choice might imply giving parents and their children enhanced opportunities to escape from the disequalizing forms of segregation (Bowles and Gintis 1974) which characterize many school systems and which have emerged from often rigid social divisions based on class, gender, and ethnic and religious identity. Although such inequalities are not the direct focus of this chapter, they have been a major concern in educational reform, as well as at the centre of much sociology of education. (See, for example, Shavit and Blossfeld 1993) We shall also consider a third related ideal of social justice which has particular salience in the context of schooling, that of democratic accountability in the control of schools (CCCS 1981, Lauder and Brown 1988). All these ideals are very much at the forefront of current debates in educational policy in late twentieth century Europe.

We shall identify a series of both convergent and divergent trends in schooling relating to concerns held in common by a number of European states, whose policies are a product both of their different historical roots and the current constraints and pressures they face. There are five principal areas for comparison. First, there is considerable variation in the degree of control which national government, as opposed to local government, exercises within the state school sector. Schools may be more or less accountable to national government. This applies crucially to the determination of financial provision and of the content of schools' curricula and pupil assessment. Second, there is the degree of parental involvement in and control over the schooling of their children. There are indications that this has undergone significant changes in recent years, at least at the level of government rhetoric. Third, parents may also choose to educate their children in private schools, the extent and nature of which may have considerable effects on the nature of state provision. Private schools may also be significantly subsidised by the state. Fourth, a major concern in all countries has been the differentiation between types of school, particularly at the secondary level. There is a marked diversity here, principally between two types of system: the comprehensive school on the one hand, catering for all pupils; and on the other, specialist schools with selective entry criteria. Associated with this differentiation is the fifth area, the nature of the curriculum itself, the degree of variation in the provision of academic learning, vocationally oriented training or a mixture of the two. For reasons of space we shall concentrate on recent developments in the United Kingdom, Scandinavia, the Netherlands, Germany and France. We shall conclude by placing these developments in the context of both continuing and new forms of inequality in educational access and outcome, considering how they relate to claims for greater social justice.

Centralized or decentralized control

One of the principal motivating forces behind the establishment and maintenance of national education systems has been the state's interest in producing a suitably qualified workforce, preserving the cultural identity of the nation and legitimizing the power of the state in the consciousness of its citizens (Dale et al. 1981). It is of little surprise, then, that national governments play an active and highly visible role in structuring and restructuring their school systems. The ways they do this, however, vary according to the relationship holding between particular national and local state apparatuses and to the weight accorded by different governments to the part they play in providing education as a public service - that is, to schooling as a form of social welfare. One can expect those governments which champion the ideals of a free market economy to seek to 'roll back the state' by reducing their political responsibilities and financial controls in the name of freedom of choice and democratic accountability, while social-democratic governments will take on a more interventionist strategy in the name of equality of opportunity. As we shall see, however, rolling back the state may involve interventionist strategies, and may be compromised by the desire to strengthen the degree to which schooling satisfies the demands for qualified labour in a market economy.

United Kingdom

Formally speaking there are three education systems serving different parts of the UK: England and Wales, Northern Ireland and Scotland. The main distinguishing features of the system in Northern Ireland are its maintenance of selective grammar schools at the secondary level and the provision of separate schools for children of Catholic and Protestant parents. In parts of Scotland too (mainly the central belt) there are separate schools for Catholic children, but the Scottish system is also distinct in terms of the age when most children start school, the more uniform spread of non-selective secondary schooling and the distinctive nature of its public examination system. Generally, however, compulsory schooling in the UK lasts from about the age 5 to 16. Whereas elsewhere in the UK post-compulsory academic courses last for two years and are the main criterion for entry into generally three-year university degree programmes, in Scotland such courses last for one year and serve as the basic qualification for university degrees usually lasting four years. In this sense British education is relatively decentralized. Nevertheless, all legislation is determined by the UK parliament, the different systems have much else in common and the latest reforms - the implementation of national curricula and standardized testing, the growth of vocational training the devolving of managerial responsibilities to individual schools and the increase in parental powers - are common to all systems, generally bringing them closer together.

Although the elaboration of these reforms has often been couched in a rhetoric of decentralizing, there have also been countervailing centralizing tendencies (Chitty 1989). Essentially the authority of local government and the professional autonomy of teachers have been significantly reduced, and national government has intervened in imposing uniform curricula and constraining individual schools to publish performance indicators. In addition the right of schools to 'opt out' of local authority control effectively places those schools which so do under the direct control of an agency of central government.

School curricula in Britain, in contrast to those in other European countries, have been traditionally more of a 'secret garden', cultivated by educationists relatively unhindered by politicians and employers (Chitty 1989). Universities, in determining their entrance requirements, have exercized considerable influence in terms of the academic content of school syllabuses. But one of the main features of recent reforms has been the reduction in the autonomy and discretion of educationists in choosing what and how they teach. This wresting of control from educationists by national government with the introduction of a national curriculum has provoked considerable conflict, and its contents have been widely debated, contested, pruned and modified over the succeeding years of its elaboration. Private schools, however, do not have to teach the national curriculum or participate in the related testing schemes.

Scandinavia

The considerable degree of economic, political and cultural homogeneity which characterizes the Scandinavian countries is reflected in their education systems, whose development was strongly influenced by Protestantism - although schooling throughout Scandinavia today is predominantly non-denominational. In all the Scandinavian countries nine years of compulsory comprehensive schooling was established in the 1960s and 1970s. In comparison with the UK, Scandinavian school systems have by tradition a more centralized structure. In terms of the locus of control, Denmark has the least centralized system, offering a greater variety than its counterparts, while schools in Sweden have been firmly located within the highly centralized welfare state system. Sweden introduced comprehensive schooling and a national curriculum for compulsory schooling in 1962, and extended the national curriculum to post-compulsory schooling in 1971. The financing and administration of schools, including rules and regulations concerning the syllabus, school texts and time-tables, was centrally controlled with the delegation of non-policy oriented functions to the regions and individual schools. Since the 1970s, however, there have been trends towards decentralization in response to political pressure and in an attempt to find more effective and cheaper local solutions to an array of emergent social problems primarily related to the downturn in the economy. During the 1980s and 1990s these trends have accelerated with major cutbacks, including half of those employed in the national government's school administration. Since 1990 teachers are no longer employed by the central government but by the municipalities. The control of education based on detailed rules and regulations has been substituted by a looser system of goals specified by Parliament and national government. Thus, although national objectives are formulated through the School Act and the national curriculum, the means to attain them are more open, and there are greater financial and decision-making powers at municipal and school levels. These reforms entail greater variation in the content of schooling and methods of instruction. Nevertheless, private schools in Sweden have to comply to a greater extent with the national curriculum than do those in the UK.

Parallel developments have also taken place in Norway and Finland. In Norway the 1980s saw the revision of earlier legislation (the 1970s' 'frame laws') to enable the transfer of funds from national to local government and to give local government greater autonomy in their use. The 1987 *Mönsterplan* also gave individual schools much greater control in the planning of their curricula (OECD 1990, Granheim and Lundgren 1991).

The Netherlands

In the Netherlands, schooling has been relatively decentralized since the mid-nineteenth century when the secular public monopoly of schooling, which discriminated particularly against the Catholics (who made up 35 per cent of the population), was also being challenged by burgeoning Calvinist interests, and was replaced by a system made up of three separate spheres - Protestant, Catholic and public or secular. This system of 'separate but equal school systems' was built into the 1917 Constitution and reflects the *verzuiling* (pillarization) of Dutch social and institutional structures still characteristic of the Netherlands today (OECD 1991b, Arends and Volman 1995). The three systems are equally funded by central government, which finances the per capita costs in both the public and much larger private sectors (see below) and controls staff/student ratios, teachers' salary scales and contracts. Central government also stipulates the minimum number of hours all schools must spend on the national curriculum and controls the public examinations for entry into secondary school. Decisions concerning teaching methods and texts, however, are decided at the level of the individual school. The ten years of compulsory schooling in the Netherlands are free, while upper secondary, post-compulsory schools, like universities, charge tuition fees (James 1991).

Germany

The basic structure of the German education system dates back to the nineteenth century and, apart from the period under Communist rule in the GDR and despite reforms in the 1960s and 1970s, remains more or less unchanged today. While there is central control over the general shape and content of the curriculum and patterns of assessment, considerable autonomy in administration is held by the *Länder* (provincial level of government); the KMK (the standing Committee of Education Ministers of the *Länder*) is responsible for periodic reviews of the curriculum, and *Länder* impose their own conditions - for example, whether or not *Gymnasium* (academic school) students study two or three subjects at the 'intensified' level. Control is also local in the sense that performance in the *Abitur* (the *Gymnasium*-leaving certificate qualifying one for university entrance) is largely dependent upon assessment of candidates' work by their own teachers. There is no national external examination (OECD 1972), although some *Länder* are moving towards a more centralized supervision of examination standards.

France

The modern French education system dates back to the late nineteenth century and is marked by a high degree of centralized control over administration, finance, curricular content and systems of formal examination. In the early 1980s, however, some financial responsibilities were transferred to provincial and local levels. The Ministry of Education's 28 provincial offices are responsible for all matters of primary and secondary education, including most private schools. All staff in state schools are civil servants paid by the Ministry of Education. The number of hours to be taught in the various schools is strictly stipulated by a National Programme Committee comprizing experts appointed by the Minister of Education. School textbooks, however, are produced by private enterprise and do not require ministerial approval, although periodic inspections seek to ensure that the content of schooling is consistent with preparation for the *Baccalauréat* (the public examination marking the end of most forms of school). The Debré Act of 1959 brought private schools in line with state schools by providing subsidies on condition that such schools meet with the Ministry's requirements (Monchablon 1994).

Summary

There is a marked diversity in the degrees and methods of control exercised by national governments over the educational policies and practices of both local government and individual schools. While all national governments are deeply involved in the elaboration of curricula designed to meet the changing demands for qualified labour, they do so in more or less interventionist ways. Whether or not such policies will increase equalities of opportunity remains to be seen. The desire to modernize curricula, increase the range and level of qualifications and expand the number of those qualified on the one hand has led to in some cases to a loss of autonomy at local levels, while on the other - in terms of the day-to-day management of schools - there are clear signs of decentralizing and arguably libertarian trends towards a greater degree of customer involvement. In addition, respect for the diversity of parental religious affiliations indicates an area in which some states, notably the Netherlands, do not intervene. The issue of parental rights and changes to them is the subject of the next section.

Degrees of parental involvement

The establishment of national education systems directly lessened the juridical rights parents exercised over their children. From the late nineteenth century throughout Europe, parents have been held legally responsible for ensuring that their children are schooled as the state dictates. Although the importance of the home environment has long and widely been recognized as affecting the educational achievements of pupils, the 'home-school partnership' has largely been one in which families are expected to support the school rather than play an active part in the elaboration of school policy and practice. We note, however, that while the relationship between parental duties and rights varies between countries, there is currently a general trend to extend parental rights, at least at the individual level of choice of school and, in some cases, by involving them directly in school management. This is discussed in particular by Husén et al. (1992), who suggest an increasing demand, particularly among middle-class parents, for fuller information about and access to what the authors term 'good' schools.

United Kingdom

British parents have until recently had little direct control over scholastic provision for their children. Apart from the minority who chose, and could afford, to send their children to fee-paying schools, most parents were obliged to send their children to the local school, the management of which was left largely to the school staff and local government. In England and Wales a few places were reserved for parents on the schools' Boards of Governors, but their role appears to have been largely passive and/or school-supportive (David 1993). In Scotland, parental representation on Boards was abolished early in the century and was not to be restored until the late 1980s. Since then the new School Boards also appear to support their schools and adopt a critical stance towards local and central government (Munn 1992).

The economic downturn of the 1970s and the growth of youth unemployment increased the weight and breadth of criticisms aimed at schools, particularly their alleged failure to train their pupils effectively for the labour market. Whether or not schools should have been held responsible in this way cannot be discussed here. But, clearly Labour and Conservative governments alike began to seek parental support in elaborating educational reforms. From the early 1980s Conservative policies stressed the role of parents as the consumers of education as a commodity in a free market. Parents' rights to send their children to non-local schools and to participate in school management were enhanced (Chitty 1989, Jones 1989). Also extended, as we discuss later, were parents' rights to private education, which plays a prominent role in the British education system.

Since the 1980s many commentators have suggested that school reforms are further privatizing education provision, although the term 'privatization' tends to be used somewhat loosely, as the following list of reforms indicates (Chitty 1989, Jones 1989, Ball 1990, CCCS 1991). The decline in levels of local government funding, as part of the national government's curtailment of state expenditure more generally, has certainly widened the gap between the state and private sectors. Parents of pupils in many schools are now asked for more financial contributions for school equipment and materials. State schools have been encouraged, and are effectively constrained, to take up funding from the private sector. A new type of school, the City Technology College, has been established with in principle funding from the private sector, although this has not proved as forthcoming as originally envisaged, and only a few of the 20 such schools planned have so far opened. Schools have been offered financial incentives to 'opt out' of local authority control, with ultimately the right to select their intake. Recent curricular reform, with greater emphasis on vocational training inspired and supported by the private sector, has rendered school learning much more responsive to prospective employers' demands. But it would be contentious, or at least premature, to label such reforms as indicators of 'privatization', and the government has strenuously denied that it is about to follow the advice of one of its advisory agencies by introducing a voucher system whereby parents will have to supplement a state grant in opting for anything other than the most basic school provision.

Scandinavia

In Sweden, Finland and Norway, the right of parents to influence their children's education has been traditionally low and remains so in comparison with Denmark, the Netherlands and some other European countries. The situation is now changing. However, in Sweden, for example, the 1994 National Curriculum strengthened parental and pupils' rights to be consulted over the selection of optional subjects. Parents also have the possibility of being represented by parents' organizations on school councils, but only in an advisory capacity. In addition, Swedish parents now have increased rights to choose to send their children to non-local schools, as long as this would not mean displacing local children; or, if they so wish, to private schools. One intention behind this greater degree of parental choice, as in Britain, was to increase the competition between schools as a means of raising their educational standards (Propositionen om valfrihet i skolan, 1992/93, p. 230). This principle of greater choice, however, is not taken by - and arguably, not available to - all parents, with those parents holding higher educational qualifications themselves being more likely to exercise this right (Skolverket 1993). Parallel developments in Norway have also taken place with the establishment of 'co-operation committees', although their effectiveness remains open to doubt (OECD 1990).

The Netherlands

In the Netherlands there are signs that *verzuiling* is being eroded by the increasing numbers of parents choosing to send their children to schools with religious identities other than their own, particularly in order to gain access for their children to schools with higher standards of academic performance. It could be argued that this is an indication of the greater freedom of choice enjoyed by parents in the Netherlands, although one should also add that the degree of freedom tends to be limited by the geographical availability of the more academic schools and to parents with higher levels of education themselves. Whatever the case, children of immigrant parents tend to be over-represented in public schools as indigenous Dutch parents prefer to send their children elsewhere - the so-called 'white flight' (OECD 1991b and 1994).

Germany

In Germany parental involvement in schooling is particularly salient for the choice of school. Although scholastic performance and teachers' assessments have an important influence, particularly in the transition from primary to secondary school, the final decision is left to parents. There is some evidence of considerable pressure from middle-class parents, mainly of German origin, seeking to gain entry for their children into the more academically oriented middle-class schools, and children of immigrant families tend to be concentrated in schools with lower academic standing (Max-Planck-Institut 1983, Leschinsky and Mayer 1990).

France

The process of decentralization in French schooling which began in 1982 was furthered by the School Act of 1989 which extended the degree of involvement by parents and voluntary organizations, but parental rights remain relatively restricted in state schools, in which they have little control over the selection process and the passage from a given year of school to the next. Progress through school is controlled by the *conseils de professeurs* (teachers' committees), although there is an appeals procedure (France 1990, Teese 1991).

Summary

Levels of parental involvement vary throughout European schools in two principal ways: the degree to which they may decide to which school to send their children, and the level of representation in school management. In those countries where parental involvement has been relatively low, notably the UK, there are trends towards increasing 'parent power', often marking a movement from schooling as a public good to schooling as a private right. This conception, and the championing of the libertarian ideal underpinning it, appear to be gaining prevalence in discourses on schooling throughout Europe. The degree to which many parents may actually influence school policy (e.g. Sweden), or exercise their rights as to choice of school (e.g. the UK) would, however, appear to be relatively limited.

Private and public funding

There are marked differences in the provision of and financial support for private schools across Europe. In most states, such provision is relatively minor compared with the numbers of children attending state schools, and (with the exception of the UK) is of limited social consequence; and where it is more common, the state in fact finances the vast bulk of provision. What is more significant for us is the relationship holding between private schools and the demand for freedom of choice (including the right to schooling within a preferred religious tradition), and the right to pay for one's children's schooling. The exercise of these rights has implications for our analysis of conceptions of social justice and the distinction between schooling as a public service or a private commodity.

United Kingdom

The relationship between scholastic provision and the social class origins of pupils has been a dominant theme in the analysis of formal education in Britain since the establishment of free compulsory schooling in the 1870s and 1980s. At that time, elementary schooling was basically all that was provided for the daughters and sons of the manual working class, while middle class children could continue with secondary education at grammar schools. The children of the bourgeoisie and landed gentry were generally schooled separately in the private sector, either with tutors and governesses at home or, particularly in the case of boys, at boarding schools (Simon 1974). Many of these constituted the so-called Public School system, whose leavers went on eventually, often after undergraduate careers at Oxford and Cambridge Universities, to hold a positions in government, the judicial system, the armed forces, the Church, industry and financial institutions in the City of London.

A Public School background still figures prominently among members of the ruling élites in Britain today, despite the expansion of schooling opportunities throughout the twentieth century (Walford 1991). For example, although few of the recent Prime Ministers attended Public School, many current Cabinet Ministers did, as did top judges, officers in the Armed Services, industrialists and financiers. Public Schools, financed by private fees but also subsidized in various ways by the government, spend considerably more per pupil than state schools and achieve generally higher results in terms of formal examination performance. Although fewer than 10 per cent of British children are schooled in the private sector, they occupy about half of the places at Oxford and Cambridge, which are regarded as the top universities in the country. The pre-eminence of the Public Schools plays a significant part in the continuing importance accorded to social class in relation to schooling in Britain today. Although Labour governments sought to restrict state subsidies to Public Schools they never sought to abolish them, while Conservative governments have strengthened the private sector through the provision of financial assistance on a means-tested basis to parents who could otherwise not afford the fees, through the Assisted Places Scheme (David 1993).

Scandinavia

In Scandinavian countries, school provision in the private sector is also small, but does not have the same social class character of the British Public School system. In Denmark about 10 per cent of pupils attend private schools, which for a long time have been supported by state finance. In Sweden only two per cent of pupils attend private schools, while in Finland and Norway the figure is still lower. In Sweden private schooling registered a decline following the introduction of comprehensive schooling in the 1950s and 1960s, although there has been a slight increase in private provision in the 1990s following more generous public funding designed to increase student choice, together with encouragement of private initiatives. The change reflects the general trend in Europe, particularly in Britain, to treat schooling less as a public service and more as a private good.

The Netherlands

In the Netherlands, the private sector in schooling predominates, although massively funded from the public purse, and has done so for a long time. The 1920 Law of Education enabled groups of parents to start their own schools and government funding was given for both initial capital outlays and maintenance costs. Such initiatives were mostly taken by religious groups. By 1990, two thirds of all Dutch elementary pupils attended private schools, as did nearly three quarters of secondary school pupils. Grants are awarded for the foundation of private schools, if they can demonstrate that they can attract sufficient pupils, at the same rate as the public sector schools. But private schools may charge additional fees for extra-curricular activities and refuse to take pupils for prescribed reasons, apart from their parents' inability to pay the additional fees (James 1991).

Germany

In Germany, despite certain similarities to other aspects of the Dutch system, private school provision is rare. Fewer than six per cent of pupils attend private general schools and fewer than seven per cent attend private vocational schools. The legal right to establish and run private schools is sanctioned by the Federal Constitution with the aim of creating diversity and freedom of choice appropriate to a liberal democracy and pluralist society. According to the School Law, all parents are entitled to send their children to private schools but these are regulated by a licence system, which is designed to ensure the quality of their educational provision and to avoid discrimination on the basis of parental income; the cost of a pupil in a private school may not exceed that in state school. The vast majority (80 per cent) of private schools are church-based. They are of two sorts. 'Substitute schools' are publicly funded and follow state school curricula, although they are free to determine their own learning objectives and teaching methods. 'Supplementary schools', usually vocational, are not controlled or funded by the state (Weiss and Mattern 1991).

France

In France about 15 per cent of the pupils attend private schools, which are predominantly Catholic. Since the nineteenth century there has been conflict between the state and the Church over educational provision, with the Church resisting the state's attempts to monopolize control. A compromise was reached with the Debré Law of 1959, which provided for state subsidies for private schools under certain conditions. The government's attempt in 1984 to abolish state subsidies to private schools met heavy opposition and the proposal was withdrawn. There are now four forms of contract between the state and private schools, which vary according to the degree of financial subsidy and state control over the curriculum with, generally speaking, smaller subsidies where there is less control (Teese 1991).

In France social selection occurs primarily in the state school sector. There are some similarities between the élite status of 'Oxbridge' (the combined universities of Oxford and Cambridge) in the UK and that of some of higher education institutions in France (*les grandes écoles*), specializing in engineering, business and administration, and recruiting a restricted number of students (six per cent) who tend to be from the upper class and have a direct route to leading posts in the private and public sectors (Monchablon 1994). French private schools also tend to be socially selective, attracting a disproportionate number of upper class children, particularly at the primary school level. There are several types: older schools of reputed academic excellence, academically selective and catering mainly for boys; less academically selective schools mainly for girls, and often focusing on the performing arts; innovative schools offering 'whole-child' approaches to learning; and schools designed for pupils with special educational needs, which are non-selective and which tend to achieve lower academic standards. There are some indications that the choice of private schooling is partly motivated by class considerations, some wealthier, predominantly white families opting for selective schools which they perceive to be less subject to industrial dispute and behaviour they deem socially deviant (Teese 1991).

Summary

While most countries run school systems which are both free and financed more or less entirely by the state for the vast majority of pupils, the provision and nature of private schooling outside the state sector varies enormously. The British Public School system of private schools mainly for the children of relatively affluent parents is exceptional, although it is also similar in some respects to private provision in France. There are some signs that schools are now seeking further finance from private interests, although it is not clear whether parents are being increasingly expected to make financial contributions towards their children's education. The extent that this is so, however, reflects the presence of both the libertarian ideal and the championing of free market forces in educational discourse, in which schooling as a private good challenges and, at present at least, may in places supplant the notion of schooling as a public service.

Comprehensive and selective schools

One of the major debates about schooling in Europe is whether to provide a common form of schooling for all pupils, or differentiated forms of specialist schooling (Husén et al. 1992). There are two main issues involved here. First, to what extent should the demand for a diversity of specialized skills from employers be met by differentiated scholastic programmes? This brings into the debate the closeness of the relationship between education (here conceived of as training for work) and the economy, which we discuss more fully later. Second, should different specialisms be provided in different schools? Responses to this question vary both between different European countries, and within them over time, and have important implications for the issues of equality opportunity and freedom of choice. Generally speaking, however, these issues only apply at the level of secondary education. Most children, apart from some of those with special educational needs and those schooled in the private sector, receive a relatively uniform elementary education starting for children of between four and six years and lasting at least until they are ten. But then there is considerable variation between countries in the ages at which the first division in the system occurs (from 10 or 11 in Germany to 16 or 17 in Denmark). There is another variation in the age at which full-time general compulsory schooling ends (in France, it may be as low as 13, for those going on to short vocational courses, while in Germany and the UK it is normally 16) (Chisholm 1992).

United Kingdom

In Britain compulsory secondary schooling is of relatively recent origin. Until the 1944 Education Act it was available only to a tiny proportion of working class children (such as the 'scholarship boys' who won places in grammar schools). After World War II, secondary schooling was made compulsory for all children, first until 14 years and then in stages up to 16 in 1972. It was, however, heavily differentiated, particularly in England, where middle class children tended to go to the more academically oriented grammar schools while working class children were generally provided with a much more basic education at secondary modern schools, with far fewer opportunities for obtaining the necessary qualifications for entry into higher education. Although selection was based on formal testing, the pass rate was geared to the number of grammar school places available, which tended to be greater in middle class catchment areas. This was, however, less true in Wales where there were proportionately more grammar school places, and in Scotland, where proportionately more pupils went to senior secondary schools, the rough equivalent of English and Welsh grammar schools, as opposed to junior secondary schools. The 1944 Act also provided for a third sort of secondary school, the technical school. In practice, however, very few technical schools were established, and secondary modern schools increasingly sought to boost the academic output of their pupils (Finch 1984).

Some educationists and politicians regarded this 'tripartite' system as too differentiated on three basic grounds. First, the post-war economy demanded a much higher general standard of education than the system provided. Second, pupils' aptitudes and abilities could not be accurately determined at 11 years of age. And, third, the system, tied so closely to parents' economic circumstances, was highly socially divisive (Fenwick 1976).

On the basis of the results of several experiments conducted by local government in unified secondary schooling, and in pursuit of equality of educational opportunity as well as a consciousness of the growing demand for more and better qualified school leavers, the Labour government in 1965 demanded the provision of comprehensive schools in all local authorities in England and Wales.

Successive Conservative and Labour governments increased the numbers of comprehensive school places, but by the 1970s new policies were being proposed, partly in reaction to the growth of youth unemployment and the suggestion that this was somehow a consequence of an alleged levelling down of standards in comprehensive schools.

When the Conservatives returned to power in 1979, radical reforms were being elaborated, although it was not until the 1988 Education Act that a drastic restructuring of the system was implemented (Chitty 1989, Jones 1989). Prior to that, however, two major if indirect steps in the process of differentiation between schools were taken. First, there was the introduction of the Assisted Places Scheme mentioned above, and second, an increase in the rights of parents to choose to which school their children should go. Parents were no longer largely restricted to enrolling their children in local schools, with the consequence that many parents, particularly those living in urban areas and with relatively high levels of education themselves, were attracted to schools with relatively high academic records of achievement. Although most parents still send their children to local schools, the consequence of increased parental choice is likely to be a greater degree of polarization between academically 'successful' and 'unsuccessful' schools, with more resources going to those schools attracting more pupils (Echols et al. 1990, David 1993).

With the 1988 Act this process of differentiation between schools was accelerated, in particular by the introduction of the right of schools to 'opt out'. Under this system, schools' Boards of Governors (or in Scotland, their School Boards) could, if they gained support from a majority of parents, break their ties with the local education authorities by becoming 'grant-maintained', being financed directly by central government. Extra funding was promised as an incentive to schools to 'opt out'. Such schools after a period of time would be eligible to introduce their own criteria of pupil selection. The likely result is further polarization between high and low achieving schools (Chitty 1989).

Another measure in the 1988 Act with implications for differentiation was the decision to publish annually examination results by school on the grounds that parents should be provided with greater knowledge of the quality of the education on offer. Opponents of this scheme have pointed out that schools themselves should not be judged alone on the examination performance of their pupils, as this ignores the close tie observed between pupils' socio-economic background and their scholastic achievement.

Scandinavia

The Scandinavian school systems had a dual character until the introduction of comprehensive schools in the 1960s and 1970s. In Sweden, children of parents in lower socio-economic groups were educated in elementary schools for six to eight years followed by vocational training in schools or at work-places. Wealthier parents sent their children to elementary school for four years followed by grammar and upper secondary schools, leading on to university. Transfer from one tier to another was rare and the choice of education by the age of 10-11 was more or less irreversible. The transition to grammar school was based on a selection process (Isling 1980, Ball and Larsson 1989).

The establishment of nine years of comprehensive school abolished the repetition of school years and final examinations. The age at which pupils were placed in differentiated study streams was the most controversial political issue in Sweden when the comprehensive school was being introduced (Marklund 1985). During the experimental phase in the 1950s, all Swedish pupils received the same education for their first six years and it was not until the last three years that the pupils were divided into subject-based lines. The choice of education was free in the sense that marks or test results did not exclude pupils from the different lines, but mobility was still restricted. In the course of the 1960s, the choice of lines was replaced by a system of optional subjects and course alternatives. Until 1980, choices made at senior level at comprehensive school played an important role in the transition to upper secondary school. After that date, all alternatives counted for the same value.

In Norway, the comprehensive school has less internal differentiation (OECD 1990), while internal study choices have for a long time played a more important role in the Finnish system (OECD 1982). In practice, pupils studying various combinations of subjects are more or less well prepared for theoretical studies at upper secondary level (Arnman and Jönsson 1983). Successive studies of pupils' choices of subject point to a quite stable social pattern with little deviation from the one characterizing the former dual school systems (Husén 1982).

Denmark has a remarkably undifferentiated school system from the start of primary school (at six or seven) through to 16, with unstreamed classes under one class teacher, but with additional specialist teachers as pupils proceed. At the end of this period optional examinations are taken in up to 11 subjects, with both internal and external assessment. Pupils are then faced with three options: to postpone the choice and stay on for a tenth year (which about 50 per cent do), to go to direct or basic vocational training, or to go to the Gymnasium for a further three years in preparation for university entrance. The curriculum in the Gymnasium is based on two single streams, in language and science, but with a common core curriculum. No vocational education is provided, but is available in commercial and technical colleges, which may also give access to higher education (Struwe, K. (ed.), 1991).

The Netherlands

The Dutch school system is still very selective, in both the private and public sectors. After eight years of pre- and primary schooling (from the age of four or five), Dutch pupils are faced with a four track secondary school system, divided into two levels, junior (or lower) and senior (or higher), and further into vocational and general courses. Thus secondary school pupils will pursue one of the following scholastic careers: LBO (junior vocational education), lasting for four years; MAVO (junior general education), also lasting for four years but with the possibility of continuing to MBO (senior vocational education); HAVO (senior general education, lasting for five years and leading to a four-year course in HBO (Higher Vocational or Professional Education); or VWO (pre-university education), lasting for six years (OECD 1991b).

The choice of secondary school in the Netherlands for pupils is heavily influenced by head teachers' assessments based on performance in national tests, but is also ultimately a matter of parental choice. Wealthier and more highly educated parents tend to prefer to send their children to VWO.

The rigidity of this system and the early age of selection led in 1968 to the passing of the Mammoth Law, which attempted to increase the degree of choice and flexibility within the system. Nevertheless, by the mid-1980s only 11 per cent of secondary pupils attended VWO and only five per cent went on to university, with another nine per cent going on to study other kinds of higher education. About 30 per cent went to LBO with the prospect of jobs in agriculture, domestic service or retail trades (James 1991).

Germany

In Germany as in the Netherlands, secondary schooling is heavily stratified, with pupils at the age of 10 being assigned, mainly on the basis of attainment but also in accordance with parental wishes, to the academically oriented *Gymnasium* (with the goal of university entrance on attaining the *Abitur*), the *Realschule* (with a general education leading to vocational and professional training and careers) and the *Hauptschule* (with a more basic level of general education leading to a dual system of apprenticeships and part-time vocational training at 16). Attempts have been made since the 1970s to build bridges between the three sorts of school, and to experiment with comprehensive education, although this aroused considerable controversy. In the 1990s Conservative-dominated *Länder* ceased such experimentation, whereas Social Democrat-led *Länder* have sought to give comprehensive schools the same status as others. Comprehensive schools have not proved very popular, attracting only six per cent of German pupils in the early 1990s. In addition, the comprehensive school system which characterized schooling in the former GDR (East Germany) was largely dismantled after unification and replaced by the more differentiated system of the former FRG (West Germany) (Lehmann 1994).

In theory French education is non-selective up to the age of 15, but in practice 12 per cent of pupils reach the end of primary school with two or even three years' delay because of non-promotion to the subsequent year(s). Pupils begin to move out of the mainstream programme into pre-vocational and pre-apprenticeship classes from the age of 13, although the major influx into such classes occurs in the last year of primary school, when 16 per cent opt for them and another four per cent leave school altogether. Non-promotion rates tend to increase in secondary school, with 11 per cent repeating the first year and 14 per cent the second year. There is another peak in non-promotion rates immediately prior to selection for the various streams in the second cycle of secondary school, when as many as 25 per cent have to repeat a year (Teese 1991).

The main point of differentiation occurs at the age of 15 when pupils complete their *collège* or lower secondary curriculum and are faced with a choice of upper secondary schools differentiated into general, technical and vocational *lycées* as well as centres for apprenticeship training. About one third leave after one year, another third go on to further vocational training and the remainder go to study for the *Baccalauréat* at either the general or technical *lycées* or (exceptionally) the vocational *lycées*. In the 1980s, in an attempt to make the traditionally academicist and socially stratified *lycée* system less elitist, the French government implemented reforms designed to enable 80 per cent school leavers to gain the *Baccalauréat* by 2000. The award now takes three forms: the BESD (secondary education *Baccalauréat*), the BTn (technical *Baccalauréat*) and the BT (technical diploma). All may lead to higher education at university level, although on a selective basis. The larger *lycées* also offer high achievers post-*Baccalauréat* preparatory courses for entry into the elite institutions of higher education, the *grandes écoles* (SOED 1992).

Summary

The nature of secondary schooling in Europe varies widely in a number of ways: whether or not there is a preponderance of a single type of comprehensive school or a hierarchy of selective schools; whether comprehensive schools coexist with selective schools; the ages at which selection takes place and the criteria on which selection is based; the degree of internal selection and streaming within secondary schools; and the ease with which pupils may transfer from one selective system to another. All these features combine in different ways to make each secondary school system unique. While responses to the pressures to match schooling to changing demands and to expand the types of qualification and numbers of those acquiring such qualifications are generally evident, these responses vary considerably. In some countries (notably in the Netherlands, France and Germany, or at least the former FRG) the system has been and remains relatively differentiated; elsewhere, however, particularly where the more egalitarian, levelling principle of the comprehensive secondary school has been implemented (if only in diluted form), standardized school provision is either being challenged (as in the UK) or dismantled (as in the former GDR). Trends are neither straightforward nor uniform. A clear general trend, however, is the push to expand the numbers both qualified for and entering further and higher education, which has had consequences for the nature of the curricula considered as appropriate for such education. We now turn to consider another aspect of curriculum development - the provision and role of vocational and technical schooling.

Academic and vocational education

The content and structure of formal education is the product of a complex and often contradictory number of forces which can be identified by the way their goals are articulated. Here we are concerned not just with issues of discrimination in terms of restrictions on equality of opportunity, but also with the tension between two other ideological precepts: on the one hand, education as a means of liberating its pupils, broadening their horizons, providing them with an appreciation or respect for 'high' culture and, on the other hand, education as a means of training its pupils for the world of work. Both precepts are evident in the curricula of all education systems, although the actual balance in this relationship varies considerably. What is remarkable in this context is the general trend in European educational reforms to reinforce the application of the latter precept, in the form of what has sometimes been called the 'new vocationalism' (Bates et al. 1984, Finn 1987).

United Kingdom

Relatively speaking, the close ties between the major universities and the Public Schools in Britain have been instrumental in fashioning schools' curricula along predominantly academic lines, since university entrance is mostly based on performance in a narrow band of basic subjects pursued until the age of 17 or 18. Those who failed in these subjects, or those who were deemed incapable of following them beyond compulsory school, left school with few or no scholastic qualifications at all. This factor was crucial in the mounting criticisms of the British school system in the 1970s by both Labour and Conservative politicians. In the 1970s, state investment in post-school training programmes was massively increased and throughout the 1980s new, vocationally oriented syllabuses were introduced into schools themselves, for the majority of pupils who were deemed to be 'non-academic'.

A variety of new courses and programmes were introduced and developed in the course of the 1980s and 1990s at both compulsory and post-compulsory levels, most notably NVQs (National Vocational Qualifications) and in Scotland, SVQs (Scottish Vocational Qualifications); and the Technical and Vocational Education Initiative (TVEI). Initially the reforms were met with considerable resistance by teachers. TVEI, in particular, was held to represent a loss of autonomy by schools and teachers themselves over what to teach and how, and to tie schooling too closely to the demands of industry (Gleeson 1989, Ainley 1990, Dale et al. 1990). Nevertheless by the mid-1990s, it had been introduced into most secondary schools. At the same time, increasing numbers of pupils have begun to combine vocational with academically more general courses in their studies, and there is mounting pressure for higher education institutions to recognize the increased variety of certificates and diplomas now available as suitable entrance qualifications. Nevertheless the traditional, highly academic qualifications remain the principal means of continuing education to a higher degree level, particularly in the older universities.

Scandinavia

In Sweden, in the middle of the nineteenth century the guild system and with it the male monopoly of vocational training were abolished. Until then women could get vocational training only as wives and daughters, but after the 1870s vocational schooling on Sundays and in the evenings was offered to all young people in work. These vocational schools were mainly attended by young men and working-class children (Kyle 1979). In the early twentieth century the expansion of industry led to the demand for better vocational training, resulting in the establishment of apprenticeship training schools to supplement the practical training young people received in the workplace. Vocational training became gradually more school-based in the 1920s and 1930s. The lack of job vacancies resulting from economic stagnation in that period decreased the opportunities for industry-based training and as a consequence many new types of vocational schools were established to fill the gap (Axelsson 1989). In the 1971 reform this variety in vocational curricular provision was incorporated into the comprehensive school, along with more academic syllabuses of varying duration. National government assumed responsibility for curriculum and syllabus and the influence of industry did not vanish but became indirect through its participation on national curriculum committees. With the rise in unemployment from the 1970s, however, pressure grew to make schooling more responsive to the demands of industry. In the 1994 curriculum reform involved an extension to three years for all upper secondary education and stipulated that those on the vocational programmes should spend 15 per cent of their study time in workplaces (Lfo 1994).

Norwegian secondary education has a similar structure to that in Sweden, while two separate systems exist in Finland and Denmark (Nord 1990). Among the Scandinavian countries, Denmark deviates conspicuously and bears a closer resemblance to Germany in its arrangements for vocational training, in that a major part of it is located in workplaces, and industry and local employers have a decisive role in designing the content and organization of vocational training. Vocationally oriented education, particularly that leading to the HHX (Higher Commercial Examination) and HTX (Higher Technical Examination) is accorded parity of esteem in Denmark. In all Scandinavian countries, however, general subjects are incorporated into vocational training as a way of increasing economic competitiveness. In Sweden all students study eight core subjects making up 30 per cent of the three years of upper secondary education. In Finland, experiments are being conducted into how to facilitate the transfer of students between the vocationally and academically oriented systems (Arnman et al. 1995).

Denmark is the only Scandinavian country in which compulsory schooling ends with examinations. Here exam marks are accompanied by the teachers' estimation of the pupils as the means of selection for upper secondary schools. The provision of upper secondary education has expanded to such an extent in Sweden and Norway that virtually all pupils are accepted on their first choice. Special arrangements are made for pupils not applying for further education.

Academic upper secondary education is very much influenced by the entrance requirements formulated by the universities (Kim 1983). Until the 1990s, this procedure was centrally administered in Sweden and Finland, while the conditions for admission to higher education vary between universities and other higher educational institutions in Denmark and Norway. In all the Scandinavian countries, examination marks serve as the most crucial selection instrument and in Sweden some of the criteria used formerly, such as labour market experience, are now being abandoned in some universities. Priority is now given to younger students qualifying from two of the purely academic upper secondary programmes, although all programmes formally give access to higher education. In relation to the number of youths in Finland applying for university studies, places are few. As a consequence, a great number of the students leaving academic upper secondary education apply for a vocational education after finishing school.

The Netherlands and Germany

In the Netherlands, as we have already seen, secondary schooling is highly differentiated along academic and vocational lines from the age of 12 or 13, with major implications for enrolment in higher education. The same applies to Germany. In 1990 about a third of German pupils finished school after nine years. The *Hauptschule* is geared to apprenticeships and is attended by many low achievers and a disproportionately high number of children of immigrant parents. A second stream is made up by the *Realschule* which attracts about 29 per cent of the age group and awards leaving certificates after 10 years of schooling. Since the 1970s the more attractive apprenticeship programmes have tended to go to those with the *Realschule* leaving certificate. Vocational training is provided separately under the joint control of the *Länder* and industry. Another 31 per cent go to the third type of school, the *Gymnasium.* It is attended by more girls than boys, although more boys who gain the *Abitur* (the university entrance qualification) go on to university than do girls. Compulsory schooling in Germany is not limited to general education, and pupils leaving both the *Hauptschule* and the *Realschule,* as well as those without school-leaving certificates, must attend courses leading to officially recognized professional qualifications (Lehmann 1994).

France

We have already indicated some aspects of vocational training in France. In addition, in 1985 the French government established a national objective to improve the levels of school pupil's qualifications by introducing the CAP (Certificate of Vocational Aptitude) or the BEP (Certificate of Vocational Studies) for all students in an age group. It has also sought to weaken the perceived barriers between technical and general education by incorporating more technical material into the syllabuses of the *lycées* and by establishing the technical *Baccalauréat* (SOED 1992).

Summary

The trend towards the vocationalization of school curricula seems to be fairly general, although it varies in terms of different starting points, with some countries having established an apparently stable marriage of vocationally and academically oriented syllabuses much earlier than others. Where schooling is or has been more selective there tends to be a greater separation of the academic from the vocational, but this is not always the case - largely we infer because of different traditions in the conceptualization of 'technical', 'vocational', 'theoretical' and 'academic' curricula and the relations between them. But there would seem to be a growing and widespread emphasis on schooling as preparation for work in a rapidly changing and depressed labour market for many pupils. Many commentators have suggested that vocationalization, rather than being a liberating force in the sense that it might enhance work opportunites for many, might result in a process of greater social differentiation and inequality, with children of parents in lower socio-economic groups more likely to be restricted to vocational training and relatively low-status jobs (Bates et al. 1984, Dale et al. 1990, Finn 1987, Gleeson 1989).

Conclusion: schooling and opportunity

In considering social justice in the context of schooling, two ideals stand out. On the one hand, there is the demand for greater social justice in terms of eradicating inequalities of access and outcome, by standardizing access to a common education system tailored to overcome broader socio-economic inequalities, based traditionally on class and urban/rural divisions, and more recently on a growing awareness of inequalities of gender, and of religious and ethnic identity, in order to increase opportunity on the basis of scholastic ability and potential for work. On the other hand, there is the demand for greater freedom of choice, brought about by differentiating within the provision of schooling to meet perceived diversities in the needs, abilities and aptitudes of pupils, and the desires and interests of their parents, and giving individual parents greater power to supplement educational provision with their own material resources. These ideals have assumed different levels of salience in different countries at different times but, in very general terms, it would seem that whereas the thrust for change until the 1970s was towards standardization, that for the last part of the century has been towards differentiation, although one can always pinpoint examples of countervailing tendencies. By and large, the relative weight accorded to these contrasting ideals of social justice is strongly influenced by major socio-economic forces, in particular the economic downturn which began in the 1970s, the growth in unemployment, especially among the young, restrictions on government expenditure and the demands of private and corporate capital to develop new forms of labour relation and production technology. It is because of these forces that we can identify as dominant the trends towards increasingly privatized, differentiated and vocationalized systems of schooling in the last years of the twentieth century These forces, however, are constantly joined and in some cases challenged by other, countervailing forces such as the demands for more meritocratic systems in which discrimination on the basis of class, gender, ethnic and religious identity is eradicated or at least reduced. There are some signs of change, particularly in the case of gender.

Without doubt, the schooling of girls and young women in much of Europe is no longer as inferior to that of boys and young men as it once was (Shavit and Blossfeld 1993). Work opportunities for women and women's scholastic qualifications have improved dramatically in many areas. This, at least in part, has been because of the recognition, however grudging, that women have central roles to play in the emergent paid workforce. Nevertheless, for many women their future work is poorly paid, often part-time, and cut off by the 'glass ceiling' of obstacles to promotion based on patriarchal attitudes of employers. The rates of female employment from different educational groups can also be related to differences in welfare state regimes and family policies pursued.

More generally, however, most recent findings suggest that there has not been an even or consistent equalization among socio-economic strata of educational opportunity, despite the expansion and elaboration of educational provision we have described. Indeed Shavit and Blossfeld's study of thirteen societies, including England and Wales, Germany, the Netherlands and Sweden, finds that only in the Netherlands and Sweden was there any real evidence of such equalization. They also state that this equalization is not attributable to the educational reforms and that '[even] in Sweden and the Netherlands, which report declines in the association, the decline is not attributable to the educational reforms, but occurred before the educational reforms' (Shavit and Blossfeld 1993, p. 21). They also refer to the claim that the Swedish model of the welfare state has been very effective in reducing the class differences in everyday life chances and life styles and suggests that it is the equalization of living conditions in Sweden which is probably the major explanation for the declining association between social origin and educational opportunity. The same is true for the Netherlands. 'In sum, these two deviant cases suggest that the long-term commitment to socioeconomic equality may lead to an equalization in the long run' (Shavit and Blossfeld 1993, p. 19). In Sweden, however, the trend towards equalization of living conditions was halted in the 1980s, with possible implications for educational equalization (Vogel et al. 1987).

But for the rest the authors suggest that educational policies seem to have a divisive effect:

> The stability in the association between social origins and educational transitions in eleven of the thirteen societies indicates that educational selection persistently favors children of privileged social origins ... whereas the proportions of all social classes attending all educational levels have increased, the relative advantages associated with privileged origins persists.... (Shavit and Blossfeld 1993, pp. 21-22)

And, for others, particularly the children of poorer and less educated parents, and especially those of families recently migrating to Europe from the Third World, scholastic provision and future work possibilities continue to be of a lower standard. This is a situation exacerbated by the present recognition through government education policies of the right of 'freedom of choice' and the current predominance of the libertarian ideal in discourses on social justice.

8   The fate of the 55-64 age group: Retirement, work or what?

Jan Petersson

Introduction

This paper focuses on the older workforce. I discuss their status in the labour market, the social policy measures they generally are confronted with, the behaviour of the group itself and the behaviour of employers in the light of the setting of various policy regimes.

Two opposing pictures can be contrasted. On the one hand, older workers confront increasing pressure to exit from the labour market and become an openly marginalized group, living on low incomes. On the other hand, they will face new opportunities for more flexible life-courses with earlier rights to draw their pension and the possibility of working under less formal conditions and therefore become a privileged group. The older workforce can be split into two categories with different fates ahead. The competent, well-educated group is in demand in the labour market. Amongst this group, exit will occur not by threat but by choice, and generous exit conditions in the form of 'parachutes' accommodate the decision to leave. These individuals jump. The uneducated group, on the other hand, is facing general depletion of their productivity as they get older. The pressure of substitution for younger workers will be high and is easily forced on unskilled workers. These individuals will be pushed. This split into two main categories of the early retired people is a theme in Laczko (1988).

Living conditions for marginalized groups has been a theme for research for sometime. One main stream connects to poverty research. Townsend (1979) introduced the term relative poverty to define those individuals that are excluded from the normal living patterns available to the population at large. Exclusion from material goods is, however, not the only dimension of marginalization. Another connects to the individual's self-esteem and quality of life in a broad sense. Especially in a 'Work Society' (like Sweden) where identity is constructed around occupation, there is a risk that exclusion from the labour force becomes associated with social stigma (Goffman 1970) - the excluded group consists of individuals rejected by the labour market. Unemployment, as shown by Jahoda (1979) and her investigations from the 1930s, may involve losing the ability to structure time and may result in passivity and produce broken marriages and problems of abuse.

In this paper the older workforce is defined as the 55-64 age group. It should be recognized that the definition and demarcation of an older workforce is nothing but a socially constructed notion. One theme of this paper is that individuals in the age group 55-64 are located in what can be called a grey zone between work and retirement, the contents of which are apt to speculation, invention and new praxis. There is an assumption that the exit process in the future is likely to be one of a more complex and gradual occurrence.

Baldwin (1990) has shown that the self-sufficiency of different groups in modern societies is intimately related to social security systems. Salonen (1993) provides evidence from Sweden to support this. In conceptualizing the fate of older workers, the concept of welfare regime (Korpi 1990, Esping-Andersen 1990) is important when examining different benefit levels and procedures for exit.

Older workers in a changing world

The European societies of the OECD are witnessing changes that affect the fate of the older workforce. First, unemployment rates have risen to above 10 per cent in many countries (see table 8.1). Especially Central/Western Europe and the Nordic countries are confronting a new reality of high (and rising?) unemployment. At the moment, one can expect these countries to look to Southern Europe to understand what adapting to high unemployment implies, and to the US and Japan for ideas about how to reverse the trend. Unemployment may well become a central and controversial issue in shaping policies within the European Union.

Table 8.1
Unemployment (%) within selected OECD countries and areas

Country	1982-90	1990	1991	1992	1993
Australia	7.8	9.6	10.8	10.9	10.8
Japan	2.5	2.1	2.2	2.5	2.6
US	7.1	6.7	7.4	7.0	6.5
Sweden	2.3	3.1	5.3	7.3	7.4
Denmark	9.1	10.4	11.1	12.4	11.7
Belgium	11.3	9.3	10.3	11.9	12.9
France	9.5	9.5	10.2	11.2	12.1
Germany*	7.4	6.7	7.7	10.1	11.3
Ireland	15.5	15.8	17.2	19.5	20.0
UK	9.7	8.3	10.1	10.7	10.4
Netherlands	9.8	7.0	6.8	8.5	9.3
Central/Western Europe	8.6	7.6	8.7	10.2	10.8
Southern Europe	12.2	11.7	12.2	13.5	13.9
Nordic countries	4.6	6.2	8.4	10.1	10.0

* From 1991 including East Germany
Source: OECD statistics

On average there has been a decline in 12.5 percentage points in the participation rate of older workers between 1965 and 1990 in OECD countries (OECD 1992). Obviously the duration of high unemployment has a particular impact on the attachment to the labour market of older workers. Further, there must be fears that this tendency will be reinforced if unemployment is not brought down. Unemployment might develop into an inter-generation issue forcing older workers out to make way for young people.

Second, the occurrence of an 'age shock' will, *ceteris paribus*, increase transfers to older people in terms of care and pensions. This development might result in no major changes in the conditions for pensioners, but it might lead to lower pensions and decreased quality of care and nursing provision. The assumption of an increasing proportion of pensioners by the year 2040 depends upon the absolute numbers of older persons, which is predictable, and upon current and future birth rates and upon the less predictable numbers of the population involved in production.

In Sweden, the 'age shock' seems comparatively mild, mainly because of (temporary) high birth-rates; to date third, behind Iceland and Ireland. A more profound 'shock' may come about in Italy, the Netherlands, Germany and Austria. But among Western European countries France could also face a problematic future for pension expenditures (see Johnson and Falkingham, 1992, p. 134).

A third complication is the issue of public finance. The societies of the West are facing deficits in state budgets and are likely to take steps to cut social expenditures. Social insurance systems are threatened with a reduction in state grants. In combination with pressures towards early exit from unemployment and pressures from demographic changes, we may expect that costs are likely to shift so that individuals and/or employers are left to finance a greater proportion of pensions.

The structure of the paper

This paper contains three parts. In the first part a model for understanding the exit 'pulls' and 'pushes' from the micro-level (behavioural) is presented. The investigation into 'pulls' and 'pushes' is important since it provides a general setting, valid in most countries. At the same time, the general setting results in different practices in different countries, mainly due to how power and influence is divided among the actors that have an interest in the issue. The second part contains a description of the Swedish pattern in terms of the model. Investigating Sweden more thoroughly is of interest, because only when a detailed investigation of one country is presented, is the actual complexity of the problem understood and differences in other countries made clearer. The choice of Sweden, of course, comes naturally to this author, but also illustrates its ambitious policies in the field. The third part presents comparative aspects.

A model for understanding early exit

The number of exits and the form they take can be understood in terms of the behaviour of three actors.

1   *The state and its intermediary bodies* In the case of Sweden these consist of executive agencies (such as Labour Market Offices, Social Insurance Offices), intermediary institutions (such as Work Environment Funds) and corporatist agencies (such as Employment Security Funds). The greater the belief in the rationality of state regulation of the market in a country, the more intermediary bodies are generally found, and they are of course of importance in characterizing the policy regime (following Esping-Andersen 1990 and others) in a country. In Sweden, the behaviour of firms has been surrounded by extensive policy measures building both on *Recht* (legal restrictions on unwanted behaviour) and *Geld* (subsidies and grants to stimulate particular behaviour).

2   *Firms* The employer has the executive power to decide on early exit in most cases. The firm engages in profit maximizing behaviour restricted mainly by the policy regime, but also by the 'conventional behaviour' of a specific country. The term 'firm' will be used interchangeably with the word

'employer' in the text to make the point that strict economic evaluations are the main ingredients of an early exit calculation.

3   *Individuals* The individual usually has a clear opinion on whether or not she/he wishes to exit early. In the case of a disability pension there is a pension 'threshold' and the individual has, in many cases, a monopoly of the knowledge necessary to presentation her/his situation in order to qualify. In such a case the individual can influence exit according to her/his preferences.

State policies

Following Olofsson and Petersson (1994), the parts of the policy regime that are relevant to early exit can be summed up under two major and opposed strategies, namely policies to prevent exit (mainly labour market policy) and policies to accommodate exit (mainly social policy).

Prevention policies aim to prevent dismissals and redundancy, while accommodation policies aim to compensate dismissed and redundant workers for the decisions of firms. The mix of the two policy elements constitutes the policy regime of a country in relation to exit and it influences the strategy of firms and the fate of individual employees. These conceptual classifications are summarized in figure 8.1

Level/ Solution	State Policy/Intention	Firm Strategy	Individual Fate
Stay at work	Prevention	Internalization	Integration
Exit	Accommodation	Externalization	Compensation

Figure 8.1 Exit policies

Let us examine the dynamics further. Firms can generally, shift the burden of the costs of older workers either onto the state or onto workers themselves by getting rid of them. They thereby externalize their costs and the organizational and individual problems. On the other hand prevention policies can force firms to internalize costs and decide to keep workers on. Consequently, the strategies of externalization and internalization are located at the level of the firm.

Individuals are generally compensated for their loss of work and thereby income in a case of exit. Generous compensation makes it easier for older workers to adjust to redundancy and for unions to accept age-specific dismissals. When the state compensates the redundant employees, or sponsors supportive arrangements (for instance, a broadening of the criteria for disability pension), it thereby also accommodates actions of firms, also making them more legitimate to individuals, as escape routes from their work situation.

The counterpart to compensation, in the eyes of the individual, is the effort to integrate her/him in the firm. This is sometimes a result of state regulation, sometimes a firm may wish to retrain an individual employee.

A model of firm behaviour

The calculations of the firm are, in the unregulated market economy, of primary importance in understanding the number of early exits. In a regulated economy these calculations are also primary, but modified by policies which aim to influence the behaviour of firms. The state can influence outcomes either through legal measures (direct steering) or economic subsidies (indirect steering).

A description of the considerations of the firm towards an early exit of individuals is given in Olofsson and Petersson (1994) and in depth in Petersson (1993). In figure 8.2, a stylized picture for the decision-considerations is given for the average unskilled or semi-skilled worker, i.e. for the individual who is threatened to be pushed (but does not wish to jump). A firm-preferred exit point (E_0) is traced. The point is located at a trade-off between Performance (P) and Requirement (R) in the model.

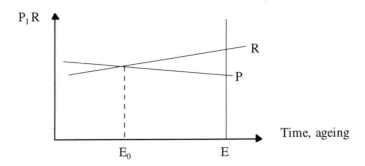

Figure 8.2 The firm preferred exit point

In figure 8.2, Performance (P) of the unskilled/semi-skilled worker decreases with age. This is supported by the fact that this type of worker often is incapacitated over time by monotonous work and/or that her/his aptitude and physical capacities deteriorate with age. As noted by Johnson and Falkingham (1992), studies in Britain in the 1950s (Clarke and Dunne 1955, Welford 1958) show that older workers were 'quite able to compete with younger workers in jobs where they were able to exercise control over the pace of their work (such as skilled manufacturing), but they found it increasingly difficult to sustain work, such as on a production line, which was conducted at an externally imposed pace' (Johnson and Falkingham, 1992, p. 98). The authors conclude that increased mechanization can be another accompanying cause to early exit.

While the Performance-line slopes downwards the Requirement-line (R) in the figure slopes upwards. In a world of a rat-race for profit, the hunt for productivity growth raises the demands on the workforce over time (i.e. with ageing). In a world of high levels of unemployment, pressures emerge on firms to let older workers go and replace them with young unemployed workers. In a world of employment protection, a rising age structure is often conceived of as a problem by firms. For these reasons the Requirement-line has an upward slope in the stylized presentation, but the analysis would be the same if the line is flat (this is the case for example for sheltered production arranged by the state). The general model may further change when different categories of employees are introduced.

If the firm-preferred exit point (E_0) is located to the left of the 'natural exit-point', i.e. the statutory pension age (E), there will be a conflict of interests between the firm and the individual and the gap constitutes the grey zone referred to above. The state can take an active part in the resolution of these conflicts either through accommodation, legitimizing the early exit in the eyes of the individual, or through prevention. Prevention can, in the context of the model, first imply that the state closes the gap either through measures that increase Performance (for example through improvements in the work environment, rehabilitation or education), or through measures that decrease Requirements (for example wage-subsidies). Second, the state can more or less empty the gap of firm influence through for example, a first in/last out principle (common in many European countries). Such a principle guards older workers against being laid off or dismissed when the workforce is cut.

The behaviour of the individual

Generally, the individual has a stand on exiting early or not. She/he may either prefer to leave early or stay on a specific job or move to another job either inside or outside the firm. Her/his calculations will be influenced by the benefits and costs of exiting early.

The major influences on the decision of the individual will be:

1   Non-economic factors. What are the benefits of having a job (structured life, work mates etc.)? What are the benefits of leaving a job (abandoning physical pain, a richer leisure time etc.)? These considerations are of course extremely individual. At the same time, they are less important, the closer to the normal pension age the early exit is being considered.

2   Economic factors. The statutory financial terms for exiting may result in a loss of income prior up to normal pension age or create a permanent loss of pension benefits after pension age has been reached, compared to what would have happened if the individual had stayed in work until pension age. The calculations in many pension systems include past work and wage profiles so that the last years of work are important. These terms, related to

the policy regimes, are supplemented by personal economic factors amongst which are the savings that the individual has accumulated and the individual settlement available from the employer regarding complementary pension agreements through individual or collective negotiation.

These considerations will shape the attitude of the individual towards exiting early, but the outcome is hard to generalize. Johnson and Falkingham (1992, p. 122) sum it up neatly by observing 'that both individual financial calculus and the pressure of social norms come to bear on the retirement decision, but in different ways and magnitudes for different people.'

In relation to the policy regime, the more generous the compensations levels for pensions are, the more likely it is that the individual will wish to exit early. The general early exit problem becomes that of 'attraction' (Marklund 1992) in the very generous welfare state. This can involve elements of dishonest behaviour, where the individual does not give the true story of her or his well-being in order to receive a disability pension while at the same time not being interested in the rehabilitation programmes that the state offers. This may make it hard and dubious for the researcher to understand what has happened after exit has taken place. As Johnson and Falkingham observe '... interview and questionnaire surveys of retired people may encourage them to give socially acceptable reasons for retirement such as ill health rather than self-interested ones such as leisure preference ...' (Marklund, 1992, pp. 96-7).

The fate of the individual is also related to the strategy of the firm. There are three possibilities at hand. First, the preferred exit point of the individual may lie to the left of the one preferred by the firm (figure 8.2 above). The main category of employees in this situation are skilled blue-collar workers and white-collar workers. They have a capacity (accumulated human capital) that the firm does not wish to loose, but they might have an agreement to exit early on good conditions or they may have saved money which makes it economically possible. In many countries statutory pension schemes contain flexible terms for early exit (often with actuarially calculated losses in future pension benefits). The second situation is where the preferred exit point of the firm and the individual coincides. This group may consist of individuals who have experienced damages to their health while at work. This is a situation in which the individual might act against the intentions of the state and in co-operation with the firm. Both actors might wish to construct a situation to allow for qualification for a disability pension rather than seek rehabilitation back into the workforce. This situation prevails when the policy regime's exit terms are generous. In cases when accommodation measures are meagre, the third position is more likely to occur. The firm wishes the individual to leave, but the individual her or himself needs to stay in the job for economic reasons. In this case the prevention policy of the state becomes a key variable. The state can either with *Geld* or *Recht* push the decision point of the firm to the right towards the statutory pension age.

Some characteristics of the Swedish Policy regime

A Work Society

Swedish Labour Market policy has almost over the whole century (but more explicitly since the 1950s) been directed towards a general commitment to full employment. The politically accepted unemployment rate was set at a maximum of roughly two per cent. This commitment ranges over all ages of the labour force, but it has had its most important effects on marginal and weaker groups in the labour market such as disabled workers, immigrants and women. In the case of the older workforce, its predominant effect is the high participation rate for older women.

Gordon (1988, p. 103) has drawn attention to this feature. Examining the participation rates in the labour market of 55-59 and 60-64 year old women, in different countries, Sweden has a record of high participation. An exclusive position in relation to other non-Nordic countries was established between 1960 and 1985, with the largest divergence occurring between 1970 and 1985. In Sweden, the participation of women, in the 55-59 age group, increased by more than 30 per cent (41.1 per cent to 74.4 per cent) between these years. The trend was the same in other European countries such as the UK (50.7 to 51.9 per cent), West Germany (32.2 to 40.2 per cent) and the Netherlands (13.9 to 20.7 per cent), but as Gordon shows, the absolute increase was smaller than that of Sweden. Of other industrialized countries, the record of Japan (48.7 to 51.0 per cent) and of the US (48.8 to 50.1 per cent) over the period, came close to the profile of the UK. Furthermore, among women in the 60 to 64 age group, Sweden was the only country among these that had an increase over the period 1970 to 1985 (from 25.7 per cent to 46.4 per cent). To conclude, women generally work and generally work longer in Sweden.

The Swedish labour market policy regime is best understood in terms of state regulation of the labour market. Regulation has aimed at shaping both the actions and outcomes of firms. It was founded on a belief in the rationality of regulation, closely linked to the ideology of the Social Democratic Party.

The Social Democratic policy has been to create a strong position for trade unions within Swedish firms and work-places and use this in the implementation, execution and control of state policies. Unions are present in the governing boards of many of the intermediary bodies that have been created to implement this policy. An important part of the Swedish policy regime is a whole range of negotiated occupational (mostly complementary) benefits (Edebalk and Wadensjö 1989).

From the perspective of 'models of welfare', or 'welfare regimes' (Korpi 1990, Esping-Andersen 1990) the commitment to full employment is an important trait of a Swedish model, but not its whole content - to understand countries in terms of welfare state regimes, social policy patterns have to be scrutinized. This implies pointing to Swedish institutional welfare, as opposed to a model of marginal welfare. Sweden is best characterized as an example of the Nordic model (Esping-Andersen 1990).

Prevention policies

If we try to categorize the prevention activities in Sweden, first, we can distinguish those that aim at preventing exit from the firm. Among these measures there are those that are preventive in a pro-active way. Among these are those which aim to create a good working environment and increasing the health of workers, through the creation of funds financed through compulsory contributions (paid by all employers) and released (to specific employers) to encourage preventive activities. A Work Environment Fund has been built up to release money when the working environment in a firm is improved through measures such as better ventilation. A Working Life Fund (no longer operating) was aimed to help disabled workers stay in a job through paying for work tools. State grants to firm based health care has encouraged activities that investigate work related damages.

Firm-based health care also involves prevention through rehabilitation in a re-active manner. Rehabilitation aims to prohibit exit from the firm through reintegration. In Sweden this became a key issue in the 'work-for-all strategy' of the early 1990s. Since 1992, firms are obliged to consider rehabilitation when an individual has been sick for four weeks in a row or when an individual shows signs of reoccurring short-term sickness or, whenever an individual asks for a rehabilitation inquiry to be performed. If rehabilitation is considered possible by the Local Insurance Office, the Office takes part in its financing. If the Office finds rehabilitation not to be possible, it processes a disability pension. In this way the Office has the power to judge whether the individual's income should be financed by the firm (wage) or by the state (pension). In times of state budget deficits the rules of entitlement to a disability pension have been tightened and the responsibility of firms to rehabilitate have become more pronounced.

In addition, prevention through a legal framework must be recognized. The first in/last out principle was made compulsory in 1974. Further, requirements to handle problems within firms through what is called 'adaption groups' exist. In these groups the employer, the union, the local Social Insurance Office together with the individual discuss possible ways out of often psycho-social problems. It has also been made difficult for management to fire employees without 'legitimate cause'. Age, pregnancy and sickness are not considered as such cause. One typical Swedish aspect in the prevention practice is the strong role given to unions in taking an active part in personnel decisions of the kind discussed.

The second category of prevention contains prevention from exit from the labour force by providing opportunities for individuals who have left one employer, for one reason or the other, to find another job. Two policy measures for job creation have been used: sheltered employment at originally a state, now a semi-privatized, foundation named the *Samhall*; and wage subsidies (up to 90 per cent) for employers who take on disabled or older unemployed people. Older workers also participate in other general labour market measures such as education. The share of older people that remain, through these measures, attached to the labour market is to be found in table 8.2. This table provides evidence that as unemployment rises (1992-3) the difficulty for the oldest age-group (60-64) of remaining attached to the labour market increases and their share in these measures increased.

Table 8.2
The share of the older workers in labour market measures in October of subsequent years

Age group	1989	1990	1991	1992	1993
55-59	13.7	12.6	14.5	12.3	15.4
60-64	1.7	2.2	2.8	3.5	7.3

Source: AMS statistics in Forsberg (1993)

Accommodation policies

Accommodation measures in the Swedish policy regime take three major forms. First a disability pension with a normal compensation level of 80 per cent of the wage (often complemented by negotiated occupational benefits) exists. Retirement on a disability pension may be full-time, but a partial exit may take place with workers continuing a half or a third time.

The disability pension has three qualification levels that have been used over the last twenty years. The first and original form is disability caused by injury at work. This includes an annuity component and together with negotiated benefits it generally yields 100 per cent compensation for lost earnings. A second form was early retirement (originally 63 and later 60) and unemployment (from 1973 to 1990). This option was implemented during economic down-turns in Sweden, as in other countries like Austria, Belgium, Denmark, Finland, France, Germany, Italy, Luxembourg, Spain and the UK (Employment Outlook 1992). A third cause of early retirement was made legitimate in 1977 - general health. This shifted the focus from the cause of disablement (work-injury) to disablement itself (Wadensjö 1991). In 1993, access to the disability pension was made less frequent and formal rehabilitation requirements within firms have been made more stringent. At the same time stricter rules for disablement have been re-established. This will mean that fewer people will qualify on the grounds of general health, but the new practice and limits have yet to be settled. The three forms have the same result, an early exit, but the route to early retirement is different among the three, although standardized within each category (Wadensjö 1991).

A second route to early retirement through accommodation is an early national pension. The Swedish pension system has a built in flexibility in between the ages of 60 and 70. Early drawing means that the pension is permanently lower, calculated on an actuarial basis. This makes it most favourable to groups in the labour market that in one way or the other can supplement this loss.

A third form in the Swedish case is a part-time pension. The part-time pension was opened up in 1976 to 60 - 64 year olds. It is on less favourable terms (1976-75 - 65 per cent; 1980-87 - 50 per cent, 1981-93 - 65 per cent and currently again lowered to 55 per cent). Besides the lower level of benefit, the age group has been narrowed to 61 - 64 year olds, from mid 1994. The increase in the numbers illustrated in table 8.3 below for the last years reflects the expectations of the less favourable conditions now in operation. The part-time pension has the double feature of both being a partial exit form and the starting point for a gradual exit-process. It has been used particularly by women. It is the third component of the 'work-for-all strategy' for older workers, since the option of part-time pension should be viewed as a partial work option rather than an exit option. Experiences in other countries provide evidence that the alternative to a partial pension is not full-time work, but complete exit from the labour market.

The three main early retirement forms and their proportions over time in Sweden are summed up in table 8.3.

Table 8.3
Disability pension, early drawing and part-time pension for individuals 60 - 64 over the period 1976-1994

Year	Population (1,000)	Disability pension %	Early drawing %	Part-time pension %
1976	481	20.2	1.7	3.1
1980	473	24.3	2.7	14.4
1984	495	27.3	3.6	9.5
1988	444	31.8	2.9	8.6
1992	415	34.4	3.6	11.6
1994	405	35.3	4.4	12.6

Source: Statistics from SCB and RFV

Olofsson (1993, p. 88) classifies the exit process through looking at two opposite solutions; abrupt or gradual withdrawal and early or late exit.

		Exit from work	
		Early	Late
	Abrupt	Germany, France, Netherlands	UK, Sweden
Transition			
	Gradual	US	Sweden

Figure 8.3 Timing of exit and form of exit in some selected countries

With its statutory retirement age at 65, Sweden belongs to the most common group. Earlier ages are found in Austria, France, Italy, Japan and New Zealand (60), later in Ireland (66) and in Denmark, Iceland and Norway (67). Nine OECD countries have a lower eligibility for women; usually by five years. However, the normal pension age in a country might be modified by mandatory take-up schemes that facilitate retirement prior to the standard age. While the Swedish abrupt exit is late in comparison with Germany, France, the Netherlands and the US, it, at the same time, has a built in flexibility which for many persons gives the withdrawal a gradual pace because of the part-time pension and the possibility for partial disability pension.

Figure 8.3 opens up two general patterns. Either exit is done through a low 'normal' pension age, or through a gradual process of decreasing the work load.

Comparative aspects in terms of differences and trends

When the fate of older workers is examined, one finds different standard solutions and patterns in different countries. According to Naschold and de Vroom (1994), this can be clarified by focusing upon the trade off between the respective responsibilities for early exit of the state, the firm and the market, and relating them to the level of participation of older workers. They find that in the former GDR and in Japan, where participation rates were and are high, the responsibility was a one sided obligation of the state and the large firm respectively. In the US and the UK, the responsibility is primarily that of the market and the outcome is that participation rates are medium. According to Naschold and de Vroom, where corporatism is strong, as in Sweden with its high level of participation and Germany and the Netherlands where there are low participation rates, the key to the difference is to be found in the type of corporatism.

The difference between the two sets of corporatist countries with respect to the labour force participation might be explained by the different subtypes of corporatism. Sweden is an example of macrolevel corporatism, whereas the Netherlands is an example of meso-corporatism. Germany is somewhere between the two models. (Naschold and de Vroom, 1994, p. 13).

At the same time as we find different settings for the older worker in different countries, their fate is changing and they are perceived of as an increasing problem. I will end this discussion by briefly surveying the outcomes and dilemmas to be found in the UK, the Netherlands, the US and Japan.

In the UK the employer is in a strong position. The strategy of the Thatcher administration was to create unrestricted, market oriented employment terms, but with high costs for purchasing exit. At the same time early retirement cases are less problematic to the state than in Sweden, since compensation levels are lower. The UK shows that the fate of the older employee in an unregulated market, depends upon the value that the employer puts on him/her. For the skilled worker the future is bright in the UK. The explanation to this is that the firm is not interested in accommodating early exit for this group. Instead the firm offers generous complementary pensions. The solution is work and a high pension. On the other hand, the unskilled and marginalized groups are left to themselves with meagre employer help and state support. Their fate becomes marginalization and poverty. The example of the UK is one of a dual solution.

In the Netherlands the situation is different. There, the individual and the firm together take on a much more pronounced responsibility for retirement arrangements, both in terms of initiative and costs. This arrangement encourages early exit. The possibility to exit is often already regulated in the employment contract. The Netherlands is a good example of a struggle over cost-sharing between the firm, the state and the individual.

The US and Japan are two different examples of secondary labour markets for older workers. In the US, many older workers on time-limited employment contracts have to arrange for a new job (at least part-time) in a second lower paid 'career'. In Japan, on the other hand, the second career is well institutionalized and officially supported by large companies. Through what is called *shukko* the older worker leaves a mother company to work in a daughter company on less demanding and less well paid conditions. Whereas in the US older workers stay in the labour market as a result of a series of positive and negative incentives built into social security, such as government employee pensions, and private pension plans (pull factors), in Japan they leave through mandatory arrangements (push factors) (Schulz, Borowski and Crown 1991). A secondary career with less payment for the older worker is a developing pattern in the US and Japan.

Conclusion

It is hard to draw any definite conclusions on the future fate of the older workforce. The one closest at hand is that to certain categories it will most likely be bleak. Prolonged high unemployment may to an even greater extent push older workers out of the market in order to bring young workers in. We might expect more pronounced efforts by the state to pursue such strategies. We already see them around, for example the Job Release scheme in the UK over the years 1977-88. However, at the same time as the state wishes to increase exit it is increasingly less willing to support this through retirement benefits. Instead we find a debate developing (very pronounced in Sweden) that is centred around lower compensation levels overall and increase in the statutory pension age.

The unemployment problem and the budget deficit problem together work in the direction of an increasing grey zone. What patterns might emerge, I am unwilling to speculate about. Guillemard and van Gunsteren (1991) argue that the possibility to place individuals in 'foreseeable trajectories of successive stages, statuses and roles, is coming apart' (p. 383). What is emerging is a 'deinstitutionalization of the life-course model' which opens up various modes of individualized identity. On the level of different countries, however, it will be possible to 'develop a system of ideal national types' according to Jacobs and Rein (1994, p. 46), i.e. to capture the essential feature of the work and retirement system of different countries. These reflections suggest that identities of older workers also should be analysed as group/class identities with national features. But the ongoing transformation in each country, along different lines, proclaims a process of continuous redefinition, Jacobs and Rein warns. Will European integration result in a convergence of the position of member states or will the current diversification continue?

Acknowledgements

I wish to thank Professor Gunnar Olofsson for intellectual stimulation and graduate student Pia Forsberg for support with statistical material. Shorter sections are copied from an unpublished paper by Olofsson and Petersson (1993).

9 Basic income: Social policy after full employment

Roswitha Pioch

Introduction

Current trends in economic and political developments ask for new discussions about the future of work and social security. Along with the common European market we are faced with border crossing capital transfers on the one hand and with border crossing labour transfers on the other hand. In consequence this new dynamic erodes old patterns of rich and poor regions as well as nations and along with that, old patterns of solidarity are changing. Alongside the old conflict line between rich and poor within one nation a new conflict line between rich and poor countries is occurring (Holz, Pioch, & Vobruba 1994). With this economic and social dynamic it is hard to predict what exactly will happen, but it might be worthwhile to think ahead about what kind of options there are for European social policy to react to, and to control, the ongoing economic and social developments. In this article I want to focus on two questions:

1   What are the problems of contemporary social protection in European countries?

2   What trends can we expect from the development of wage work and social security and what does this mean for European social policy?

In trying to give an answer to the first question I will focus on some structural problems I identify especially in wage centred social security systems, the prototype of which is the welfare system in Germany. In the second part of my article I will compare current trends in the development of the labour market, as they occur along with European integration, with optional perspectives of social reforms. I especially take into consideration the proposal for a guaranteed basic income as a strategy to expand the labour market.

Contemporary social protection schemes

Today, in almost all countries we can distinguish two basic types of social protection schemes, i.e. social insurance and social assistance. However, the way in which these two basic forms of social protection are related to each other varies widely. Social protection can be strongly insurance based with a general social assistance scheme acting as a supplementary safety net. Or social assistance can play a more dominant role, for example through specific schemes that cover specific groups of the population. Furthermore, insurance systems vary greatly too: insurance-based benefits may be either flat-rate or earnings related (Schulte 1994).

Throughout all the existing social security schemes we find some kind of link between formal wage employment and participation in social protection schemes. However, the prototype of a wage centred social security system is the German social security system which is based on the principle of social insurance in such a way that the group of people protected is primarily defined by reference to their status in the labour market (Vobruba 1990). First, the level of the contribution to social insurance depends on income. Second, the social benefits received in case of emergency differ according to the income related contributions paid. In this way, wage centred social security systems are mainly financed by the waged workers' payments. They are not financed by taxes.

Furthermore the principle of social insurance is extended by the principle of solidarity. This is the case for example in the sector of health care. The economic capacity of the insured person is taken into account and the better off pay higher contributions than those who earn less. But everybody is entitled to receive the same medical services. Because these higher contributions are not matched by higher benefits, this form of financing involves a redistribution of income.

Apart from social insurance the German social security system provides social assistance to those who are not entitled to claim social benefits based on their previous contributions while in paid work. Either they have never been employed and therefore never contributed, or their income was so low that their contributions do not entitle them to sufficient social benefits to cover their basic needs. However, a right to receive public welfare does not exist. Evidence of need has to be proved through means testing (Lampert 1991, Frerich 1987).

Social security and the primacy of the labour market

In all societies social protection is organized with awareness and recognition of the primacy of the labour market. In fact, all social protection schemes provide some kind of work incentives to ensure the priority of the labour market as an income source. However, there are different modes of combining social security while recognising the priority of the labour market. The connection between social protection and the labour market can be either very tight or rather flexible. Historically we can observe that in those countries, as in Germany and Austria, where the development of governmental social protection began very early we find the primacy of the labour market very thoroughly obtained (Alber 1988).

In Germany, the connection between the social security system and the labour market is based on three conditions (Vobruba 1989):

1   The priority of waged work is ensured through the condition of prior wages being required to gain entitlement to social benefits, following the proverb: 'First you work, then you eat'.

2   Receipt of benefit is conditional upon no adequate job being available and only lasts until a job becomes available. The priority of the labour market is guaranteed as receipt of welfare benefits is meant to be the exception.

3   Social benefits are based upon income while in the labour market. Income differences in the labour market are extended into the area of social benefits through the principle of equivalence. Again, the primacy of the labour market is acknowledged in the social protection scheme.

This wage centredness of the social security scheme has two consequences. First, social benefits are focused on waged workers. Second, those who receive social benefits are focused on waged work. On the one hand, the labour market is controlled and regulated by social policy measures, and on the other hand people are controlled by these very protection schemes.

Is the assumption of the normality of waged work still a reality?

In contemporary European societies we are faced with a situation where receiving social benefits depends on waged work but as an adequate basis for social security for all citizens this condition is becoming increasingly problematic.

The social construction of waged work and wage centred social security relies on specific assumptions about the 'normal' life of waged workers (Mückenberger 1985). It is assumed that people are working in full-time jobs and that their wages are sufficient to cover all basic needs. Furthermore one supposes that work biographies are continuous. If at all, they include only very few interruptions. And finally, it is assumed that the man is the head of the family. The economic and social position of women depends on their husbands' work and income.

However, one can observe more and more that these 'normal' standards no longer exist in reality. For the last ten or fifteen years a variety of jobs has been developing: part-time jobs; time limited jobs; and jobs with flexible working time. Due to these institutional changes we can not take one single work form for granted any longer. Furthermore, alongside the trends to pluralism and individualism we suggest there are structural changes taking place in people's work biographies. A significant number of people do not have a continuous life-career anymore, following the conventional pattern of education, work and retirement (Kohli 1989). This means, wage centred social security provide reliable protection for those who are still working in 'normal' jobs. However, as much as the institutional and individual changes create work forms and work biographies apart from the normal standard of wage work, for those who do not fulfil the normality assumption of waged work, waged centred social protection schemes become inadequate ways of providing social security.

The selectivity of wage centred social security systems can already be seen, if we look at the economic situation of women. Women, who do not want to be dependent upon their husbands' income, are disadvantaged by wage centred social security systems. As long as women still take on the role of raising children, very likely they will not have a continuous work biography. Because of the 'normal' assumptions of wage centred social security, and because women on average are paid less than men, in wage centred social security systems women receive lower benefits than men (Soerensen 1992).

Besides these structural gaps, the major problem of wage centred social security systems is that, in Europe, the labour market does not offer full time jobs for everybody. In consequence, everybody does not have the opportunity to fulfil the standard of full-time waged work, even if they want to. In Germany, following reunification, the situation has become especially problematic (Bäcker & Steffen 1992).

Even five years after German unification all the major economic research institutes agree that a substantial improvement in the economic situation is not in sight. This is not just an economic problem, but also a political problem. People in Eastern Germany feel politically disappointed. They feel excluded and due to this a mystification of the 'good old times in the GDR' might spread out.

The economic decline in Eastern Germany was dramatic. Compared with 1989, in 1991 gross domestic product (GDP) had dropped by 34.8 per cent. The decline in productivity in Eastern Germany was even higher than in other East European countries. In Poland and Hungary, GDP declined between the same years by around 9 per cent, in Czechoslovakia by around 16 per cent. The deindustrialization process in Eastern Germany is continuing. So, a major socio-economic problem which comes from German unification is mass unemployment. Two thirds of the financial aid, given to Eastern Germany in 1992, was spent on unemployment benefits. While in 1989 there were about 9 million employed people in the GDR, two years later only 5.8 million people had jobs and the unemployment rate at that time was as high as 15 per cent. It is estimated that, without any labour market subsidy the unemployment rate would be 35 per cent. In addition to that, one needs to consider that demand for labour varies regionally, sectorally and by gender. In particular there has been a lot of work reduction in the metal and textiles industries. Also, women account for 63 per cent of the unemployed while in Western Germany 'only' 46 per cent (Bialas and Ettl 1993).

The failure of the full employment strategy

Besides the specific situation deriving from German unification, during the past two decades the goals of the modern welfare state - full employment and social security - have continually not been achieved. In 1975 unemployment in Germany hit one million, in the eighties - two million and in 1995, the unified Germany had more than three and a half million of registered unemployed (2,610,332 in the former FRG and 1,063,617 in the former GDR (*Sozialpolitische Umschau*

10.4.1995)). For the last twenty years the unemployment rate has been growing in all European countries and Japan. Only in the United States has the picture been different (see Petersson in this book).

Increasing unemployment implies that the primacy of wages as an income source can no longer be taken for granted. In consequence, more and more people are in danger to fall into poverty. The risk of unemployment, however, differs widely among the working population. Unemployment is especially high amongst unskilled employees. In Germany in 1989 their unemployment rate (13.8 per cent) was twice as high as the average unemployment rate (Scharpf 1995). Therefore any considerations about how to balance social protection with the on-going developments of the labour market need to take the extent of unemployment among unskilled workers into account. Most of these people are young and tend to be long term unemployed.

In order to discuss different political options in response to the increasing social and economic problems which are due to the labour market situation, one has to ask why the full employment strategy has been failing. There are several answers to this question. First, there are changing relationships between different societies (Scharpf 1993):

1   In all industrial nations the influence of national policy on economic developments has been declining. The internationalization of the capital markets makes a national regulation of the economy as it was intended by Keynes very difficult.

2   The integration of the world market has caused increasing economic competition for Western European industry from low wage countries like South-eastern Asia.

Second, as already mentioned above, there are developments within societies, such as demographic changes, the ageing of society, individualization, and so on.

If the connection between social protection and wage work comes out of balance, because of the specific developments in the economy, there are two main ways of readjusting it. Either the on-going developments in the labour market can be stopped and the capacity of the labour market can be improved or the social protection scheme has to be adjusted to the labour market situation.

Supporters of the former way aim to reestablishing full employment through government policy. They assume that economic growth, full employment and comprehensive social protection are still achievable, and that their absence can be blamed on misguided, short-sighted government policies (Coates and Brown 1993, Cripps and Ward 1993). Through a variety of government measures, such as job creation schemes, further education programmes, early retirement and parental leave the potential of the labour market should be increased in order to recreate full employment (for an overview see Schmid 1994).

While liberal approaches search for evidence that full employment can be achieved by further extension and flexibilization of working time, those, who follow social democratic traditions argue in favour of reducing working hours (Bäcker & Hanesch 1993). Indeed, the unions have tried to reduce working time and slow down the increase in unemployment. However, there are serious doubts that the strategy of reducing working time can go on for ever. At some point the reduction of working time will neither be in the interest of the employers nor in the interest of the employees. This means that unemployment and its socio-political consequences can not be prevented through a redistribution of current work (Vobruba 1990).

In order to reestablish full employment, we also find other options aimed at expanding the labour market. Under the conditions of the integration of the world market and the completion of the European Single Market, the price competition between countries with relatively high wage levels and those with comparably low wage costs makes an expansion of labour demands in the former countries very unlikely. In reaction to this some plead for a strategy of wage reduction. However, even with a very modest wage policy, there would be no way of lowering wages in Northern European countries to the level of Southern Portugal let alone Thailand. If at all, increasing the numbers of jobs in countries with high wage levels will be through innovations in production and high productivity. But, this will not address the problem of high unemployment amongst unskilled workers (Scharpf 1995).

The Swedish strategy has been to address unemployment through increasing employment in the public sector. But this is an expensive solution and has limits within tight state budgets and a limited acceptance by tax payers.

Another option still exists, that of expanding the number of jobs in the low-wage sector. The United States have shown that it is possible to increase the number of low paid jobs. However, the question remains whether there is a way of increasing employment in the low wage sector without losing the high standard of social security that has been built up in Northern European countries.

All in all, the supporters of full employment remain rather vague about their concepts. But assuming there is a way of achieving full employment, one could ask who has an interest in a successful full employment strategy? It seems to be evident, that decreasing unemployment goes with increasing inflation. This is what the Philipps Curve shows us (Phelps, 1967). Thus, we have to suppose that there will be very little political support for paying the costs for a successful full employment strategy. We can assume that stable money markets are much important than the interests of the unemployed. Maybe this also explains the gap between strong verbal commitments to full employment on the one hand and vague ideas about how to achieve it on the other (Vobruba 1995).

Summing up, there is not much evidence that full employment will be recreated in the immediate future and that if a balance between social protection and the labour market is to be found, one needs to look for another way. If the labour market cannot be readjusted to the social security system, adapting the social protection scheme to the changed situation in the labour market seems to be inevitable. However, in order to control the developments in the labour market one needs to look for a way of improving social security and positive employment effects at the same time.

The concept of a negative income tax or the idea of a so called guaranteed basic income addresses this demand. A basic income would be given to any citizen without a job regardless of his or her prior work record. At the same time employment effects are created as the receipt of the basic income can be combined with income from low paid jobs. This concept has been discussed internationally for a long time not only in Germany (Opielka & Vobruba 1986, Vobruba 1989, Biedenkopf 1986, for an overview see Wolf 1992) but also in Beveridge countries as in Britain and the Netherlands (Roebroek & Hogenboom 1989, Walter 1989, Parker 1989). Discussion of it has intensified recently (Scharpf 1993, 1995, Vobruba 1993, 1995, Hüther 1994). Negative income tax replaces the high wage costs due to the existing wage centred social security system through a simple tax system. It separates the wage costs from the costs of social security. Therefore, entrepreneurs could offer all kind of jobs which until now, they considered as not profitable because of the high social security payments related to wage payments. For employees, low paid working places will become attractive as soon as they can legally combine social benefits with income from waged labour. This is exactly the point where contemporary wage centred welfare systems offer nothing more than a trap (Scharpf 1993).

The welfare state as a trap

Under conditions of high unemployment, contemporary social security systems in Western Europe become a trap. The welfare state becomes part of the problem that it was supposed to solve.

Regardless of the standard of social security provided in any individual country, the relationship between income from paid work and that from social benefits throughout Europe means that this is the case (Jordan et al. 1992). In Germany 'social assistance' is relatively high. Because all income is taken into account in calculating entitlement to social benefits, it is only in a person's interest to take on a job when their net income in work is well above that which they would receive from social security. As long as social benefits cannot be combined with low paid work, there is no incentive to take either a low paid job or part-time work. Contemporary social security creates a gap between unemployment and the labour market which it is difficult to jump over. Where there is persistently high unemployment a bridge needs to be built between income while unemployed and income from employment. It is this which the idea of a guaranteed income, provided through a negative income tax seeks to do.

How does a basic income work?

In most proposals, a guaranteed basic income is constructed as a negative income tax. Negative tax and positive tax are terms referring to the financial budget of the state. Negative tax refers to the circumstance under which the state has to pay something; it has a negative effect on the state budget. Positive tax means that the state receives money; it has a positive effect on the state budget. The central point of negative income tax as a labour market instrument is that it creates the possibility of combining social benefits with income from work. Someone who has no income sources at all receives a basic income. In the case where a person earns some income from waged work, a specific amount would be subtracted from the total sum of the basic income, but unless the income is higher than a certain limit, the person still receives part of the basic income. In this way it is worthwhile to take on a low paid job whereas in contemporary social security systems any income from waged work would mean the withdrawal of almost all social benefits.

The difference between social assistance and negative income tax is best illustrated figuratively (Scharpf 1993).

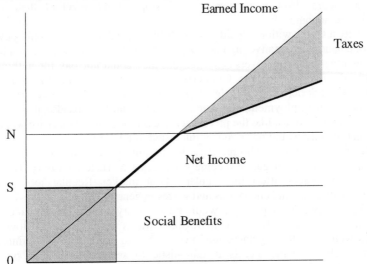

Figure 9.1 The social assistance model

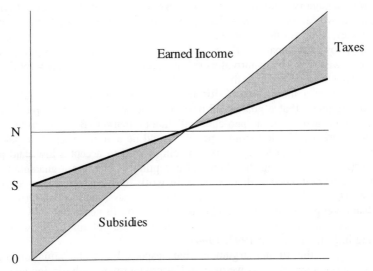

Figure 9.2 The negative income tax model

Figure 9.1 shows the social assistance model, figure 9.2, the negative income tax model. Each model needs an operational definition of the level of a subsidised income (S) and the level of an acceptable net income (N) where the duty to pay taxes begins. The definition of these levels will be a political decision. Under a negative income tax scheme, those who do not have any income receive a full subsidised income. Anybody who works, but has less money than the level of the acceptable net income, is still entitled to claim an income subsidy. This subsidy reduces as income from work increases and stops at the level of the socially acceptable net income.

In this way a sector with low paid jobs with an acceptable income could develop. On the one hand, the negative income tax provides a work incentive for employees and on the other hand employers can offer jobs they could not pay for without the wage subsidy of a basic income. Of course, this concept is not appropriate to solve the employment deficits in highly developed industrial sectors. However, instead of just financing unemployment, the labour market could be expanded this way by subsidising jobs in areas, like the private service sector, where otherwise wages are so low that nobody would be seriously interested in taking a job.

Critics of this proposal, who are close to the unions, are afraid of uncontrolled deregulation through a negative income tax (Bäcker & Hanesch 1993). They fear that subsidised wages affect the regular labour market. Regular jobs will be displaced by insecure and cheap jobs and wages in general will just go down.

Indeed, to prevent this happening it would be necessary that the Unions take on an active role. It would be their role to regulate wages in the expanded low wage sector as well as in the regular labour market and to participate in defining the level of a subsidised income. Is it unrealistic to see the unions as powerful enough? It depends. If a negative income tax fulfils its employment effects, than one can assume that with increasing employment, the labour force will increase as well.

This way, a negative income tax could be adapted to meet the structural changes in work that we can observe in all European countries. It enables people to take on a broad variety of forms of work, such as 'normal' work, different forms of flexibility, low and unpaid work. Social security would thus no longer privilege one type of waged work as 'normal work'. It would offer equal security for different forms of waged work, creating the freedom to choose to work.

This would be a major benefit for the autonomy of the individual. It is a common argument that a guaranteed basic income would enable people to accept low paid jobs and create a 'neo-classical' labour market. But the point is that through a guaranteed basic income, people would be able to accept low paid jobs voluntarily. There is a difference between being forced to accept a low paid job in order to survive and having the choice of accepting it. Because a guaranteed basic income can be combined with income from work, it would create an autonomy which would enrich the motivation of the labour supply (van Parijs 1990). On the other hand, people would also be able to refuse dirty or senseless jobs at a low price or even at any price. For instance, they could refrain from working in polluting industries (Nissen 1993, 1994).

This leads to the further argument that, especially in the situation of the transformation of societies, as we have in Eastern Germany, a basic income would

156

provide the material basis to choose. This is not just an individual enrichment, but also very important from a collective perspective. For instance, presently one can observe that in conflicts over whether a factory should be shut for ecological reasons, workers consistently vote for their jobs even in polluting industry (Nissen 1993). With the material security of a basic income people could afford to take a long term perspective and could take economic and ecological perspectives into consideration. In this sense a basic income can be considered as a precondition for the modernization of societies (Vobruba 1991a).

Who might support a basic income?

There are two arguments often raised against the idea of a basic income. First, a basic income is seen as not financially viable. Secondly, doubts about the social acceptance of such a reform are formulated. According to the first point, the costing of a basic income depends very much on the specific proposal and the estimated employment effects deriving from a negative income tax. Those schemes which propose replacing all benefits based on social insurance with a basic income involve larger financial transfers than those which aim to replace only social assistance through a negative income tax. For the latter, several economic research studies have proved the economic viability of a negative income tax (for Germany see Hüther 1990, 1994, Scharpf 1995, for the UK see Parker 1989).

Asking about the acceptance of reform plans in social policy, such as the introduction of a negative income tax, one needs to look at the empirical interests of those who would be affected by it. All surveys show broad public acceptance of the welfare state. However, support for the welfare state has its limits. Recent empirical studies show clearly that there is an upper limit above which people would not accept a further expansion of the welfare state (Roller 1992). But on the other hand, recent studies also show that people in all nations have very clear images of a bottom line for welfare state activities (Kelley & Evans 1993, Haller 1989). In other words, people accept neither unlimited cuts in social benefits for the poor nor a further expansion of the welfare state due to the failure of the full employment strategy, where the income gap between rich and poor grows. These results can be used to argue that the conditions for social reform exist (Pioch & Vobruba 1994). In particular a negative income tax would address people's desire to prevent welfare gaps by providing a much smoother transition from unemployment to employment and the possibility to move up the income scale.

Another question which might be asked is, would a basic income improve the situation of women in the labour market? Looking at the proposal for a guaranteed basic income from a feminist perspective might raise some scepticism, as it might prevent women from participating actively in the labour market once they receive their basic income (Blickhäuser & Molter 1986, Beer 1987). On the other hand, the positive effect of a basic income for women would be that they would be able to choose what they want to do. Because through a negative income tax, different income sources can be combined, it might become easier for women to get into the labour market, if they wanted to (Schreyer 1987).

However, political change depends on the actors involved in political bargaining such as political parties, organisations and interest groups. The trade unions are in a difficult position in relation to a basic income. On the one hand the unions' members are waged workers. As long as their earnings are high and stable, a wage centred social policy might be considered as being in the interest of their key members. In the short term, this is right. On the other hand, if the trade unions tolerate growing poverty then they may weaken their own bargaining position, because those who are threatened by poverty may cause deregulation from below. Therefore trade unions are faced with the problem of integrating the short and the long term interests of their members. In the long run it seems that, because of its employment effects, a basic income would strengthen the bargaining position of trade unions (Nissen 1988).

Regarding the political parties, a basic income is not simply an idea of the left or the right of the political spectrum. In Germany there are basic income proposals in the Christian Democratic Party as well as among the Liberals and the Green Party. The following four-fold scheme serves to differentiate social reform plans (Nissen 1990). Basically, there are two criteria to analyse different welfare reform plans. First, in which direction do they want to change the structure of the social security system? Second, in which direction do they want to change the level of welfare benefits?

Level	Low	High
Wage-centered	I	III
Universal	II	IV

Figure 9.3 Social reform plans

Presently in Germany the employers' association opts for keeping the wage centred social security system, but lowering the level of social benefits. This position is indicated by field I. The trade unions as well as the Social Democrats aim to improve the standard of social security within the contemporary protection scheme as shown by field III. Both fields II and IV contain basic income proposals. The Liberals have already made public that they support a negative income tax in a way where the subsistence income is low and has to be supplemented by private insurance. On the contrary, field IV indicates those proposals which design the basic income as a labour market instrument and at the same time a way of improving social protection.

Social protection and integration in Europe

Presently all member states of the European Union provide varying degrees of protection against the principal social risks of illness, maternity, invalidity, occupational accident and disease, old age, death with surviving dependants, unemployment and costs of children. However, in 1994 guaranteed income schemes and social assistance schemes which are primarily intended to relieve poverty and to support a minimum level of subsistence exist in only eight of the twelve EU Member States: in Belgium *minimum de moyen's d'existence*, in Denmark *social bistand*, in France *revenu minimum d'insertion* and *aide sociale*, in Ireland Supplementary Welfare Allowance, in Luxembourg *revenu minimum garanti*, in Netherlands *Sociaal Bijstand*, in Germany *Sozialhilfe*, and in the United Kingdom Income Support and Family Credit. These schemes are mostly general minimum income schemes, i.e. they are available on principle to the whole population or at least to large categories of the population, even if in practice entitlement to benefits is subject to various conditions - in particular age, nationality, length of residence and labour market attachment (Schulte 1994).

However, all these general minimum income schemes are means tested in order to ensure the primacy of the labour market. There exists no scheme where a specified amount of money is given to any citizen irrespective of any further condition besides citizenship or residence in the particular Member State. As the concept of a guaranteed basic income breaks the link between the labour market and social protection, it is unrealistic to expect a sudden introduction of a negative income tax in any of the member states of the European Union. Nevertheless one could imagine integrating tax and transfer schemes step by step (Hüther 1994, Scharpf 1995).

Perspectives for European social policy

Looking at Europe the growth of unemployment will be one of the major problems the European integration process has to cope with. First, in all countries we can expect an increasing number of women entering the labour market. Second, the labour supply side will be expanded by migration.

Therefore European social policy is faced with the three political options: a failing employment strategy; deregulation; or the expansion of the labour market through basic secure low income jobs (Vobruba 1991b). Of course, it is hard to predict which of these three options is most likely. There are good reasons not to be very optimistic that common European social policy necessarily means better social security. Nevertheless, in the White Paper on Growth, Competitiveness and Employment of the European Commission, member states are advised to consider introducing a negative income tax in order to make it possible to accumulate income from different sources, i.e. social benefits and low-wage jobs (Commission of the European Community 1993). This provides evidence of the relevance of the proposal of a guaranteed basic income in the future of European social policy. Along with that, in Germany, the Expert Commission on Economic Development has already recommended the integration of the social insurance scheme with a negative income tax (Sachverständigenrat 1993/94). At least, the discussion of a basic income might point to the different options that there are and their consequences.

All in all, the process of German integration illustrates the problems of a wage centred social policy. Furthermore, a guaranteed basic income would provide a more appropriate social security system, since it enables people to choose between a variety of forms of work. In giving people the chance to participate in the labour market at least on the basis of secure low paid jobs, a basic income would be a necessary precondition for the modernization and integration of European countries.

10 The additional use of social policy in the modernization and transformation of societies

Georg Vobruba

Introduction

In his presidential address delivered at the ninety-third meeting of the American Economic Association in 1980, Moses Abramovitz (1981, pp. 2-3) pointed out:

> The enlargement of the government's economic role, including its support of income minima, health care, social insurance, and the other elements of the welfare state, was, ... - up to a point - not just a question of compassionate regard for the unfortunate, and not just a question of reducing inequalities of outcome and opportunity, though that is how people usually think of it. It was, and is - up to a point - a part of the productivity growth process itself.

Statements of this kind are rare. A different view dominates the present political discussion. Social security has come under pressure in all Western capitalist market economies as well as in the new reform countries in Middle and Eastern Europe. Cuts in public social expenses are recommended in order to enforce economic performance and international competitiveness.

In the following I will argue that the usual construction of a contradiction between social security and economic performance is misleading. I will develop the argument that, quite to the contrary, social security is a precondition for economic success. My starting point is that beyond its socio-political effects, there is an additional use of social policy. More concretely, social policy plays an important role in the modernizing process of market economies. There is an 'economic significance of social policy' and as such social policy may be a precondition for economic success in the new reform countries in Middle and Eastern Europe.

Despite all the risks of a diagnosis from outside, my impression of the present intellectual and political situation in the new reform countries in Middle and Eastern Europe is that such an interpretation of social policy as a precondition for economic success should come into discussion. I do not want to step into any details of this diagnosis. I will rather start immediately by presenting some aspects of the discourses of the 'economic significance of social policy' (Vobruba 1988, Vobruba 1991a). What is their general characteristic?

Usually economic efficiency and social security are treated as a contradiction with economics on the one side and the welfare state on the other. This dualism suggests opposition and invites confrontation. The arguments endorsing the systemic primacy of economics are well preserved within this dualism. The thesis of a one-sided dependency of the welfare state on the economic system is strongly supported. The status of the former is subsequently reduced, at best, to a necessary evil. But even arguments aimed at proving the necessity of social security for the most part fit the dualism of economics and the welfare state. This applies to all those arguments that defend the necessity of welfare state intervention in a purely normative fashion. The argument is usually presented as if socio-political problems, measured in terms of socio-political goals, give rise to a need for welfare action. Compared to this well-established discourse, debates about the 'economic value of social policy' play only a marginal role. But the discussion isn't new at all. At the beginning of the European welfare states, economic modernization through social policy was important. It is due to the expected modernization effects, that the economic latecomers, as Germany and Austria, were the socio-political avant-garde. Later, in the beginning of the world economic crisis after 1929, there was an intensive discussion on the 'economic significance of social policy'.

The general aim of this discussion can be understood as trying to avoid the zero sum conception[1] of the relationship between the economy and social policy and thus to attribute a universalistic status to the interest in social policy by exploring an additional use of social policy and additional interests in it. The key argument therefore was to improve living conditions as a precondition for improved economic performance. It was, as we can see in retrospect, a strategy where the stakes were high. The tragedy was that, although some of the arguments in Germany won through, it was only after the destruction of democracy. In our days one often can hear that the new reform countries are faced with economic problems comparable with those experienced after the world economic crisis of 1929. If this is true, it is a strong incentive to pick up the discussion from that time and to learn from it.

The discussions on the economic significance of social policy undermine the dualism of economics and the welfare state by thematizing a double-sided feedback loop: 'Social policy without economic policy is as impossible as economic policy without social policy.' This is the quintessence of Goetz Briefs' (1930, p. 170) agenda-setting address on the occasion of the XIth General Assembly of the *Gesellschaft für Soziale Reform* in Berlin in 1929.

The discourses that can be put under the general heading of 'the additional use of social policy' share an interest in what effects social security may have beyond the group of individuals who benefit directly. From a functionalist point of view, these discourses are interested in discovering 'latent functions' (Merton 1949) of social security, the effects beyond their immediate socio-political aims. This means from the point of view of a theory of action that these discourses are trying to explore the additional interests in social security - interests beyond those of the immediate beneficiaries. Thus, the strategic sense of analysing the additional use of social policy becomes clear. The aim is to discover the additional benefits and additional beneficiaries of social policy in order to create a rational foundation for a broad consensus supporting the promotion of the welfare state.

To systematically examine the additional use of social policy, I will refer to three systemic levels upon which the benefits may become manifest. These levels are: the individual enterprise; the macroeconomic level; and the social system. On these systemic levels the, actual or potential, beneficiaries of social security play different roles. I will refer to them as 'worker', 'income user'; and 'citizen'. The main question can now be more precisely formulated. How does social security modify the behaviour of beneficiaries (in their different roles) in such a way that there are corresponding positive economic effects at the different systemic levels?

Benefits for the use of labour power and technology

What are the positive effects of social security at the level of the individual enterprise? The economic effects which result from the ways that social security changes the behaviour of employees are a traditional and prominent topic in social scientific and political debates. 'What we spare the worker we spare ourselves' was a famous phrase of the German industrialist Krupp. During the world economic crisis the economic significance of social policy was programmatically emphasized in the proceedings of the *Gesellschaft für Soziale Reform* (1930 and 1931). Participants sought to demonstrate that a social policy able to prevent existential distress, in addition to its immediate socio-political significance, is an economic factor in the sense that it preserves the quality of labour power.

> Social policy as the doctrine of man's economic value takes into account particularly this side of the economic process. Therein lies its economic function and its attraction. By increasing the quality of human labour power it creates the very preconditions for economic progress ... (Schröder (1930, p. 205), a leader of the association of German white collar workers, Berlin).

163

The enlightened interest of the enterprise could only be pursued through explicit measures which protected labour power from the unchecked grip of entrepreneurial interests.

> All such laws take the form of placing restrictions on labour. Their purpose, however is the opposite: They are adopted in order to achieve a higher rather than a lower level of labour performance. And to achieve better performance in the long run! (Potthoff, 1931, p. 16).

A discussion of the necessity of physically protecting workers in order to secure functional employees is no longer carried on today. Instead, the considerations are about social security as a precondition for modernization by enabling flexibilization and facilitating technological innovation.

> The existence of unemployment insurance can increase ... the allocative efficiency of the labour market, e.g. by increasing mobility and thus the adaptability of the labour market to a new technological factor mix or to new demand profiles. A 'generous' unemployment insurance consequently may then be understood as a productive subsidy for such mobility processes. Moreover, the willingness to accept temporary job offers or jobs with a known high (e.g. seasonal) unemployment risk would probably increase in the presence of 'generous' insurance benefits; such jobs also need to be done, and their support, if not subsidization, thus contributes to the flexibility of the labour market. (Schmid, Reissert & Bruche, 1987, p. 205)

The new discussion on flexibilization and deregulation in general stresses the point that such projects require a socio-political embedding in order to be feasible. Guy Standing for instance concludes on the basis of such considerations 'that growing labour flexibility must be encouraged in ways that do not undermine, but actually increase, personal income security.' (Standing, 1986, p. 88) The German *Deregulierungskommission*, a commission of independent economic experts established by the German *Bundesregierung*, equally postulates not the dismantling, but the reorganization of social security parallel to deregulation. Considering that the *Deregulierungskommission* (1991, p. 6) interprets German unification as 'a colossal deregulation' for the former GDR, one might see that the idea of complex combinations of deregulation and socio-political stabilization (Vobruba 1991b) is of great importance for the development of the new reform countries.

Fritz Tarnow, at the time chairman of the German Woodworkers Association, posed an important question when he asked:

Does anybody believe that the large scale rationalization of the economy could be carried out at all without the existing forms of social security? That, for example, in the current concentration in banking several thousand redundant bank employees would leave quietly their old jobs and lie down in the streets to starve? (Tarnow, 1930, pp. 188-9)

It is not the availability of technology which is the most important limiting factor for the development of productivity in the economy as a whole. 'The politically much more difficult problem is how to absorb, compensate, and socially regulate the inevitable displacement of labour.' (Zapf, 1983, p. 298, Abramovitz 1981) This may be an important point for the former planned economies. Victims of technological innovation may have a lower resistance to change where social benefits provide some protection to their living standards. Thus social benefits may facilitate the process of technological change by modifying the behaviour of some of the losers from the changes.

Benefits on the macroeconomic level

What are the positive effects of social policy at the macroeconomic level? The question is what modifications in consumers' behaviour are brought about by social security, and what are their macroeconomic effects[2]?

Social security enables consumers to spend more money, more consistently, than would be the case in the absence of such protection. This is the basis of the 'purchasing power argument' that trade unions counterposed to the issue of 'social welfare costs' raised by employers in the social policy debate towards the end of the Weimar Republic (Preller, 1978, p. 388). 'In the face of the economic crisis, which is primarily caused by a lack of sales, the political intervention in the process of income distribution is a measure that contributes to an increase in mass consumption and thereby also benefits the economy.' (Tarnow, 1930, pp. 194, 195) These are the practical conclusions drawn from the theoretical insight into the twofold character of wages: elements of costs and of purchasing power. Each entrepreneur perceives wages as costs, but all entrepreneurs contribute to purchasing power through wages. Thus, purchasing power is a collective good: all use it but no one will produce it. This is a 'classical' situation requiring external intervention by the state.

In his plan for post-war social policy in Great Britain, Sir William Beveridge pointed out programmatically:

If unemployment benefits are set as high as possible while preserving a flexible labour market and incentives for the individual to look for work rather than to stay at home, the purchasing power of the working classes at the beginning of a crisis will be protected and the severity of the depression will be reduced. (Beveridge, 1942, p. 252)

Martin Pfaff has demonstrated the countercyclical rates of growth in social expenditures and GNP for Sweden, the old countries of the Federal Republic of Germany, Austria and the United States. He concludes that social expenditures have a stabilizing effect (Pfaff, 1989, p. 131ff.).

The effects of social security on purchasing power are not restricted to the volume of social benefits that is provided directly. It goes beyond this since social security also affects the wage level as a *de facto* minimum wage. Social security, in interplay with the organizational power of trade unions (Nissen 1988), works against 'the industrial reserve army' and thus against 'dirty competition' among the suppliers of labour power. It thereby prevents the occurrence of deflationary spirals that would be destructive for the economy as a whole (Kregel 1980). With respect to these stabilizing effects, Henry Ford II suggested, 'if trade unions did not exist, they would have to be invented.'

Social policy as a 'buffer'

What are the positive effects of social security at the level of society as a whole? What are the changes in behaviour produced by social policy that have significance for the society as well as for the economy?

Let me refer to some insider diagnoses of the main problems of development in the former planned economies.

> A basic feature typical of real socialism is the strong interrelation between the economy, the political and the welfare function of the state. The interrelation leads to the loss of identity of each sphere: their objectives and principles become vague and confused, a fact that results in the poor performance of each of them. (Kolarska-Bobinska, 1990, p. 63)

Under the ideology of the 'priority of politics' a confusion of systemic function took place, leading to a low degree of economic performance and a low level of social security.

> Politics have dominated the economy, and the economy has dominated, albeit in a covert, non-explicit way, social policy. What is more, since the advent of the crisis, the social elements built into the economy (the employment policy, the price policy etc.) may be blamed for inefficiencies of the economy. (Ferge, 1989, p. 9)

Similar diagnoses can be made for the other planned economies.

166

'A confusion of systemic function' is the problem diagnosis in terms of system theory. So I refer first, briefly, to the systemic effects of social policy, and then, in more detail, to the changes in behaviour through social policy, which are relevant for the success of the transformation of the former planned economies into market economies.

The most important systemic effect of social policy in this respect is to operate as a 'buffer' between different subsystems within society. Thus social policy supports processes of social differentiation and functional specialization. In particular, social policy enables the economic system to concentrate on the economic aim of 'efficient production' and to relieve it of additional tasks. On the individual level the result is to cutback the overload of functions of the single working place. One cannot expect any longer, that a working place secures subsistence, provides *kindergarten* places and the entrance to organized holidays, and shapes one's sense of life. On the collective level, social policy relieves the economic system of distributional conflicts. This can be proved by the negative correlation between the degree of social security and the degree of strike activities (Hibbs 1978, Paloheimo 1984). This last point leads to the second question. What behavioural modifications produced by social policy are relevant for the success of the transformation into market economies?

Transformation of planned economies

Economic transitions start with a journey through a desert, or 'economic transitions start with a valley of tears' (Dahrendorf 1990, p. 41). Such metaphors focus on a social problem and they introduce a political solution. First, the old planned economy has to be destroyed, and then a market economy can be built. In the meantime the living conditions for the majority inevitably will decline. Furthermore it is necessary to postpone individual claims, in order to support economic transformation. In the long run this will be in the interests of all. There is a green land behind the desert, there is a good place on the other side of the valley. Therefore temporary renunciations are in the individual's interest. It is rational to wait.

One of the problems discussed most intensively in the period of transformation of the former planned economies is the problem of the compatibility between the time horizon of the transformation and the time horizon of people's desire.

> One might describe the processes of transformation in Middle and Eastern Europe as a complicated agreement offered to the people by the new elites: civil rights, full personal and political freedom now and a well functioning economy in the expectable future in exchange for tolerance of the costs and risks of transformation as well as the abandonment of the right to economic equity.' (Smolar, 1990, p. 74)

Everyone has to postpone his or her own economic interests and wait for collective economic success.

'Waiting' is the crucial point in such agreements. Arpad Göncz, the President of Hungary, stresses, 'that the whole country is impatient and discontented.' (*Süddeutsche Zeitung*, 2 5 1991) Prime Minister Jan Krzysztof Bielecki draws a similar picture for Poland: 'Since two years we realize the Transformation towards a market economy ... People will hold out only if they are able to see some sense in their sacrifices.' (*Süddeutsche Zeitung*, 11 10 1991. S. 34) Since amelioration is expected during the transformation to market capitalism, there is a common call for foreign investment: 'We are lacking domestic capital, therefore we need it from outside.' (Bielecki) 'We would appreciated to see a big concurrence, a big crush of foreign capital, which we have not yet at the moment.' (Göncz)

The common need of foreign investments in the new reform societies causes a fundamental problem. There is competition between these societies for investment rather than competition between investors. On the investors' side such a situation leads to the expectation that the political need for investment will lead inevitably to lower prices (of real estate etc.) and higher subsidies. Transnational investors wait for, economically, rational reasons. But the new national political actors who are now under the pressure of the expectations of their voters can hardly wait, and are forced to improve the conditions for investment, thus confirming the investor's expectations. The German *Sachverständigenrat* in his annual report (*Jahresgutachten*, 1990/91, p. 66) mentioned the growing public debate about subsidies for investment and, as it calls it, *Investitionsattentismus* as the main problem of the transformation of the Eastern economies in general and of the former GDR in particular.

Unlike investors, politicians act under pressure of time. This time pressure is caused by the simultaneity of the political transformations from bureaucratic dictatorships into democracies and the economic transformations from planned economies into market economies (Hankiss, 1990, p. 183, Przeworski 1991)[3]. To put it simply, the newly achieved right to vote implies the political risk that people vote against the projects of economic transformation. The degree of this risk depends upon the capacity of the people to wait for the fruits of economic transformation in basically two ways (Vobruba 1994):

1   Public opinion must be strongly convinced that temporary renunciations are in the individual interest of all. People must be willing to wait.
2   Material living conditions should not fall below a certain level. At least the fear of starvation must be excluded. People must be able to wait.

As a result, the political management of transformation runs into a time problem. The problem can be characterized as combining the longer time horizon of the economic transition with the shorter horizon of interests, claims etc.. If one accepts this as a description of the problem of transformation in general, two kinds of solutions appear:

1   Shortening the time period of the transformation process.
2   Extending the time horizon of the individual interests.

Shocks and speed

In the first case, the political rhetoric and the strategies centre around the imagination of shocks and speed. The former US Secretary for Foreign Affairs, James Baker, recommended 'shock therapy' for Albania. Facing the economic problems in the (former) USSR, Vaclav Klaus, the Prime Minister of the Czech Republic, stressed that half a reform is worse than no reform. The advocates of shock therapies and the speed-up programmes themselves describe this strategy as 'highly risky' (Pellicani, 1991, p. 57), but they emphasize that there is no alternative. 'Better no reform, than an incrementalist one' said Vaclav Klaus. The last five years in the USSR are often seen as a good example of the negative results of hesitant reform.

> It is my firm belief that people would by far prefer to face a single, radical shock and the ensuing trauma if they were really convinced that the situation would improve as a result rather than to suffer the hopeless torture, the slow but steady economic deterioration and economic and social spasms we are now undergoing. (Kornai, 1990, p. 161)

The recommendation, in this case for Hungary, is that the unavoidable deterioration of living conditions must come at one stroke, in order to achieve ameliorations in a relatively short time period. Consequently the discussions on how to perform the transformations of the former planned economies centre around the problem of time. Bronislaw Geremek stresses, that 'Poland's problem number one is acceleration' (Ash, 1990, p. 28). The advocates of shock therapy have one strong argument, but only one argument. There is no alternative. That's why the risks of this strategy have to be accepted.

Let us first ask what the specific risks of shock therapy are? I am unable to list all of them, as there are many and they will change from country to country. All I can do is to offer a general interpretation of the problem generating mechanism. The main problem of shock therapy is that vicious cycles appear. This can be the case, because 'hard measures' do not only solve problems, but create new ones. Otherwise shock therapies would not be risky. Therefore, up to this point, the advocates of shock therapies agree. Amongst the problems which result may be a decline of purchasing power, growing strike activities, governmental instability and politicians' claims for 'temporarily special powers'. The harsher the measures are to solve the original problems, to speed up the solutions and solve the new problems, the more new problems arise.

Thus a fundamental danger of shock therapy is that the argument that there is 'no alternative' leads to a one-dimensional political strategy with growing problems requiring 'more of the same.' In that way economic and political vicious circles are created: Insufficient success of the harsh economic measures leads to harsher measures, insufficient success of the 'special powers' leads to more extensive 'special powers'. This process may end in the temporary suspension of democracy which in retrospect may turn out to be irreversible[4]. Thus even if shock therapy is well founded in economic theory, the practical result can be that while the operation is successful, the patient is dead.

Capitalism and democracy

There are two lessons from this. First, the success of the transformation depends upon the economy, but pure economic theory is a false way of thinking and misleads the politics of transformation (Schmähl 1994). A theory including economic processes and their social and political framework is needed. Such a sociological theory of transformation is still missing. Second, the vote for shock therapy stems from a false alternative. It is not 'radical reforms or hesitation' but 'radical reforms with or without a socio-political buffer'.

German unification with its simultaneous and sudden introduction of the market economy and the welfare system can be seen as a case in point (Ganßmann 1993, Mangen 1994). This leads to the second way of coping with the time problem, extending the time horizons of the individuals through social policy.

Unlike the majority of politicians the group of economic experts of 'The World Institute for Development Economics Research' (WIDER) advocate an economic shock and socio-political buffers.

> Stabilization cannot wait, nor can price liberalization. Step by step price liberalization, of the sort envisioned in the now defunct five hundred day programme, triggers purchases of goods in anticipation of price increases, which in turn leads to shortage, economic chaos, and strong political pressure on the government to delay the increases. (Blanchard et al., 1991, p. xii)

Simultaneously they call for 'a targeted basic needs programme for those parts of the population most likely to be impoverished' (Blanchard et al., 1991, p. 30, Barr 1994, Sipos 1994)[5]. 'A reserve must be set aside before the stabilization begins in order to provide assistance to those temporarily in difficulties.' (Kornai, 1990, p. 201) This is not just a recommendation from a 'humanitarian point of view'

(Kornai, 1990, p. 200); it is, to quote Abramovitz, (1981, p. 2) 'not just a question of compassionate regard for the unfortunate'.

The need to combine the liberalization of the economy with the socio-political stabilization of the people's living conditions is the strategic result of theorizing social policy as a means of supporting functional differentiation. More specifically, social policy enables the economic system to concentrate on its economic functions for the society, by freeing the work place from additional socio-political tasks[6]. This is, as we have seen before, the essence of the discussion on the additional use of social policy. It is the theoretical argument behind the thesis that social policy enables economic and ecological modernization (Nissen 1992), and it leads to the conclusion that socio-political buffers are a requirement for the simultaneous success of the economic and political transformations in the new reform societies (Vobruba 1991a). Social policy supports the economic transformation by enabling people to wait. Furthermore social policy lowers the danger of vicious cycles: in an economic sense, insofar as social policy stabilizes purchasing power and in a political sense, insofar as social policy reduces conflict in society. This happens, not by providing justice in the sense of income equality, but by facilitating the acceptance of growing income inequalities, which are problematic as well as necessary.

Again the requirement is to alter the interpretation of society from a zero sum game to a positive sum game (Bohmann & Vobruba 1992).

> People must alter their way of thinking. Enrichment has long been considered something shameful. A fallacy has reached the marrow of people's bones: if someone gets more, then it is because he took it away from others. (Kornai, 1990, pp. 181-2)

Inequality of incomes can be in the interest of the disadvantaged, if this inequality leads to an income situation in which they will get more than before. Inequality combined with higher efficiency can be better than income equality combined with lower efficiency. Inequality can be a precondition for higher efficiency and thus reasonable for the disadvantaged (Vobruba, 1983, p. 176). That is the reason why one should 'refrain from comforting the poor members of Hungarian society by declaiming with resounding phrases against the "rich".' (Kornai, 1990, p. 204) Meanwhile this is a very common argument in theory. But in order to accept the argument in practice, one has first to demonstrate that inequality leads to higher economic performance and is in the interest of all. This, again, is a question of time.

Finally, if the differences between the time period of the transformation process and of individual interests is the main problem in the politics of transformation, and if a pure shock therapy is 'highly risky', and if the strategies of speeding up the transformations are self-defeating, then the extension of the time horizons of individuals, i.e. socio-political measures in order to enable then to wait, are an investment by political actors in the governability of transforming societies. In order to make the transformation a success they must focus on the capacity of people to wait. Thus, one may distinguish between political actors who promote a transformation into stable capitalism and democracy, and others, who will tolerate new dictatorships, even including markets.

Conclusion

What is the additional use of social policy? With regard to individual problems, social security basically provides some degree of freedom from the constraints of the labour market. Social security extends individual options and thus provides a central promise of modernity: the promise of free choice for everyone - a task for the development of the society which was passionately emphasized both by the political liberals and in the early work of Karl Marx. From a more 'technocratic' point of view this widening of individual options also means that social security enables the individual to accept the inevitable consequences of rationalization, deregulation and of economic modernization. I do not see social policy as a blue-print for solving all conflicts related to the modernization of market economies and even less for solving all conflicts related to the transformation from planned to market economies, but it facilitates the transformation by compensating for at least some of its costs.

With regard to collective development, social policy supports processes of functional differentiation and functional specialization by its 'buffer function'. This 'buffer function' obviously plays an important role in the process of modernization in the former planned economies. Usually our times are seen as a new 'Schumpeter era'. And most probably many observers will see the present situation in the former planned economies as the golden hour of Schumpeter's idea of 'creative destruction'. So let me refer to Schumpeter too. To paraphrase Schumpeter (1975, p. 146), one may say that introducing social policy as a means to improve economic performance is no more paradoxical than the observation that cars equipped with breaks can be driven faster than those without.

Notes

1   The differences between such interpretations in the first world economic crisis after 1929 and the second world economic crisis after 1974 are discussed in Bohmann & Vobruba 1992.

2   The effects of social security on savings are discussed in Feldstein 1974. For an empirical critique of the Feldstein thesis see Berthold & Külp 1987.

3   Unlike the majority of the authors I would like to argue, that this simultaneity not only creates problems but creates short-term opportunities

as well, another reason to take the problem of speed seriously (Vobruba, 1991a, p. 142).

4   Kornai (1990, pp. 206-7) tries to solve the dilemma between 'the need for a strong government' on the one hand and the danger of a 'repressive authoritarian administration' on the other by interpreting elections as 'self-bound'. 'The operation must be done, but the Hungarian people as the patient must give their consent through the voice of their elected representatives.' It is notable that the transformation is seen as an operation. This implies that people are under anaesthetic - another picture for a temporary solution which creates time pressure. The operation must be done before the patient comes out of the anaesthetic.

5   The authors claim an important aim, limiting 'the extent of long term unemployment and the process of disenfranchisement', but they recommend a dubious measure - generous unemployment benefits 'for a limited period of time, say six months, after which they drop sharply.' (Blanchard et al., 1991, p. 90). The authors state that this is the lesson they have learned 'from the Western European experience of the last two decades.' (Blanchard et al., 1991, p. xix) Unfortunately they do not tell us which lesson they mean. Anyhow it is not true that 'most Eastern European countries have open-ended unemployment benefit systems.' (Blanchard et al., 1991, p. 90) On the contrary, due to the fact that in the planned economies there existed no (officially acknowledged) unemployment, these countries did not have unemployment benefits at all until the beginning of the transformation.

6   For Russian people for instance this is still a very strange idea.

Bibliography

Abramovitz, M. (1981), 'Welfare Quandaries and Productivity Concerns', *American Economic Review*, Vol. 71, pp. 1-17.

Aglietta, M. (1976), *Régulation et crises du capitalisme*, Calman-Lévy: Paris.

Ainley, P. (1990), *Training Turns to Enterprise: Vocational Education in the Market Place*, Hillcole Group Paper 4, Tufnell Press: London.

Alber, J. (1984), 'Versorgungsklassen im Wohlfahrtsstaat', *Kölner Zeitschrift für Soziologie*, Vol 36, Nr. 1.

Alber, J. (1988), *Vom Armenhaus zum Wohlfahrtsstaat. Analysen zur Entwicklung der Sozialversicherung in Westeuropa*, Campus Verlag: Frankfurt,M. & New York

Altmann, N. (1992), 'Japanische Arbeitspolitik - eine Herausforderung?', in Hans-Böckler-Stiftung (ed.), *Lean Production - Schlanke Produktion*, HBS: Düsseldorf.

Andersen, J. and Larsen, J. (1995), 'The Underclass Debate - a Spreading Disease?', in Mortensen, N. (ed.), *Social Integration and Marginalisation*, Samfundslitteratur: Frederiksberg.

Andersen, S. and Eliassen, K. (1994), *Making Policy in Europe: The Europeification of National Policy-making*, Sage: London.

Anderson, B. (1983), *Imagined Communities*, Verso: London.

Aranowitz, S. (1993), *Roll over Beethoven. The Return of Cultural Strife*, Wesleyan University Press: Hanover.

Arends, J. and Volman, M. (1995), 'Equal Opportunities in the Netherlands and the Policy of the ILEA' in Dawtrey, L., Holland, J., Hammer, M. and Sheldon, S. (eds.) *Equality and Inequality in Education Policy*, Multilingual Matters: Clevedon.

Arnman, G. and Jönsson, I. (1983), *Segregation och svensk skola. En studie av utbildning, klass och boende*, Arkiv Förlag: Lund.

Arnman, G., Kutscha, G. and Young, M. (1995), 'The Experimental Reform of Upper Secondary Education in Finland. International Evaluation Report' in *Experimental Reform of Upper Secondary Education of Finland* Report 5, Ministry of Education: Helsinki.

Ash, T. G. (1993), *In Europe's Name: Germany and the Divided Continent*, Cape: London

Ash, T. G. (1990), 'Après le déluge, nous', *Transit*, Heft 1, pp. 11-34.

Ashenfelter, A. and Johnson, G. E. (1969), 'Bargaining theory, trade unions, and industrial strike activity', *American Economic Review*, Vol. 59, pp. 35-49.

Axelsson, R. (1989), 'Upper Secondary School in Retrospect: The Views of Former Students' *Uppsala Studies in Education 30*, Almqvist and Wiksell International: Stockholm.

Bäcker, G. & Hanesch, W. (1993), 'Nicht den Kernbestand des Sozialstaates in Frage stellen', *Frankfurter Rundschau*, 11. 8. 1993

Bäcker, G. & Steffen, J. (1992), 'Reichtum im Westen - Armut im Osten? Neue Gesellschaftsspaltungen machen soziale Mindestsicherung erforderlich', *WSI-Mitteilungen*, 44. Jg., 5/1991, pp. 292 - 307

Bader, V. M. and Benschop, A. (1989), *Ungleichheiten*, Leske & Budrich: Opladen.

Baethge, M. (1991), 'Arbeit, Vergesellschaftung, Identität', *Soziale Welt*, No. 1.

Baglioni, G. (1990), 'Industrial Relations in Europe in the 1980s', in Baglioni, G. and Crouch, C. (eds.), *European Industrial Relations. The challenge of Flexibility*, Sage: London.

Bamber, G. J. and Lansbury, R. D. (1987), *International and comparative industrial relations*, Allen & Unwin: London.

Baimbridge, M., Burkitt, B. and Macey, M. (1994), 'The Maastricht Treaty: exacerbating racism in Europe?', *Ethnic and Racial Studies*, Vol. 17, No 3, July, pp. 420-41.

Baldwin, P. (1990), *The Politics of Social Solidarity*, Cambridge University Press: Cambridge.

Ball, S. (1990), *Politics and Policy Making in Education*, Routledge: London.

Ball, S. and Larsson, S. (eds.), (1989) *The Struggle for Democratic Education, Equality and Participation in Sweden*, Falmer: London.

Barkin, S. (ed.) (1983), *Worker militancy and its consequences; the changing climate of western industrial relations*, Praeger: New York.

Barr, N. (1994), 'Income Transfers: Social Insurance', in Barr, N. (ed.), *Labor Markets and Social Security in Central and Eastern Europe. The Transition and Beyond*, Oxford University Press: Oxford.

Bates, I., Clarke, J., Cohen, P., Finn, D., Moore, R. and Willis, P. (1984), *Schooling for the Dole? The New Vocationalism*, Macmillan: London.

Batstone, E., Boraston, I. and Frenkel, S. (1978), *The social organization of strikes*, Basil Blackwell: Oxford.

Beck, U. (1983), 'Jenseits von Stand und Klasse?', in Kreckel, R. (ed.), *Soziale Ungleichheiten*, Schwartz: Göttingen.

Beck, U. (1992), *The Risk Society*, Sage: London.

Beckenbach, N. et al. (1973), *Klassenlage und Bewußtseinsformen der technisch-wissenschaftlichen Lohnarbeiter*, Europäische Verlagsanstalt: Frankfurt/Main.

Beckenbach, N. et al. (1975), *Ingenieure und Techniker in der Industrie*, Europäische Verlagsanstalt: Frankfurt/Main.

Beechey, V. (1978), 'Women and Production', in Kuhn, A. and Wolpe, A. M. (eds.), *Feminism and Materialism*, Routledge: London.

Beer, U. (1987), 'Sozialpolitische Perspektiven für Frauen am Beispiel "Mindesteinkommen und Probleme einer feministischen Sozialstaatsanalyse"', Opielka, M. & Ostner, I. (eds.), *Umbau des Sozialstaats*, Klartext: Essen, pp. 177-93.

Bell, D. (1986), *The Cultural Contradictions of Capitalism*, Basic Books: New York.

Berger, P. A. (1986), *Entstrukturierte Klassengesellschaft?*, Westdeutscher Verlag: Opladen.

Berger, P. A. and Hradil, S. (1990), *Lebenslagen, Lebensläufe, Lebensstile*, Schwartz: Göttingen.

Berger, S. (1994), 'Nationalism and the Left in Germany', *New Left Review*, No 206, July/August, pp. 55-70.

Berthold, N. & Külp, B. (1987), *Rückwirkungen ausgewählter Systemme der Sozialen Sicherung auf die Funktionsfähigkeit der Marktwirtschaft*, Duncker & Humblot: Berlin.

Betz, H-G. (1993), 'The new politics of resentment: radical right-wing populist parties in Western Europe', *Comparative Politics*, Vol. 26, No 4, July, pp. 413-27.

Beveridge, Sir William (1943), *Der Beveridgeplan*, Europa Verlag: Zürich, New York.

Bialas, C. & Ettl, W. (1993), 'Wirtschaftliche Lage, soziale Differenzierung und Probleme der Interessenorganisation in den neuen Bundesländern', *Soziale Welt*, 44 (1), pp. 52-74

Biedenkopf, K. (1986), 'Führt die Kostenentlastung der Unternehmen zu Mehrbeschäftigung? Plädoyer für die Trennung von Arbeits- und Sozialverhältnis', in Maier, H. E. & Schmid, T. (eds.), *Der goldene Topf. Vorschläge zur Auflockerung des Arbeitsmarktes*, Berlin, pp. 142-255.

Billiet, J. (1993a), 'Measurement for some scales in the survey on political attitudes and behaviour connected with the general elections (24 Nov. 1991) in Flanders', *ISPO Bulletin 1993/6*, Leuven.

Billiet, J. (1993b), *Ondanks beperkt zicht*, VUB-Press: Brussel.

Billiet, J. and De Witte, H. (1993) 'Attitudinal Dispositions to Vote Right Wing: The Case of Vlaams Blok', *ISPO Bulletin 1993/9*, Leuven.

Billiet, J., Swyngedouw, M. and Carton, A. (1993), 'Protest, ongenoegen en onverschilligheid op 24 November... en nadien', *Res Publica*, 2.

Bischoff, J. et al. (1982), *Jenseits der Klassen?*, VSA: Hamburg.

Bjorgo, T. and Witte, R. (eds.) (1993), *Racist Violence in Europe*, Macmillan: Basingstoke.

Blanchard, O. et al. (1991), *Reform in Eastern Europe*, Cambridge, Massachusetts: The MIT Press.

Blickhäuser, A. & Molter, M. (1986), 'Garantierte Lebenssicherung für Frauen. Bemerkungen zur Mindesteinkommensdiskussion', in Opielka, M. & Vobruba, G. (eds.), *Das garantierte Grundeinkommen. Entwicklung und Perspektiven einer Forderung*, Fischer Taschenbuch Verlag: Frankfurt/M., pp. 106-17.

Blossfeld, H.-P., Gianelli, G. and Mayer, K. U. (1993), 'Expansion of the Tertiary Sector and Social Inequality', in Esping-Andersen, G. (ed.), *Changing Classes. Stratification and Mobility in Post-Industrial Societies*, Sage: London.

Bogdanor, V. and Woodcock, G. (1991), 'The European Community and Sovereignty', *Parliamentary Affairs*, Vol. 44, No 4, October, pp. 481-92.

Boh, K., Bak, M. and Clason, C. (eds.) (1990), *Changing Patterns of European Family: A Comparison of 14 Countries*, Routledge: London.

Bohmann, G. & Vobruba, G. (1992), 'Crises and their Interpretations', *Crime, Law and Social Change* Vol. 17. pp. 145-63.

Bourdieu, P. (1979), *La distinction*, Les Editions de Minuit: Paris.

Bourdieu, P. (1985) *Sozialer Raum und 'Klassen'*, Suhrkamp: Frankfurt/Main.

Bourdieu, P. (1987), 'What makes a social class?' *Berkeley Journal of Sociology*, Vol. 32.

Bowles, S. and Gintis, H. (1976), *Schooling in Capitalist America*, Routledge & Kegan Paul: London.

Braverman, H. (1974), *Labor and Monopoly Capital*, Monthly Review Press: New York.

Briefs, G. (1930), 'Der wirtschaftliche Wert der Sozialpolitik', *Schriften der Gesellschaft für Soziale Reform*, Heft 83, pp. 144-70.

Brown, G. and Wright, T. (1995), *Values, Visions and Voices, An Anthology of Socialism*, Mainstream Publishing: Edinburgh.

Bruegal, I. (1979), 'Women as a reserve army of labour: a note on recent British experience', *Feminist Review*, No. 3.

Camilleri, J. and Falk, J. (1992), *The end of Sovereignty? The Politics of a Shrinking and Fragmenting World*, Edward Elgar: Aldershot.

Carter, F., French, R. and Salt, J. (1993), 'International migration between East and West in Europe', *Ethnic and Racial Studies*, Vol. 16, No 3, July, pp. 467-91.

Carton, A., Swyngedouw, M., Billiet, J. and Beerten, R. (1993), *Source Book of the Voters' Study in connection with the 1991 General Election*, S.O.I.-K.U.L: Louvain.

CCCS - Centre for Contemporary Cultural Studies (1981), *Unpopular Education: Schooling and Social Democracy in England since 1944*, Hutchinson: London.

CCCS - Cultural Studies Education Group II (1991), *Education Limited: Schooling and Training and the New Right Since 1979*, Unwin Hyman: London.

Cernigoj-Sadar N. (1990), 'Psycho-social dimensions of paid work and family life', in Boh, K., Bak, M. and Clason, C. (1990), *Changing Patterns of European Family: A Comparison of 14 Countries*, Routledge: London.

Chisholm, L. (1992), 'A Crazy Quilt: Education, Training and Social Change in Europe' in Bailey, J. (ed.) *Social Europe*, Longman: London.

Chitty, C. (1989), *Towards a New Education System: the Victory of the New Right?*, Falmer: London.

Clarke, F. and Dunne, A. C. (1955), *Ageing in Industry*, Nuffield Foundation: London.

Coates, K. & Barratt Brown, M. (eds.) (1993), *A European Recovery Programme: Restoring Full Employment*, Spokesman: Nottingham.

Commission of the European Communities (1989) *Women of Europe Supplement No 30*, Office for the Official Publications of the European Communities: Luxembourg.

Commission of the European Communities (1993), *Growth, Competitiveness, Employment - The challenges and ways forward into the 21st century*, Luxembourg.

Cripps, F. & Ward, T. (1993), *Europe Can Afford to Work: Strategies for Growth and Employment in the European Community*, Spokesman: Nottingham.

Crompton, R. (1993), *Class and Stratification. An Introduction to Current Debates*, Polity Press: Cambridge.

Crouch, C. and Pizzorno, A. (1978), *The resurgence of class conflict in western Europe since 1968*, Macmillan: Basingstoke.

Curtice, J. (1993), 'Satisfying Work: if you can get it', *10th BSA Report: International Attitudes*, Dartmouth Publishing Co.: Aldershot.

Dahrendorf, R. (1959), *Class and Class Conflict in Industrial Society*, Routledge & Kegan Paul: London.

Dahrendorf, R. (1964), 'Recent Changes in the Class Structure of European Societies', *Daedalus*, Vol. 93.

Dahrendorf, R. (1990), 'Politik, Wirtschaft und Freiheit', *Transit*, Heft 1, pp. 35-47.

Dale, R. Bowe, R., Harris, D., Loveys, M., Moore, R., Shilling, C. Sikes, P., Trevitt, J. and Valsecchi, V. (1990), *The TVEI Story: Policy, Practice and Preparation for the Workforce*, Open University: Milton Keynes.

Dale, R., Esland, G., Fergusson, R. and MacDonald, M.(eds.), (1981) *Education and the State* , Falmer: London.

Dalton, R. J. (1988), *Citizen Politics in Western Democracies*, Chatham House: Chatham.

David, M. (1993), *Parents, Gender and Education Reform*, Polity: Cambridge.

Davies, J. (ed.) (1993), *The Family: is it just another lifestyle choice?*, Welfare Series No 15, IEA Health and Welfare Unit: London.

De Witte, H. (1990), *Conformisme, Radicalisme en Machteloosheid*, HIVA: Leuven.

De Witte, H. (1994), 'Schijn bedriegt. Over de betekenis en de strategie van het Vlaams Blok', *De Gids op Maatschappelijk Gebied*, Vol. 85, No. 3.

Dennis, N. and Erdos, G. (1993), *Families without Fatherhood*, Welfare Series No 12, IEA Health and Welfare Unit: London.

Deppe, F. (1993), 'Gestaltungskompetenz und Gegenmacht' *Sozialismus*, No. 2.

Deregulierungskommission (1991), *Marktöffnung und Wettbewerb*, mimeo: Bonn.

Deschouwer, K. (1987), *Politieke partijen in België*, Kluwer: Antwerpen.

Deschouwer, K. (1993), 'Nieuwe breuklijnen in the politiek? Herverkaveling van het partijenlandschap', *Kultuurleven*.

Deschouwer, K. and Stouthuysen, P. (1984), 'L'électorat d'Agalev', *Courier Hebdomadaire du CRISP*, No. 1061.

Devine, J. and Wright, J. (1993), *The Greatest of Evils. Urban Poverty and the American Underclass*, Aldine de Gruyter: New York.

Dex, S. and Shaw, L. (1986), *British and American Women at Work*, Macmillan: Basingstoke.

Dogan, M. (1994), 'The decline of nationalisms in Western Europe', *Comparative Politics*, Vol. 26, No 3, April, pp. 281-305.

Dörre, K., Neubert, J., Wolf, H. (1993), 'New Deal' im Betrieb?' *SOFI-Mitteilungen Nr 20*, Soziologisches Forschungsinstitut: Göttingen.

Eatwell, R. (1994), 'Why are Fascism and Racism reviving in Western Europe?', *Political Quarterly*, Vol. 65, No 3, July-Sept., pp. 313-25.

Echols, F., McPherson, A. and Willms, J. (1990), 'Parental Choice in Scotland' *Journal of Educational Policy*, Vol.5, No.3, pp. 207-222.

Edebalk, P. G. and Wadensjö, E. (1989), *Arbetsmarknadsförsäkringar*, DS 1989:68: Stockholm.

Edwards, R. (1979), *Contested Terrain*, Basic Books: New York.

Eichenberg, R. and Dalton, R. (1993), 'Europeans and the European Community: the dynamics of public support for European integration', *International Organization*, Vol. 47, No 4, Autumn, pp. 507-34.

Elchardus, M. (1991a), *Een tijd voor waarden en normen*, Koning Boudewijnstichting: Brussel.

Elchardus, M. (1991b), 'Flexible men and women. The changing temporal organization of work and culture: an empirical analysis', *Social Science Information*, 30, 4.

Elchardus, M. (1994a), 'Gekaapte deugden. Over the nieuwe politieke breuklijn en the zin van limieten', *Samenleving en Politiek*, 1, 1.

Elchardus, M. (1994b), 'In praise of rigidity: on temporal and cultural flexibility', *Social Science Information*, 33, 3.

Elchardus, M. and Heyvaert, P. (1991), *Soepel, Flexibel en Ongebonden*, VUB Press: Brussels.

Elchardus, M., Deschouwer, K., Pelleriaux, K. and Stouthuysen, P. (1993), 'Hoe negatief kan vrijheid zijn? Ongeloof, vrijzinnigheid en populistische ontvoogding', in Swyngedouw et. al. (eds.), *Kiezen is verliezen*, Acco: Leuven.

Erbslöh, B. et al. (1988), 'Klassenstruktur und Klassenbewußtsein in der Bundesrepublik Deutschland', *Kölner Zeitschrift für Soziologie und Sozialpsychologie*, Vol. 40.

Erbslöh, B. et al. (1990), *Ende der Klassengesellschaft?*, Transfer Verlag: Regensburg.

Erdmann, E-G. (1985), 'Die Verbindlichkeit von Tarifnormen ist unverzichtbar', *Wirtschaftsdienst*, V, pp. 222-4.

Erikson, R. and Goldthorpe, J.H. (1992), *The Constant Flux*, Clarendon Press: Oxford.

Esping-Andersen, G. (1990), *The Three Worlds of Welfare Capitalism*, Polity Press: Cambridge.

Esping-Andersen, G. (1990), *The Three Worlds of Welfare Capitalism*, Polity Press: Cambridge.

Esping-Andersen, G. (1993), 'Post-Industrial Class Structures: an Analytical Framework', in Esping-Andersen, G. (ed.), *Changing Classes*, Sage: London.

European Centre (1993), 'Welfare in a Civil Society', *Report for the Conference of European Ministers Responsible for Social Affairs - United Nations European Region* , European Centre: Vienna.

European Parliament (1991), *Committee of Inquiry on Racism and Xenophobia, Report of the findings of the Inquiry*, European Parliament: Strasbourg.

Featherstone, M. (1991), *Consumer Culture and Postmodernism*, Sage: London.

Feldstein, M. (1974), 'Social Security, Induced Unemployment, and Aggregate Capital Accumulation', *Journal of Political Economy*, Vol. 82, No. 5, pp. 905-26.

Felling, A. and Peeters, J. (1984), 'Conservatisme in Nederland nader bekeken', *Mens en Maatschappij*, 4.

Fenwick, I. (1976), *The Comprehensive School 1944-1970: The Politics of Secondary School Reorganization*, Methuen: London.

Ferge, Z. (1989), 'Unemployment in Hungary', Paper presented at the Conference on Comparative Research in Social Policy, Labour Markets, Inequality and Distributive Conflict (ISA Research Committee 19) Stockholm.

Ferner, A. and Hyman, R. (1992), 'Introduction. Industrial Relations in the New Europe: Seventeen Types of Ambiguity', in Ferner, A. and Hyman, R. (eds.), *Industrial Relations in the New Europe*, Basil Blackwell: Oxford.

Finch, J. (1984), *Education as Social Policy*, Longman: London.

Finch, J. and Groves, D. (1983), *A Labour of Love*, Routledge: London.

Fincher, R. (1993), 'Women, the State and the Life course in Urban Australia', in Katz, C. and Monk, J. (eds.), *Full Circles: Geographies of Women over the Lifecourse*, Routledge: London.

Finn, D. (1987), *Training Without Jobs: New Deals and Broken Promises*, Macmillan: London.

Flanagan, S. C. (1987), 'Value Change in Industrial Societies', *American Political Science Review*, 81, 4.

Flanagan, S. C. and Beck, P. A. (eds.) (1984), *Electoral Changes in Advanced Industrial Democracies*, Princeton: Princeton University Press.

Ford, G. (1994), 'Europe's limited plan to tackle racism', *Searchlight*, November.

Ford, G. (ed.) (1992), *Fascist Europe. The Rise of Racism and Xenophobia*, Pluto Press: London.

Forsberg, P. (1993), *De äldre och arbetsmarknaden - en statistisk översikt*, Dept of Sociology, Lund University: Lund.

France (1990), *Education pour tous. Politiques et stratégies rénovées pour les années 1990*, Ministre de l'Education Nationale de la Jeunesse et des Sports: Paris.

Franklin, M., Marsh, M. and McLaren, L. (1994), 'Uncorking the Bottle: Popular Opposition to European Unification in the Wake of Maastricht', *Journal of Common Market Studies*, Vol. 32, No 4, December, pp. 455-72.

Frerich, J. (1987), *Sozialpolitik. Das Sozialleistungssystem der Bundesrepublik*, Oldenbourg: München & Wien.

Gallagher, T. (1994), 'The Regional Dimension in Italy's Political Upheaval: Role of the Northern League 1984-1993', *Parliamentary Affairs*, Vol. 47, No 3, July, pp. 456-68.

Ganßmann, H. (1993), 'After Unification: Problems Facing the German Welfare State', *Journal of European Social Policy*, Vol. 3 No. 2, pp. 79-90.

George, S. (1991), *Britain and European Integration since 1945*, Blackwell: Oxford.

Gershuny, J. (1994), 'Occupational trajectories: the importance of longitudinal evidence in understanding change in social stratification', *Plenary address to Friesland Academy Conference*, October 12.

Gibbins, J. R. (1989), 'Contemporary Political Culture: an Introduction', in Gibbins, J. R. (ed.), *Contemporary Political Culture, Politics in a Postmodern Age*, Sage: London.

Giddens, A. (1973), *The Class Structure of the Advanced Societies*, Hutchinson University Library: London.

Giddens, A. (1990), *The Consequences of Modernity*, Stanford University Press: Stanford.

Giddens, A. (1991), *Modernity and Self Identity*, Cambridge University Press: Cambridge.

Glasner, A. (1992), 'Gender and Europe; cultural and structural impediments to change', in Bailey, J. (ed.), *Social Europe*, Longman: Harlow.

Gleeson, D. (1989), *The Paradox of Training: Making Progress out of Crisis*, Open University: Milton Keynes.

Glendinning, C. and Millar, J. (eds.) (1992), *Women and Poverty in Britain: the 1990s*, Harvester Wheatsheaf: Hemel Hempstead.

Goffman, E. (1970), *Stigma: notes on the management of spoiled identity*, Penguin: Harmondsworth.

Goldthorpe, J. H. et al. (1968), *The Affluent Worker: Industrial Attitudes and Behaviour*, Cambridge University Press: Cambridge.

Goodin, R. (1995), 'Conjectures on the Nation State', *Government and Opposition*, Vol. 30, No 1, Winter, pp. 26-34.

Gordon, M. S. (1988), *Social Security Policies in Industrial Countries: A Comparative Analysis*, Cambridge University Press: Cambridge & New York.

Grahl, J. and Teague, P. (1994), 'Economic Citizenship in the New Europe', *Political Quarterly*, Vol. 65, No. 4, October-December, pp. 379-96.

Granheim, M.K. and Lundgren, U.P. (1991), 'Steering by Goals and Evaluation in the Norwegian Education System. a Report form the EMIL Project' *Curriculum Studies* , Vol.23, No.6.

Grunberg, G. and Schweisguth, E. (1990), 'Libéralisme culture et libéralisme économique', in Boy, D. and Mayer, N. (eds.), *L'électeur Français en question*, CEVIPOF, Parijs.

Guilemard, A-M. and van Gunsteren, H. (1991), 'Pathways and their prospects: A comparative interpretation of the meaning of early exit', in Kohli, M et. al. (eds), *Time for Retirement*, Cambridge University Press: Cambridge, pp. 362-87.

Guillemard, A-M. (1989), 'The Trend Towards Early Labour Force Withdrawal and the Reorganization of the Life Course: A Cross-national Analysis', in Johnson, P. et al. (eds.), *Workers versus Pensioners. Integrational justice in an ageing world*, Manchester University Press: Manchester and New York, pp. 163-80.

Haas, E. (1993), 'Nationalism: An Instrumental Social Construction', *Millennium: Journal of International Studies*, Vol. 22, No 3, pp. 505-45.

Hagelstange, T. (1988), *Die Entwicklung von Klassenstrukturen in der EG und in Nordamerika*, Campus: Frankfurt/New York.

Haller, M. (1988), 'Die Klassenstruktur im sozialen Bewußtsein. Ergebnisse vergleichender Umfrageforschung zu Ungleichheitsvorstellungen', in Haller, M., Hoffmann-Nowottny, H.-J. & Zapf, W. (eds.), *Verhandlungen des 24. Deutschen Soziologentags, des 11. Österreichischen Soziologentags und des 8. Kongresses der Schweizerischen Gesellschaft für Soziologie in Zürich*, Campus: Frankfurt & New York, pp. 447-69.

Hamilton, R. F. (1972), *Class and Politics in the United States*, John Wiley & Sons: New York.

Hankiss, E. (1990), 'Zwischen zwei Welten. Wertewandel in Ungarn', *Transit*, Heft 1, pp. 167-184.

Harding, S., Phillips, D. and Foggarty, M. (1986), *Contrasting Values in Western Europe*, Macmillan: Basingstoke.

Hargreaves, A. and Reynolds, D., (eds.), (1989), *Education Policies: Controversies and Critiques*, Falmer: London.

Hearn, J. (1992), *Men in the Public Eye*, Routledge: London.

Hedetoft, U. (1994), 'The State of Sovereignty in Europe: Political Concept or Cultural Self-Image', in Zetterholm, S. (ed.), *National Cultures and European Integration*, Berg: Oxford.

Hellemans, S. (1990), *Strijd om the moderniteit*, KADOC-studies 10, Universitaire Pers Leuven: Leuven.

Hellemans, S. (1993), 'The Nieuwe Sociale Bewegingen in the Belgische politiek. Een impressie', *Res Publica*, 2.

Herkommer, S. & Bierbaum, H. (1979), *Industriesoziologie*, Enke: Stuttgart.

Herkommer, S. (1983), 'Sozialstaat und Klassengesellschaft', in: Kreckel, R. (ed.), *Soziale Ungleichheiten*, Schwartz: Göttingen.

Herkommer, S. (1991), 'Individualisierung und Klassenverhältnis', in Deppe, F. et al., *Eckpunkte moderner Kapitalismuskritik*, VSA: Hamburg.

Herkommer, S. (1991), 'Subjektivierung der Arbeit', *Sozialismus*, 4/91.

Herkommer, S. (1992), 'Klassen und Lebensstile. Bourdieus Beitrag zur Klassenanalyse', in Meyer, H. (ed.), *Soziologen-Tag Leipzig 1991*, Akademie Verlag: Berlin.

Herkommer, S. and Mühlhaus, M. (1992), 'Klasse, Geschlecht, Individualität', in Thomas, M. (ed), *Abbruch und Aufbruch*, Akademie Verlag: Berlin.

Hibbs, D. A. (1978), 'On the political economy of long run trends in strike activity', *British Journal of Political Science*, Vol. 8, pp. 153-175.

Hinrichs, K., Roche, W., and Sirianni, C. (1991), *Working Time in Transition. The Political Economy of Working Hours in Industrial Nations*, Temple University Press: Philadelphia.

Hobsbawm, E. (1990), *Nations and Nationalism since 1780*, Cambridge University Press: Cambridge.

Holz, K., Pioch, R., & Vobruba, G. (1994), 'Verteilungskonflikte in politischen Integrationsprozessen', in Eichener, V. & Voelzkow, H. (eds.) *Europäische Integration und verbandliche Interessenvermittlung*, Metropolis: Marburg, pp. 575-97.

Hondrich, K. O. and Koch-Arzberger, C. (1992), *Solidarität in der modernen Gesellschaft*, Fischer Taschenbuch: Frankfurt/Main.

Hradil, S. (1987), *Sozialstrukturanalyse in einer fortgeschrittenen Gesellschaft*, Leske & Budrich: Opladen.

Hradil, S. (1992), 'Sozialstruktur und gesellschaftlicher Wandel', in Gabriel, O. W. (ed), *Die EG-Staaten im Vergleich*, Westdeutscher Verlag: Opladen.

Hradil, S. (1993), 'New German Social Structure Analysis', *Schweizerische Zeitschrift für Soziologie*, 19, pp. 663-88.

Hunt, S. J. (1993), 'Racist Trends in European Politics', *Talking Politics*, Vol. 6, No 1, Autumn, pp. 52-6.

Hunter, J. D. (1991), *Culture Wars. The Struggle to Define America*, Basic Books: New York.

Husén, T. (ed.), (1982), *Grundskolan under 20 år*, Skolöverstyrelsen: Stockholm.

Husén, T., Tuijnman, A. and Wills, W. (1992), *Schooling in Modern European Society*, Pergamon: Oxford.

Hüther, M. (1990), *Integrierte Steuer-Transfer-Systeme für die Bundesrepublik Deutschland, Normative Konzeption und empirische Analyse*, Berlin.

Hüther, M. (1994), 'Ansatzpunkte für einen Umbau des Sozialstaats', *Wirtschaftsdienst*, 3/94, pp. 127-35.

Huyse, L. (1992), 'Politiek in the jaren negentig', *The Nieuwe Maand*, 35, 10.

Ignazi, P. and Ysmal, C. (eds.) (1992), 'Extreme Right-Wing Parties in Europe', *European Journal of Political Research*, 22, 1.

ILO (1991), *Year book of labour statistics*, International Labour Organisation: Geneva.

IMSF (1973), *Klassen-und Sozialstruktur der BRD 1950-1970* , 2 Vols, Institut für Marxistische Studien und Forschungen: Frankfurt/Main.

Inglehart, R. (1977), *The Silent Revolution: Changing Values and Political Styles among Western Publics*, Princeton University Press: Princeton.

Inglehart, R. (1984), 'The Changing Structure of Political Cleavages in Western Society', in Dalton, R. J., Flanagan, S. C. and Beck, P. A. (eds.), *Electoral Changes in Advanced Industrial Democracies*, Princeton University Press: Princeton.

Inglehart, R. (1987), 'Value Change in Industrial Societies', *American Political Science Review*, 81, 4.

Inglehart, R. (1989), 'Observations on Cultural Change and Postmodernism', in Gibbins, J. R. (ed.), *Contemporary Political Culture, Politics in a Postmodern Age*, Sage: London.

Inglehart, R. and Flanagan S. C. (1987), 'Value Change in Industrial Societies', *American Political Science Review*, 81.

Isling, Å (1980), *Kampen för och emot en demokratisk skola. 1. Samhällsstruktur och skolorganisation*, Sober Förlag: Stockholm.

Jacobs, K. and Rein, M. (1994), 'Early Retirement, Stability, Reversal, or Redefinition', in Naschold, F. and de Vroom, B. (eds.), *Regulating Employment and Welfare*, de Gruyter: Berlin & New York, pp. 19-49.

Jacobs, K., Kohli, M. and Rein, M. (1991), 'The evolution of early exit: A comparative analysis of labour participation patterns', in Kohli, M. et al. (eds.), *Time for Retirement*, Cambridge University Press: Cambridge, pp. 36-66.

Jaffré, J. (1995), 'année faste pour le Front national', *Le Monde*, 17 June 1995.

Jahn, D. (1989), 'Changes in the Political Culture - Challenges to the Trade Union Movement: the Debate on Nuclear Energy in Swedish and German Trade

Unions', in Gibbins, J. R. (ed.), *Contemporary Political Culture, Politics in a Postmodern Age*, Sage: London.

Jahoda, M. (1979), 'The impact of Unemployment in the 1930s and the 1970s', *Bulletin of the British Psychological Society*.

James, E. (1991), 'The Netherlands: Benefits and Costs of Privatized Public Services - Lessons from the Dutch Educational System' in Walford, G. (ed.) *Private Schools in Ten Countries: Policy and Practice*, Routledge: London.

Johnson, P. and Falkingham, J. (1992), *Ageing and Economic Welfare*, Sage: London.

Jones, D. T. (1992), 'Lean Production fordert die Fertigungstechnik heraus', *VDI-Nachrichten*, No. 7.

Jones, K. (1989), *Right Turn: The Conservative Revolution in Education*, Hutchinson Radius: London.

Jordan, B., James, S., Kay, H. & Redley, M. (1992), *Trapped in Poverty? Labour-market Decisions in Low-Income Households*, Routledge: London.

Jürgens, U. (1992), 'Lean Production in Japan: Mythos und Realität', in Hans-Böckler-Stiftung (ed.), *Lean Production - Schlanke Produktion*, HBS: Düsseldorf.

Jürgens, U., Malsch, T., and Dohse, K. (1989), *Moderne Zeiten in der Automobilfabrik*, Springer: Berlin & Heidelberg.

Katz, M., ed. (1993), *The 'Underclass' Debate*, Princeton University Press: Princeton.

Keating, M. (1990), 'Minority Nationalism and the State: the European Case', in Watson, M. (ed.), *Contemporary Minority Nationalism*, Routledge: London.

Kelley, J. & Evans, M. D. R. (1993), 'The Legitimation of Inequality: Occupational Earnings in Nine Nations', *American Journal of Sociology*, No. 1/93, Vol. 99, pp. 75-125.

Kellner, D. (1992), 'Popular culture and the construction of postmodern identities', in Lash, S. and Friedmann, J. (eds.), *Modernity and Identity*, Blackwell: Oxford.

Kelly, J. E. and Nicholson, N. (1980), 'The causation of strikes; a review of theoretical approaches and the potential contribution of social psychology', *Human Relations*, Vol. 33, pp. 853-83.

Kerr, C. (1954), 'Industrial conflict and its mediation', *American Journal of Sociology*, Vol. 60, pp. 230-45.

Kim, L. (1983), *Att välja eller väljas. En studie av tillträdesreglerrna och övergången från gymnasieskola till högskola*, UHÅ: Stockholm.

King, M. (1993), "The impact of Western European border policies on the control of 'refugees' in Eastern and Central Europe", *New Community*, Vol. 19, No 2, January, pp. 183-99.

Kitchelt, H. (1989), *The Logics of Party Formation, Ecological Politics in Belgium and West Germany*, Cornell University Press: Ithaca.

Kitchelt, J. and Hellemans, S. (1990), *Beyond the European Left. Ideology and Political Action in the Belgian Ecology Parties*, Durham: London.

Klocke, A. (1993), *Sozialer Wandel, Sozialstruktur und Lebensstile in der Bundesrepublik Deutschland*, Lang: Frankfurt/Main.

Knight, C. (1990), *The Making of Tory Education Policy in Post-War Britain 1950-1986*, Falmer: London.

Knowles, K. (1954), 'Strike-proneness and its determinants', *American Journal of Sociology*, Vol. 60, pp. 213-29.

Koch, M. (1994), *Vom Strukturwandel einer Klassengesellschaft*, Westfälisches Dampfboot: Münster.

Kohli, M. (1989), 'Institutionalisierung und Individualisierung der Erwerbsbiographie. Aktuelle Veränderungstendenzen und ihre Folgen', in Brock, D. et al. (eds.), *Subjektivität im gesellschaftlichen Wandel*, Juventa: München, pp. 249-78.

Kohli, M., Rein, M., Guillemard, A-M. and van Gunsteren H. (eds.) (1991), *Time for Retirement*, Cambridge University Press: Cambridge.

Kohn, M. L. (1977), *Class and Conformity: A Study in Values*, University of Chicago Press: Chicago.

Kohn, M. L. and Schooler, C. (1978), 'The Reciprocal Effects of the Substantive Complexity of Work and Intellectual Flexibility: A Longitudinal Assessment', *American Journal of Sociology*, 84.

Kolarska-Bobinska, L. (1990), 'Socialist Welfare State in Transition: the State, the Market and the Enterprise in Poland', in Deacon, B. and Szalai, V. (eds.), *Social Policy in the New Eastern Europe*, Avebury: Aldershot.

Kornai, J. (1990), *The Road to a Free Economy*, W. W. Norton & Company: New York & London.

Korpi, W. (1990), *The Development of the Swedish Welfare State in a Comparative Perspective*, The Swedish Institute: Stockholm.

Kreckel, R. (1990), 'Klassenbegriff und Ungleichheitsforschung', in Berger, P. A. and Hradil, S. (eds), *Lebenslagen, Lebensläufe, Lebensstile*, Schwartz: Göttingen.

Kregel, J. A. (1980), 'Market and Institution as Features of a Capitalistic Production System', *Journal of Post-Keynesian Economics*, Vol. 3, pp. 32-48.

Kronauer, M., ed. (1993), 'Unemployment in Western Europe', *International Journal of Political Economy*, Vol. 23, No. 3.

Kyle, G. (1978), *Gästarbeterska i manssamhället. Studier om industriarbetande kvinnors villkor i Sverige*, Publica: Stockholm.

Laczko, F. (1988), 'Between work and retirement: becoming "old" in the 1980s', in Bytheway, B. (ed.), *Becoming and Being Old*, Sage: London, pp. 24-40.

Laffan, B. (1992), *Integration and Cooperation in Europe*, Routledge/UACES: London.

Lampert, H. (1991), *Lehrbuch der Sozialpolitik*, 2, Auflage, Springer Verlag: Berlin.

Lash, S. and Friedmann, J. (eds.) (1992), *Modernity and Identity*, Blackwell: Oxford.

Lash, S. and Urry, J. (1994), *Economies of Signs and Space*, Sage: London.

Lauder, H. and Brown, P., (eds.) (1988), *Education in Search of a Future*, Falmer: London.

Lehmann, R. (1994), 'Germany: System of Education' in Husén, T. and Poslethwaite, N. (eds.) *International Encyclopedia of Education*, Pergamon: London.

Leinberger, P., Trucker, B. (1991), *The New Individualists: the generation after the organization man*, Harper Collins: New York.

Leschinsky, A. and Mayer, K. (eds.) (1990), *The Comprehensive School Experiment Revisited: Evidence from Western Europe*, Verlag Peter Lang: Frankfurt am Main.

Lfo (1994), *Läroplan för de frivilliga skolformerna*, Utbildningsdepartmentet: Stockholm.

Lipset, S. M. (1959), 'Democracy and Working Class Authoritarianism', *American Sociological Review*, 24, pp. 482-502.

Lipset, S. M. (1963), *Political Man, The Social Basis of Politics*, Doubleday: Garden City.

Lipset, S. M. and Rokkan, S. (1967), *Party Systems and Voter Alignment*, The Free Press: New York.

Macey, M. (1992), 'Greater Europe: Integration or Ethnic Exclusion', in Crouch, C. and Marquand, D. (eds.), *Towards Greater Europe*, Blackwell: Oxford, pp. 139-53.

Maffesoli, M. (1985), *La connaissance ordinaire. Précis the sociologie comprehensive*, Meridiens, Paris.

Magone, J. (1994), 'The Territorial Politics of the European Union and Southern Europe (1986-1994): The Rise of Regionalist and Nationalist Politics', Unpublished Paper, *Beyond Boundaries? Citizens, Cultures and Languages in the New Europe Conference*, University of Salford, 11-12 November.

Mair, P. (1984), 'Party Politics in Contemporary Europe: A Challenge to Party', *West European Politics*, 7.

Mair, P. (1989), 'Continuity, Change, and the Vulnerability of Party', *West European Politics*, 12.

Mangen, S. (1994), 'The Impact of Unification', in Clasen, J. and Freeman, R. (eds.), *Social Policy in Germany*, Harvester Wheatsheaf: Hemel Hempstead, pp. 42-57.

Mann, M. (1993), 'Nation-States in Europe and Other Continents: Diversifying, Developing, Not Dying', *Daedulus*, Vol. 122, No 3, pp. 115-40.

Marklund, S. (1985), *Skolsverige 1950-1975, Differentieringsfrågan*, 4, Utbildningsförlaget: Stockholm.

Marklund, S. (ed.) (1992), *Rehabilitering i ett samhaellsperspektiv*, Studentlitteratur: Lund.

Marquand, D. (1994), 'Reinventing Federalism: Europe and the Left', *New Left Review*, No 203, January/February, pp. 17-26.

Marx, K. (1953), *Grundrisse der Kritik der politischen Ökonomie*, Dietz: Berlin.

Marx, K. (1956), *Das Kapital, III, Marx Engels Werke, Vol. 25*, Dietz: Berlin.

Max-Planck-Institut für Bildungforschung (1983), *Between Elite and Mass Education*, Albany: New York.

Merton, R. (1949), *Social Theory and Social Structure*, The Free Press: New York.

Miller, S. M. and Reissman, F. (1961), *Working-Class Authoritarianism: A Critique of Lipset*, British Journal of Sociology, 12.

Minkenberg, M. (1992), 'The new right in Germany. The transformation of conservatism and the extreme right', *European Journal of Political Research*, Vol. 22, No 1, July, pp. 55-81.

Minkenberg, M. (1992), 'The New Right in Germany: the transformation of conservatism and the extreme right', *European Journal of Political Research*, 22, 1.

Minkenberg, M. and Inglehart, R. (1989), 'Neoconservatism and Value Change in the USA: Tendencies in the Mass Public of a Postindustrial Society', in Gibbins, J. R. (ed.), *Contemporary Political Culture, Politics in a Postmodern Age*, Sage: London.

Monchablon, A. (1994), 'France: A System of Education' in Husén, T. and Poslethwaite, N. (eds.) *International Encyclopedia of Education*, Pergamon: London.

Mort, F. (1988), 'Boys Own; masculinity, style and popular culture', in Chapman, R. and Rutherford, J. (eds.), *Male Order: Unwrapping Masculinity*, Lawrence and Wishart: London.

Mückenberger, U. (1985), 'Die Krise des Normalarbeitsverhältnisses', *Zeitschrift für Sozialreform*, 31. Jg., Heft 7, pp. 415-34 und Heft 8, pp. 457-75.

Müller-Jentsch, W. (1986), *Soziologie der industriellen Beziehungen*, Campus: Frankfurt/New York.

Munn, P. (1992), 'Devolved Management of Schools and FE Colleges' in Paterson, L. and McCrone, D. (eds.) *Scottish Government Yearbook 1992*, Unit for the Study of Government in Scotland: Edinburgh.

Murray, C. (1990), *The Emerging British Underclass*, Welfare Series No 2, IEA Health and Welfare Unit: London.

Nagelkerke, A. (1994), 'Institutional Responses to Changing Conditions in European Systems of Industrial Relations', in Dijck, J. J. J. van and Groenewegen, J. P. M. (eds.), *Changing Business Systems in Europe. An Institutional Approach*, VUB Press: Brussels.

Naschold, F. and de Vroom, B. (eds.) (1994), *Regulating Employment and Welfare. Company and National Policies of Labour Force Participation at the End of Worklife in Industrial Countries*, de Gruyter: Berlin & New York.

Nissen, S. (1988), 'Jenseits des Arbeitsverhältnisses. Sozialpolitische Positionen der Tarifparteien zwischen Mitglieder- und Verbandsinteresse', *Zeitschrift für Sozialreform*, 34, Jg., Heft 11/12, pp. 695 - 709.

Nissen, S. (1988), 'Jenseits des Arbeitsverhältnisses. Sozialpolitische Positionen der Tarifparteien', *Zeitschrift für Sozialreform*, 34, Jg. Heft 11/12, pp. 695-709.

Nissen, S. (1990), 'Zwischen lohnarbeitszentrierter Sozialpolitik und sozialer Grundsicherung: Sozialpolitische Reformvorschläge in der parteipolitischen Diskussion', in Vobruba, G. (ed.), *Strukturwandel der Sozialpolitik. Lohnarbeitszentrierte Sozialpolitik und soziale Grundsicherung*, Suhrkamp: Frankfurt/M., pp. 233-99.

Nissen, S. (1992), 'Citizenship im Modernisierungsprozeß', in Nissen, S. (ed.), *Modernisierung nach dem Sozialismus*, Metropolis: Marburg, pp. 199-220.

Nissen, S. (1993), *Umweltpolitik in der Beschäftigungsfalle*, Metropolis, Marburg.

Nissen, S. (1994), 'Arbeitsplatzangst und politischer Immobilismus. Soziale Sicherheit und politische Partizipation als Vorraussetzungen staatlicher Handlungsfähigkeit', *Zeitschrift für Sozialreform*, 40. Jg., Heft 12, p. 781-96.

Noll, H. (1993), 'Lebensbedingungen und Wohlfahrtsdisparitäten in der Europäischen Gemeinschaft', in Glatzer, W. (ed.), *Einstellungen und Lebensbedingungen in Europa*, Campus: Frankfurt/New York.

Noll, H. and Habich, R. (1990), 'Individuelle Wohlfahrt. Vertikale Ungleichheit oder horizontale Disparitäten?', in Berger, P. A. and Hradil, S. (eds.), *Lebenslagen, Lebensläufe, Lebensstile*, Schwartz: Göttingen.

Nord (1990), *Skola och förvaltning i Norden*, Nord: Köpenhamn.

OECD (1972), *Reviews of National Policies for Education: Germany*, Organization for Economic Co-operation and Development: Paris.

OECD (1982), *Reviews of National Policies for Education: Finland*, Organization for Economic Co-operation and Development: Paris.

OECD (1990), *Reviews of National Policies for Education: Norway*, Organization for Economic Co-operation and Development: Paris.

OECD (1991a), *Quarterly labor force statistics*, Organization for Economic Co-operation and Development: Paris.

OECD (1991b), *Reviews of National Policies for Education: The Netherlands*, Organization for Economic Co-operation and Development: Paris.

OECD (1992), *Employment Outlook*, July, Organization for Economic Co-operation and Development: Paris.

OECD (1994), *School: A Matter of Choice*, Organization for Economic Co-operation and Development: Paris.

OECD (1995), *Quarterly labor force statistics*, Organization for Economic Co-operation and Development: Paris.

Offe, C. (1985), *Disorganized Capitalism: Contemporary Transformations of Work and Politics*, Polity Press: Cambridge.

Olofsson, G. (1993), 'Gradual Withdrawal and Partial Exit among Older Workers', in Forsberg, P. and Olofsson, G. (eds.), *Den äldre arbetskraften och arbetsmarknaden*, Dokumentation av en forskarkonferens, Dept of Sociology, Lund University: Lund.

Olofsson, G. and Petersson, J. (1993), *Seven Swedish Cases*, Working Paper 1993:4, Socialhögskolan: Lund.

Olofsson, G. and Petersson, J. (1994), 'Sweden: Policy Dilemmas of the Changing Age Structure in a "Work Society"', in Naschold, F. and de Vroom, B. (eds.), *Regulating Employment and Welfare*, de Gruyter: Berlin & New York, pp. 183-245.

Opielka, M. & Vobruba, G. (eds.) (1986), *Das garantierte Grundeinkommen. Entwicklung und Perspektiven einer Forderung*, Fischer Taschenbuch Verlag: Frankfurt/M.

Paloheimo, H. (1984), 'Distributive Struggle and Economic Development in the 1970s in Developed Capitalist Countries, *European Journal of Political Research*, 12, pp. 171-90.

Paquette, J. (1991), *Social Purpose and Schooling: Alternatives, Agendas and Issues*, Falmer: London.

Parker, H. (1989), *Instead of the Dole. An enquiry into integration of the tax and benefit system*, Routledge: London.

Parsons, T. (1971), *The System of Modern Societies*, Prentice Hall: Englewood Cliffs.

Pearson, R. (1992), 'The Geopolitics of People Power: The Pursuit of the Nation-State in East Central Europe', *Journal of International Affairs*, Vol. 45, No 2, Winter, pp. 499-518.

Pelleriaux, K. (1994), *Sociografie van the AGALEV-kiezer*, Unpublished manuscript, Centrum voor Sociologie, Vrije Universiteit Brussel: Brussel.

Pellicani, L. (1990), 'Preconditions for Soviet Economic Development' *Telos*, No. 84, pp. 43-57.

Petersson, J. (1993), 'Äldre arbetskraft och uttåget från arbetsmarknaden,' in FKF Debatt, *De ekonomiska trygghetssystemen - i ett historiskt och internationellt pespektiv*, Försäkringskasseförbundet: Stockholm.

Pfaff, M. (1989), 'Zur ökonomischen Bedeutung der Sozialen Sicherung', in Vobruba, G. (ed.), *Der wirtschaftliche Wert der Sozialpolitik*, Duncker & Humblot: Berlin, pp. 123-147.

Phelps, E. (1967), 'Phillips Curves, Expectations of Inflation and Optimal Unemployment Over Time', *Economica*, 34, pp. 254-81.

Phillip, A. (1994), 'European Union immigration policy: Phantom, Fantasy or Fact?', *West European Politics*, Vol. 17, No 2, April, pp. 168-91.

Pinder, J. (1991), *European Community. The Building of a Union*, Oxford University Press: Oxford.

Pinder, J. (1994), 'The European Elections of 1994 and the future of the European Union', *Government and Opposition*, Vol. 29, No 4, Autumn, pp. 494-514.

Pioch, R. & Vobruba, G. (1994), 'Gerechtigkeitsvorstellungen im Wohlfahrtsstaat. Eine Sekundäranalyse zur Akzeptanz wohlfahrtsstaatlicher Maßnahmen', in Döring, D. et al., *Gerechtigkeit im Wohlfahrtsstaat*, Schüren: Marburg, pp. 114-65.

Piore, M. and Sabel, Ch. (1984), *The Second Industrial Divide: Possibilities for Prosperity*, Basic Books: New York.

Poole, M. (1986), *Industrial relations: origins and patterns of national diversity*, Routledge and Kegan Paul: London.

Potthoff, H. (1931), 'Der Mensch als Wirtschaftswert: Der wirtschaftliche Wert der Sozialpolitik', *Schriften der Gesellschaft für Soziale Reform*, Heft 84/85, pp. 1-18.

Poulantzas, N. (1974), *Les classes sociales dans le capitalisme d'aujourdhui*, Seuil: Paris.

Preller, L. (1978), *Sozialpolitik in der Weimarer Republik*, Athenäum: Kronberg/Ts.

Projekt Klassenanalyse (1973, 1974), *Materialien zur Klassenstruktur der BRD*, 2 Vols, VSA: Berlin.

Propositionen om valfrihet i skolan (1992/3), *Valfrihet i skolan*, Utbildningsdepartmentet: Stockholm.

Przeworski, A. (1991), *Democracy and the Market*, Cambridge University Press: Cambridge.

Rapoport, R. (1990), 'Ideologies about Family Forms: towards diversity', in Boh, K., Bak, M. and Clason, C. (eds.), *Changing Patterns of European Family: A Comparison of 14 Countries*, Routledge: London.

Reider, H. L. (1989), 'Party Decline in the West; A Skeptic's View', *Journal of Theoretical Politics*, 3.

Reif, K. and Schmitt, H. (1980), 'Nine Second-Order National Elections: A Conceptual Framework for the Analysis of European Election Results', *European Journal of Political Research*, Vol. 8. No. 1, pp. 3-44.

Reimer, B. (1989), 'Postmodern Structures of Feeling: Values and Lifestyles in the Postmodern Age', in Gibbins, J. R. (ed.), *Contemporary Political Culture, Politics in a Postmodern Age*, Sage: London.

Roberts, G. (1994), 'Extremism in Germany: Sparrows or Avalanche?', *European Journal of Political Research*, Vol. 25, No 4, June, pp. 461-81.

Roberts, G. and Edwards, A. (1991), *A New Dictionary of Political Analysis*, Edward Arnold: London.

Roebroek, J. & Hogenboom, E. (1989), *Basisinkomen: Alternatieve Uitkering of Nieuw Paradigma?*, Katholieke Universiteit: Brabant.

Roller, E. (1992), *Einstellungen der Bürger zum Wohlfahrtsstaat der Bundesrepublik Deutschland*, Westdeutscher Verlag: Opladen.

Ross, A. M. (1948), *Trade Union Wage Policy*, University of California Press: Berkeley.

Ross, A. M. and Hartman, P. T (1960), *Changing patterns of industrial conflict*, John Wiley: New York.

Rutherford, J. (1990), *Identity, Community, Culture, Difference*, Lawrence and Wishart: London.

Rutherford, J. (1992), *Men's Silences: Predicaments in Masculinity*, Routledge: London.

Sachverständigenrat (1993/94), *Jahresgutachten 1993/94 des Sachverständigenrates zur Begutachtung der gesamtwirtschaftlichen Entwicklung*, Deutscher Bundestag, 12. Wahlperiode, Drucksache 12/6170.

Salonen, T. (1993), *Margins of Welfare - A Study of Modern Functions of Social Assistance*, Hällestad Press: Torna Hällestad.

Scharpf, F. W. (1993), 'Umbau des Sozialstaats: Von der Finanzierung der Arbeitslosigkeit zur Subventionierung niedriger Erwerbseinkommen', *Gewerkschaftliche Monatshefte*, 7/1993, pp. 433-43.

Scharpf, F. W. (1995), 'Nicht Arbeitslosigkeit, sondern Beschäftigung fördern', in Meyer, H.-W. (ed.), *Sozial gerecht teilen - ökologisch umsteuern? Beiträge zur Reformdiskussion im Deutschen Gewerkschaftsbund und seinen Gewerkschaften*, Band 2, Bund Verlag: Köln, pp. 24-41.

Schmähl, W. (1994), 'On the Economic Significance of Social security in the Process of Transformation from a Socialist Economy to a Market Economy', *EISS Yearbook 1993*, Acco Leuven.

Schmid, G. (1994), 'Übergänge in die Vollbeschäftigung: Formen und Finanzierung einer zukunftsgerechten Arbeitsmarktpolitik', *Aus Politik und Zeitgeschichte*, B 12-13, pp. 9-23.

Schmid, G., Reißert, B. & Bruche, G. (1987), *Arbeitslosenversicherung und aktive Arbeitsmarktpolitik*, Sigma: Berlin.

Schmitt, R. (1989), 'From "Old Politics" to "New Politics": Three Decades of Peace Protest in West Germany', in Gibbins, J. R. (ed.), *Contemporary Political Culture, Politics in a Postmodern Age*, Sage: London.

Schopflin, G. (1991), 'Nationalism and National Minorities in East and Central Europe', *Journal of International Affairs*, Vol. 45, No 1, Summer, pp. 51-65.

Schreyer, M. (1987), 'Mindesteinkommen - Stolper- oder Meilenstein für eine grüne Zukunft?', in Opielka, M. & Vobruba, G. (eds.), *Das garantierte Grundeinkommen*, Fischer Taschenbuch Verlag: Frankfurt/M., pp. 158-69.

Schröder, T. (1930), 'Aussprache zum Vortrag von Dr. Goetz Briefs: Der wirtschaftliche Wert der Sozialpolitik', *Schriften der Gesellschaft für Soziale Reform*, Heft 38, pp. 204-6.

Schulte, B. (1994), *The Provision of Minimum Protection Within Member States of the European Union*, Paper presented at the European Conference on Historical and Comparative Sociological Research, London, 16-18 December 1994.

Schulz, J. H., Borowski, A. and Crown, W. H. (1991), *Economics of Population Ageing - The 'Graying' of Australia, Japan, and the United States*, Auburn House: Westport.

Schumann, M. et al. (1992), 'Hat 'lean production' eine Chance?' *SOFI-Mitteilungen Nr 19*, Soziologisches Forschungsinstitut: Göttingen.

Schumpeter, J. A. (1975), *Kapitalismus, Sozialismus und Demokratie*, Francke: München.

Scott, J., Braun, M. and Alwin, D. (1993), 'The Family Way', *10th BSA Report: International Attitudes*, Dartmouth Publishing Co.: Aldershot.

Seton-Watson, H. (1977), *Nations and States*, Metheun: London.

Shavit, Y. and Blossfeld, H-P., (eds.), (1993), *Persistent Inequality: Changing Educational Attainment in Thirteen Countries*, Westview: Oxford.

Shorter, E. and Tilly, C. (1974), *Strikes in France 1830-1968*, Cambridge University Press: Cambridge.

Simon, B. (1974), *The Two Nations and the Educational Structure 1780-1870*, Lawrence & Wishart: London.

Sipos, S. (1994), 'Income Transfers: Family Support and Poverty Relief', in Barr, N. (ed.), *Labor Markets and Social Security in Central and Eastern Europe. The Transition and Beyond*, Oxford University Press: Oxford, pp. 226-259.

Skolverket (1993), 'Val av skola. Rapport om valfrihet iniom skolpliktens ram läsåret 1992/93', *Skolverkets Rapport* No.40: Stockholm.

Smith, A. (1979), *Nationalism in the Twentieth Century*, Martin Robertson: Oxford.

Smith, A. (1995), *Nations and Nationalism in a Global Era*, Polity Press: Cambridge.

Smolar, A. (1990), 'Durch die Wüste. Die Dilemmas des Übergangs', *Transit*, Heft 1, pp. 65-78.

SOED (1992), *Upper Secondary Education in Scotland* (The Howie Report), HMSO: Edinburgh.

Soerensen, A. (1992), 'Zur geschlechtsspezifischen Struktur von Armut', in Leibfried, S. & Voges, W. (eds.), 'Armut im modernen Wohlfahrtsstaat', *Kölner Zeitschrift für Soziologie und Sozialpsychologie*, Sonderband 32, pp. 345-66.

Sorrentino, C. (1990), 'The Changing Family in International Perspective' *Monthly Labor Review*, March.

Standing, G. (1986), 'Measuring Labour Flexibility with Security: An Answer to British Unemployment', *International Labour Review*, Vol. 125, No. 1, pp. 87-106.

Statistical Office of the European Communities (1992), *Europe in figures*, Office for the Official Publications of the European Communities: Luxembourg.

Stevenson, O. (1994), 'Paid Work and Unpaid Work: Women who care for adult dependants', in Evetts J. (ed.), *Women and Careers*, Longman: Harlow.

Strasser, H. and Goldthorpe, J. H. (eds.), (1985), *Die Analyse sozialer Ungleichheit*, Westdeutscher Verlag: Opladen.

Streeck, W. (1987), 'Vielfalt und Interdependenz: Uberlegungen zur Rolle von intermediären Organizationen in sich ändernden Umwelten', *Kölner Zeitschrift für Soziologie und Sozialpsychologie*, 39, 4.

Streeck, W. (1987), 'The Uncertainties of Management in the Management of Uncertainty: Employers, Labor Relations and Industrial Adjustment in the 1980s', *Work, Employment and Society*, No. 1.

Struwe, K. (ed.) (1991), *Schools and Education in Denmark*, Det danske selskab: Copenhagen.

Swyngedouw, M. (1992), *Waar voor je waarden. The opkomst van Vlaams Blok en Agalev in the jaren tachtig*, ISPO, Sociologisch Onderzoeksinstituut: Leuven.

Tarnow, F. (1930), 'Aussprache zum Vortrag von Dr. Goetz Briefs: Der wirtschaftliche Wert der Sozialpolitik', *Schriften der Gesellschaft für Soziale Reform*, Heft 38, pp. 188-96.

Teese, R. (1991), 'France: Catholic Schools, Class Security and the Public Sector' in Walford, G. ed. *Private Schools in Ten Countries: Policy and Practice*, Routledge: London.

Therborn, G. (1987), 'Auf der Suche nach dem Handeln. Geschichte und Verteidigung der Klassenanalyse' *Prokla* 66.

Therborn, G. (1995), *European Modernity and Beyond*, London: Sage.

Thompson, P. (1983), *The Nature of Work*, Macmillan: London.

Toivonen, T. (1990), 'The New Rise of Self-Employment and Industrial Structure', in: Clegg, St. R. (ed.), *Organization theory and class analysis*, de Gruyter: Berlin/New York.

Topf, R. (1989), 'Political Change and Political Culture in Britain, 1959-87', in Gibbins, J. R. (ed.), *Contemporary Political Culture, Politics in a Postmodern Age*, Sage: London.

Townsend, P. (1979), *Poverty in the United Kingdom*, Penguin Books: Harmondsworth.

van Parijs, P. (1990), 'The Second Marriage of Justice and Efficiency', *Journal of Social Policy*, 19, pp. 1-25.

Verdery, K. (1993), 'Nationalism and National Sentiment in Post-Socialist Romania', *Slavic Review*, Vol. 52, No 2, Summer, pp. 179-203.

Vester, M. et al.(1993), *Soziale Milieus im gesellschaftlichen Strukturwandel*, Bund: Köln.

Vianello, M. and Siemienska, R. (1990), *Gender Inequality: a comparative study of discrimination and participation*, Sage: London.

Vobruba, G. (1983), *Politik mit dem Wohlfahrtsstaat*, Suhrkamp: Frankfurt.

Vobruba, G. (1988), 'The Economic Significance of Social Policy' English Version of *Discussion Paper FS I 88-11*, Science Center Berlin.

Vobruba, G. (1989), *Arbeiten und Essen. Politik an den Grenzen des Arbeitsmarkts*, Passagen Verlag: Wien.

Vobruba, G. (1991a), *Jenseits der sozialen Fragen*, Suhrkamp: Frankfurt/M.

Vobruba, G. (1991b), 'Futures of Work and Security', in Room, G. (ed.), *Towards a European Welfare State?*, SAUS Publications: Bristol, pp.57-71.

Vobruba, G. (1993), 'Lohn aus zwei Töpfen. Arbeitslosigkeit: Wie die Beschäftigung gesteigert werden kann und trotzdem die Kosten der Betriebe sinken', *Die Zeit*, No. 37, 10.9.93, p. 27.

Vobruba, G. (1994), 'Transnational Social Policy in Processes of Transformation', in de Swaan, A. (ed.), *Social Policy beyond Borders*, Amsterdam University Press: Amsterdam.

Vobruba, G. (1995), 'Arbeit und Einkommen nach der Vollbeschäftigung', *Leviathan*, 23. Jg., Heft 2, pp. 154-64.

Vobruba, G. (ed.) (1990), *Strukturwandel der Sozialpolitik. Lohnarbeitszentrierte Sozialpolitik und soziale Grundsicherung*, Suhrkamp: Frankfurt/M.

Vogel, J., Andersson, L-G., Davidsson, U. and Häll, U. (1987), *Ojämlikheten i Sverige, SCP Rapport no.51*, SCB förlag: Stockholm.

Wadensjö, E. (1991), 'Early Exit from the Labour Force in Sweden', in Kohli, M et al.(eds.), *Time for Retirement*, Cambridge University Press: Cambridge, pp. 284-323.

Walby, S. (1990), *Theorizing Patriarchy*, Blackwell: Oxford.

Walford, G. (ed.) (1991), *Private Schooling: Tradition, Change and Diversity*, Chapman: London.

Wallace, W. (1990), 'Introduction', in Wallace, W. (ed.), *The Dynamics of European Integration*, Pinter/RIIA: London.

Walter, J. A. (1989), *Basic Income. Freedom from Poverty, Freedom to Work*, Marion Boyars Publisher: London.

Watson, P. (1993), 'Eastern Europe's Silent Revolution Gender', *Sociology*, Vol. 27, No 3.

Weiss, M. and Mattern, C. (1991), 'Federal Republic of Germany: The Situation and Development of the Private School System', in Walford, G. (ed.) *Private Schools in Ten Countries: Policy and Practice*, Routledge: London.

Weißgerber, F. (1991), 'Eine Belegschaft von Unternehmern', *Automobil-Produktion*, December (special issue on VW Wolfsburg).

Welford, A. T. (1958), *Ageing and Human Skill*, Oxford University Press: London.

Winter, L. (1990), 'Die Arbeiterklasse der EG - Entwicklungstendenzen', in Leisewitz, A.and Pickshaus, K. (eds.), *Gewerkschaften, Klassentheorie und Subjektfrage*, IMSF: Frankfurt/Main.

Wolf, J. (1992), 'Sozialstaat und Grundsicherung. Ein Bericht über den Forschungsstand', *Leviathan*, 3/1992, pp. 386-410.

Womack, J.P., Jones, D.T., and Roos, D. (1990), *The Machine that Changed the World*, Rawson: New York.

Wright, E. O. (1978), *Class, Crisis and the State*, New Left Books: London.

Wright, E. O. (1985), *Classes*, Verso: London.

Wright, E. O., ed. (1989), *The Debate on Classes*, Verso: London.

Zapf, W. (1983), 'Entwicklungsdilemmas und Innovationspotentiale in modernen Gesellschaften', in Matthes, J. (ed.), *Krise der Arbeitsgesellschaft? Verhandlungen des 21. Deutschen Soziologentages in Bamberg 1982*, Campus: Frankfurt, pp. 293-308.

Zetterholm, S. (1994), 'Cultural Diversity and Common Policies', in Zetterholm, S. (ed.), *National Cultures and European Integration*, Berg: Oxford.